The Five Biblical Scrolls

The Five Biblical Scrolls

A Modern Reader's Guide to Ecclesiastes, Esther, Song of Songs, Ruth, and Lamentations

ANDREW VOGEL ETTIN

CASCADE *Books* • Eugene, Oregon

THE FIVE BIBLICAL SCROLLS
A Modern Reader's Guide to Ecclesiastes, Esther, Song of Songs, Ruth, and Lamentations

Copyright © 2025 Andrew Vogel Ettin. All rights reserved. Except for brief quotations in critical publications or reviews, no part of this book may be reproduced in any manner without prior written permission from the publisher. Write: Permissions, Wipf and Stock Publishers, 199 W. 8th Ave., Suite 3, Eugene, OR 97401.

Cascade Books
An Imprint of Wipf and Stock Publishers
199 W. 8th Ave., Suite 3
Eugene, OR 97401

www.wipfandstock.com

PAPERBACK ISBN: 979-8-3852-2163-9
HARDCOVER ISBN: 979-8-3852-2164-6
EBOOK ISBN: 979-8-3852-2165-3

Cataloguing-in-Publication data:

Names: Ettin, Andrew Vogel [author].

Title: The five biblical scrolls : a modern reader's guide to Ecclesiastes, Song of Songs, Ruth, and Lamentations / Andrew Vogel Ettin.

Description: Eugene, OR: Cascade Books, 2025 | Includes bibliographical references and index.

Identifiers: ISBN 979-8-3852-2163-9 (paperback) | ISBN 979-8-3852-2164-6 (hardcover) | ISBN 979-8-3852-2165-3 (ebook)

Subjects: LCSH: Bible.—Five Scrolls—Criticism, interpretation, etc. | Bible.—Ecclesiastes—Criticism, interpretation, etc. | Bible.—Esther—Criticism, interpretation, etc. | Bible.—Song of Solomon—Criticism, interpretation, etc. | Bible.—Ruth—Criticism, interpretation, etc. | Bible.—Lamentations—Criticism, interpretation, etc.

Classification: BS1309 E88 2025 (paperback) | BS1309 (ebook)

05/21/25

For my family

Contents

	Introduction	ix
1	Ecclesiastes/Qohelet	1
2	Book of Esther	25
3	Song of Songs/Shir ha-Shirim	68
4	Book of Ruth	103
5	Lamentations/Eykhah	134
6	Coda	165
7	For Further Reading	175
	General Index	181
	Scripture Index	185

Introduction

How does religion talk about passionate love? About catastrophic suffering? About spiritual confusion or life's apparent meaninglessness? How does it not simply command us but more internally teach us to know the heart of the stranger or to value risking one's own life in the jaws of malice? Where are the sacred texts, what is the canonized scripture, that will lead us by word and example through the entanglements of love and hate, loneliness and terror, friendship and risk, destruction and desire? How do we find the pulse of normal human living—its ordinariness along with its vital moments—sanctified through holy words? The five biblical books that Jewish tradition has appointed for reading on five major holy days offer us a *vade mecum*, a companion and guide, for these journeys of the mind, spirit, and emotions that conventional religious expression typically ignores or shuns.

Why consider these texts together? If we think of them as a set, they make an odd collection indeed. Ecclesiastes, Esther, Song of Songs, Ruth, and Lamentations: here are five scriptures that appear to have nothing in common except that each is a remarkable literary work—truly, every one of them a literary masterpiece—each is in Hebrew, and each has had enormous influence on the arts as well as religion. For centuries they have inspired and touched audiences beyond the Jewish realm, richly informing both Christian and secular culture. Indeed, apart from the Psalms, no texts from the Jewish Bible have been set to music as often as Song of Songs and Lamentations, including major works by leading composers of church music. Apart from the Psalms, few biblical books have been as widely quoted as Ecclesiastes, for which there always seems to be "a time and place under heaven." The stories and main characters of both Ruth and Esther have often been admired and even loved by people with no commitment to Judaism or Jewish culture, often readers who might otherwise identify themselves as secular.

Still, these books' diversity of genres, styles, and spiritual outlooks seems to mark them each as singular when we first consider them, rather than being connected through any cultural or spiritual resemblances among them that we might seek. Frequently, religiously motivated readers are nonplussed by works such as these. They are not oracular like the words of the prophets, nor do they reverberate with divine pronouncements from Mount Sinai or the Mount of Olives. How (such readers might want to know) do they belong to "Holy Scripture?" Among the Jewish biblical writings that are mandated scriptural readings for holidays, as these five books are, they are very unusual in containing no prophetic teachings and no religious laws except for laws of Purim proclaimed near the end of the Book of Esther. What is sacred about them? What is the religious message one can learn or teach from each of these texts, and to whom could one possibly teach it?

Answering these questions will take us deeper into understanding each of the books; more than that, it will also take us deeper into understanding how life's experiences become sacred. Those are some of the reasons for this book, which aims to be inspirational and instructive for the adventurous seekers along with teachers and readers who may explore any or all of the Five Scrolls themselves, in a group or with a class, be that in an academic or congregational setting, or privately as part of their own exploration of literature, religion, or ideas.

Above all else, each of these five books or "scrolls" is a great work of literature, enjoyable to read in the ways that every great literary work is, engaging a reader regardless of the events depicted or any real or imaginary historical context, or for that matter regardless of the reader's religious beliefs or absence of them. In a similar spirit, the commentaries that follow are essayistic, not formulaic. The hope is that they will be enjoyable and interesting to read, and that the book will be more an inquisitive, engaged companion to the biblical texts than a textbook about them.

In this book, all the translations are the author's, except as noted. To facilitate reading for non-specialists, all Hebrew quotations are transliterated phonetically. Modern authorities referred to in the text are cited, along with others, in the bibliographic section "For Further Reading."

Even though (as noted below) there are benefits to other ways of looking at the five scrolls in relation to one another, the order of this discussion follows the sequence of today's Jewish calendar. Therefore, Ecclesiastes comes first, followed by Esther, Song of Songs, Ruth, and Lamentations, with a concluding Coda offering a contemporary perspective

INTRODUCTION

and a suggested overarching concept for the entire collection of Megillot (that is, scrolls), as they are known in Hebrew. Individual chapters will occasionally reference others of these books, but each chapter may be read independently. They do not necessarily have to be read in the printed order.

TERMINOLOGY

Let us begin with some nuances of terms. Precision is important, and each culture's names for its writings will teach us something about how that culture understands those writings. For instance, the term "New Testament" explicitly places that particular group of writings in relation to an older corpus, a prior body of writings that logically were then designated as "Old Testament." As we know, the two testaments transmitted in Christian tradition became known collectively as the Bible. The Latin word *biblia*, denoting a text, comes from Greek, where *biblia* is a plural form, thus introducing an ambiguity: is the work at hand a collection of texts, a plurality, or is it a unity? The early Christian scholars who so named the *Kainē Diathēkē* or *Novum Testamentum* might instead have simply called it The Life and Teachings of Jesus or the Biblia Christiana, the Christian Bible, rather than "New Testament." Instead, they purposefully chose a phrase that places this new body of writing in relationship to an extant one on which it depends and from which it partially derives meanings, both positive and negative. What becomes the Holy Bible of Christians are therefore these two bodies of works, "testaments," yoked together as if they comprise a single, coherent religious communication.

By contrast, the canon of Jewish sacred scripture generally corresponding to Christianity's so-called "Old Testament" has two names in Hebrew. One is Miqra, meaning "that which is read" (i.e., publicly proclaimed). The other is the more common term Tanakh, an acronym representing the three sections of canonized texts: **T**orah (often called Law in English, but more properly meaning Enlightenment), **N**evi'im or Prophets, and **K**etuvim or Writings. For Jewish people there is no Hebrew "Old Testament." There is a Hebrew Bible or, one might say, there are The Jewish Scriptures or the Tanakh.

I generally refer to the Hebrew Bible as the Tanakh. When I use the term "Old Testament," I mean the Hebrew Bible as Christians reconstruct and use it, including the reordering of the three major sections so as to place the Prophets, and specifically placing Malachi's prophecy of Elijah's reappearance before "the great and awesome day of God," right before Matthew's genealogy of Jesus at the beginning of the New Testament.

Jewish terminology preserves the historic diversity of this body of writings, which in ancient times consisted of a collection of individual scrolls for each of the books. It is an assemblage of heterogeneous material that became the canon (that is, the measuring stick or rule) that religious authorities accepted as inspired writings, beginning first with the five books of the Torah (Genesis through Deuteronomy), next the collection of Nevi'im beginning with Joshua and concluding with Malachi, finally the diverse other texts in poetry and prose that (as we shall see) expressed divine inspiration, according to the consensus of rabbis in the first and second centuries CE.

Though one might be tempted to call the Tanakh a chorus, that musical metaphor is not quite apt. In a chorus the voices must balance and harmonize with one another. Taken as a whole, therefore, the Tanakh is not a chorus; instead, it is more like a family reunion, where some tell quiet anecdotes or offer advice, others boom out their experiences and opinions; often there is singing, sometimes an off-color anecdote; memories may be challenged, contradictions struggled over or left unresolved. The Tanakh will not focus on a single storyline or point of view. Its congregation of voices turns into a bricolage of viewpoints, and it is not ashamed to seek for enlightenment in dark places or to call that search a sacred act.

Although disparate in so many ways, the five books on which we are concentrating, the shortest books among the Ketuvim, nevertheless share a distinction within Hebrew scriptures because each was designated many centuries ago, at least by talmudic times (second to sixth centuries CE) as the special reading for one of the major Jewish holy days, apart from the so-called High Holy Days (*Yomim Nora'im*, Days of Awe) of Rosh Hashanah and Yom Kippur. Collectively they are known and often published together in modern times as the Five Scrolls or Megillot (plural of *megillah*).

Their titles as they appear in common parlance express points of interpretive difference, which we shall consider more specifically as we take up each of the books. Briefly, however, we can outline at the outset where differences occur. "Song of Songs" neatly translates the Hebrew title Shir ha-Shirim. "Canticles" (a word derived from Latin) is the preferred Catholic designation while "Song of Solomon" is the more familiar Protestant usage, occasionally met as well in Jewish writings, albeit that title implies an ascription to King Solomon that few modern scholars would countenance. More conventionally, Lamentations or, as the Church generally calls it, The Lamentations of Jeremiah, is simply titled in the original Hebrew by the first word of the text, *eykhah*, meaning "how." That is in keeping with a common Jewish practice for naming texts (for instance, for Hebrew readers the book called Genesis is Bereishit, which is the text's first word). The book known in Hebrew as Qohelet (sometimes transliterated as Kohelet) takes its title from a word used as if it is the narrator or putative author's proper name, indicated by the speaker's own reference to himself in the first line. In English it is most often designated by the Greco-Roman term Ecclesiastes, meaning something like "convener" or perhaps preacher. Traditional Jewish and Christian commentators alike dubiously ascribe authorship to one of Israel's most famous kings, Solomon, treating "Qohelet" as a pseudonym.

Esther is commonly regarded as quintessentially "the megillah" inasmuch as it is the only one of the five still customarily read in the synagogue from an actual scroll rather than a bound book; it is also the only book in the Jewish biblical canon that may be read from a scroll bearing ornaments and illustrations. For this reason scrolls of Esther, along with their often-decorative cases of wood or metal, have been collected for their artistic value as well as studied for their illuminations of such historical details as styles of attire that reflect the customs and artistic imagination of the time and place of the scroll's origin.

Ecclesiastes/Qohelet, which is read in the fall at Sukkot (Festival of Booths or Tabernacles), comes first in the liturgical year, followed in about five months by Esther at Purim (Feast of Esther or Lots), Song of Songs a month after that at the beginning of Pesach/Passover, Ruth fifty days later for Shavuot/Pentecost (Festival of Weeks), and lastly Lamentations at Tisha b'Av/Ninth Day of Av, commemorating the destruction of the first and second Temples in Jerusalem along with other historical catastrophes besetting the Jewish people. Disparate as they are in style and content, the books do not form easily into a logical sequence.

The synagogal reading of these works on the relevant holy days was standard at least by talmudic times. There is no explicit explanation of how this came about, though we can speculate that was an attempt to integrate the third of the three Tanakh sections—Torah, Nevi'im/Prophets, and Ketuvim/Writings—into liturgical use.

The five books comprising the Torah are read sequentially during the year, supplemented by the haftarah ("completion"), passages drawn from various prophets and chosen for their verbal or thematic connections with the Torah section or the time in the liturgical year. By and large, each week every synagogue in the world will read all or some of the same Torah and haftarah sections, regardless of the congregation's denomination. But the third portion of the Tanakh might have had no regular liturgical role aside from numerous psalms that were incorporated into regular worship. Adding pertinent short books to the services for Sukkot, Pesach, and Shavuot distinguished and elaborated the observances of these three major holidays instituted in the Torah, which are collectively called Shalosh Regalim ("Three Pilgrimage Festivals"). Choosing another two would yield five books selected from the Ketuvim, thus balancing the five books of the Torah as well as the five books of the Psalms. One of those two additional books had to be Lamentations because the destruction of the Temple and Jerusalem along with continued mourning for them by Jews in exile and the hope of eventual restoration are major themes throughout Jewish history and worship. The fifth had to be Esther, for Purim was both an enormously popular holiday enjoyed by children as well as adults and an important festival of Jewish liberation from potential genocide.

The celebration most obviously omitted from this roster is Hanukkah. Thematically, it is similar to Purim; though there are significant differences in their stories and meanings, one could imagine Hanukkah being selected for special liturgical treatment, such as a lengthy reading, beyond the few special blessings designated for it. However, one major difference and a critical impediment to using a special reading to honor Hanukkah in the same way as these other holidays is that there is no megillah for it. The story of Hanukkah was transmitted textually in the four books of the Maccabees, which Jewish tradition did not canonize; they are not included in the Tanakh. One possible reason for their exclusion was those books' rather uninspiring focus on military campaigns and political infighting, though another was surely the later era's disillusionment with the dynasty of the Maccabees. Yet a third reason was that only the first of the four books exists in a Hebrew version, the others being preserved (ironically) only in Greek.

However, perhaps the most significant factor was a crucial lacuna in the Maccabean chronicles. By the time the order of the synagogue services was set, the rabbis had elevated as the major element in the Hanukkah narrative "the miracle of the oil," that is, the story that when the Temple was liberated, cleansed and rededicated, the small flask of sanctified pure olive oil that seemed barely able to light the menorah for one night lasted for eight, thus the eight days of festivities. This tale appears for the first time in the Mishnah (codified in the late second century CE), having been mentioned nowhere in the books of the Maccabees. Whether it was an orally transmitted legend or a metaphoric invention of the rabbis to transform a military campaign into a religious miracle, we do not know. What we do know is that for the rabbis shaping a religious celebration of the festival, there would be no point in reading a narrative about Hanukkah without that crowning anecdote that was unattested by any source beyond the Mishnah itself.

It is their function in synagogue worship that makes the Megillot especially compelling to study and discuss as a group rather than solely as individual works. While a cycle of set weekly readings from the Torah and prophets is a long-established feature of both Jewish and Christian lectionaries, here we have the pairing of entire biblical books with annual observances to which each book is linked by content and theme, with the public reading of the text (traditionally in its entirety) being an integral part of the day's worship service.

True, taken as a group they make a diverse—some might say mismatched—set. The genres are different, to begin with: Shir ha-shirim and Eykhah are poetic, while Ruth and Esther are prose narratives, and Qohelet is a collection of observations and sayings. They also stand in different relationships to the religious days they help commemorate. Esther and Eykhah are explicitly and inextricably linked to Purim and Tisha b'Av respectively by their subject matter, while the other three are more loosely associated with their festivals through imagery and themes. Clearly, the sages (be they priests, scribes, rabbis, or some other learned coterie) who devised these additions to the liturgy thought not just literally but also metaphorically and analogically about texts. The notion of bringing an additional "offering" to the worship obligations for these special sacred days, corresponding to the additional sacrificial offering biblically mandated on holy occasions, must have been so compelling that the liturgists sought out companion readings for the services.

The liturgical use of these works compels commentary and discussion. One wants to examine how each book complements the observance with which it is paired. How is the public reading of the text incorporated into the liturgy? What special traditions, musical or otherwise performative, are generally associated with the reading, and how do these express the community's understanding of the text? How does the meaning of each of the holy days shape interpretations of its megillah? How might the megillah text define a community's understanding of the holy day? These are among the topics this book explores.

THE FIVE SCROLLS AS A CANON

While the vast number of critical analyses on each of the Megillot attests to the value of studying any one of them alone, seeing them together as a distinguishable canon within the entire biblical corpus offers them as a topic for study, if not exactly providing a ready-made syllabus. For although the Torah, the first five books of the Tanakh, implies a logical sequence for discussion based on its own internal sequences of narratives and revelations from the beginning of Genesis to the conclusion of Moses' life at the end of Deuteronomy, no such logic drives the order of discussing the five Megillot. They form no intrinsic chronological, thematic, literary, or theological series. They do nevertheless follow a liturgical sequence based on the order in which they are read on their five Jewish holidays.

Standard Tanakh editions begin the third major unit, Ketuvim/Writings, with Psalms, followed by Proverbs and Job, after which come the five scrolls, which we might expect to be printed in the sequence in which they are read during the Jewish year. That would mean starting with Qohelet/Ecclesiastes, the appointed reading for Sukkot, the joyful fall festival coming two weeks after the new year begins at Rosh Hashanah. However, in the Tanakh the order begins instead with Song of Songs, which is recited at Passover, surely reflecting the older biblical order of months according to which Aviv ("Spring," now called Nisan in Hebrew) was counted as the first month and the one in which Passover is observed, while the month that begins with Rosh Hashanah (the New Year) and includes Sukkot is the seventh month according to the Torah.

Studying and discussing these texts, we might choose to apply our own ingenuity in devising sequences if only to provide a through-line for interpreting them. By default we might choose simply to follow their order in the Jewish liturgical calendar, as this book does. That entails separating from one another the two narrative books with female protagonists, Esther and Ruth, that might well benefit from being looked at

INTRODUCTION xvii

adjacently, in addition to starting the sequence with the disconcerting moral and theological ambiguities of Qohelet/Ecclesiastes and finishing in the profound grimness of Eykhah/Lamentations. But that order of texts is familiar to Jewish readers, and one is not bound to read these books only according to the modern Jewish calendrical order.

A different tactic would be to arrange the texts by literary types in order to appreciate the resulting conversations of styles, tones, and dramatic situations. From this approach, it would be sensible to begin with the pair of short stories whose plots and characters seem readily accessible, Ruth and Esther, then switch genres to the poetic texts of Song of Songs and Lamentations, finally turning to the philosophical musings (and one might say the ethical opacity) of Ecclesiastes.

Concentrating instead on thematic ideas could generate other sequences for richer possibilities of discussion. For example, since Song of Songs, Ruth, and Esther all engage with plots involving love, desire, marriage, security, and power, particularly in the light of gender awareness and recognizing imbalances of authority and agency, those three books might be brought into conversation with one another, while Ecclesiastes and Lamentations could be viewed as poetic meditations on life, loss, and history, with Esther perhaps serving as a bridge between the two sets because of its engagement with history (or at least a fictive version of political history) and the themes of vulnerability and gender-based manifestations of influence and authority.

Similarly, the books all explore at some level the topics of public exposure, defenselessness, weakness, danger, and exile, themes that are relevant to personal experiences and particularly to Jewish history but, as we increasingly understand, to many individuals and groups, not all of them Jewish. After all, in early Christian churches Lamentations became a Holy Week reading and liturgical musical experience, projecting mourning for Jerusalem onto mourning for the crucifixion of the Christian savior, and it has remained so across the centuries. One does not have to be Jewish to perceive valor and value in the personal devotional story of Ruth and Naomi or the cannily strategic exercise of political influence by the seemingly passive "good wife" Esther. Verses from Ecclesiastes have entered into popular usage and the common storehouse of proverbial wisdom. Passages and scenes from Song of Songs are deeply embedded in the history of literature and music celebrating both love and nature.

The five books might be viewed as giving different angles of vision on all these recurrent issues and more in life and politics. They are diverse enough, and each is rich enough in itself, to be a treasury for contemplation or discussion. Whether read individually or collectively, with other people or by oneself, once or (better yet) again and again over the years, they repay our attention with gifts of sometimes resonant and sometimes elegantly spare language, profound emotions ranging from despair to exultation, and insights about life that the books communicate either explicitly or obliquely. We can read them for pleasure one at a time in the same way we read all literature. We can absorb them as devotional texts, part of our religious experiences and development. We can study them as literary classics, as cultural icons, and as spiritual guidebooks. We can explore them as a cross-section of an ancient culture's sophisticated, muti-genre literary environment.

In sum, how one organizes one's reading depends on what "story" one wants to make of the texts. This is true even if one decides to claim that there is no "story" aside from the independent artistic expression represented by each of them and that therefore any sequential organization of studying them is arbitrary.

We can also read them solely in translation, if need be, albeit preferably with some well-chosen glances to the Hebrew originals. A translation is not a simple, uninflected carrying-over (*trans-lating*, literally) from the original into our own vernacular. Every translation constitutes an interpretation of the work, expressing its particular meanings through the shading of particular words and the implications of tone.

Some specialists see reading a text in translation as aesthetically and intellectually limiting because a translation is necessarily a "second-hand" version of the original. But the plain meaning of the original language (what is termed in Hebrew *p'shat*) is seldom direct or lacking in nuances and overtones, nor is English (the target language of translation in this case) always well suited to capture precisely the meaning of the Hebrew text. In contrast, if one chooses carefully, one can welcome the translation as another well-informed commentator in the room, a knowledgeable, insightful reader whose stylistic choices might sometimes be misleading (in other words, different from ours), narrow or tendentious, but often cannily helpful in illuminating something essential in the text.

These generalizations include not only modern renditions but also the ones that arose long ago in some Jewish milieu, namely, the Aramaic targumim and the Greek Septuagint, the former intended for Jews whose vernacular language was Aramaic and the latter for Hellenistic Jews in Egypt and elsewhere who primarily spoke and wrote Greek. The

Septuagint became in time a vital textual source of the Christian Old Testament. Grammatical and lexical commentaries along with midrashim (rabbinic homiletic expositions) also come into play, explaining implications of words and phrases. Yet one also must acknowledge that at many places there are obscurities and uncertainties within the Hebrew as well. Often, while studying a passage, any attentive and inquisitive reader might pause, whether in private reading or in discussion, to hover over a verbal or stylistic detail, comparing two or three modern translations as well as targumim and the Septuagint against one's own sometimes different perceptions of the original Hebrew or the presumed sense of the passage and the literary moment. The study thus becomes a conversation not only over the received texts but over the received traditions of interpretation.

It is extremely important to keep in mind some broad dimensions of Jewish scriptural commentaries. In contrast to the emphasis frequently found among Protestants of adhering to the "literal word of the Bible," Jewish readers view the "literal word of the Bible" as inherently in need of explication and the meaning of any passage of Tanakh as requiring interpretation. That is true even for the most traditional and seemingly literal-minded Jewish practitioner. One might encounter a stringently Orthodox Jew who believes, as other religious literalists do, that the world was made in six days as we experience days, that evolution is a blasphemous fiction, and that the world is less than six thousand years old; however, he or she believes that not because the biblical text seems to say it literally but because certain rabbinic interpreters whose authority is not to be questioned presented those ideas as verities many centuries ago.

Jewish readings of texts, therefore, embrace a myriad of interpretive approaches, no one of which negates any other approach, no matter how contradictory. If the resulting interpretations can coexist easily, well and good. If not, they stand as alternatives, each one available for the potential insight that it can offer. The reader looking to understand a given passage in the Tanakh, be it a commandment or law or be it an episode of biography or history, might consult the Talmud or midrash from late antiquity, the mystical kabbalistic tradition exemplified by the Zohar, or any number of subsequent commentaries of such major interpreters as Rashi, ibn Ezra, Maimonides, and Nachmanides and find multiple interpretations offered sequentially, each sometimes introduced by the phrase *davar akher*, literally "another word." These alternatives are on offer paratactically, not hierarchically. That is, they are given as equal to one another in their potential merit.

Studying five diverse, relatively short texts (the widely used Jewish Publication Society bilingual edition of the Megillot that also includes the Yom Kippur special reading, Jonah, is only 121 pages), one might choose to read all of them in the same edition. One can also make a case for selecting a different translation for each work. In this way one experiences a variety of translational styles as well as different approaches to biblical commentary and contextualization. The appendix about texts "For Further Reading" offers remarks on some recommended individual translations and commentaries.

Still, to know and appreciate these books well also means gaining more information about them. For each text discussed in this study, several questions are considered, not necessarily in this order.

What is the canonicity of the text? So far as can be determined, at what point did the book become part of the Tanakh? Was there any controversy about its inclusion? What does Jewish tradition teach about its authorship, date, and place of origin and on what evidence? What are the opinions of modern scholars about these questions, and on what do they base their conjectures?

What are both the fictive and the likely historical contexts? In what era and place is the work ostensibly set? Based on internal evidence such as linguistic and stylistic traits, allusions or other contextual frames of reference, what do modern scholars view as the likely date and place of composition? What are the implications of each of those eras and locations?

How does the work fit a literary context, including genre and stylistics? How does the book resemble other works from early Hebrew, ancient Near Eastern, or Hellenic literature in form, style, or content? Does its vocabulary or formal characteristics show unique or unusual characteristics? In what ways might it be described as "typical" and in what ways singular?

What is the structure of each work? That entails the organization of incidents and shape of the plot where appropriate, the organization of chapters or segments and their relationship to one another, consistency or changes in tone.

How is our understanding deepened and sharpened by literary analyses focusing on characters, plot, drama, language, and other stylistic traits?

What is the work's theological stance? What are the text's religious affirmations, its views of the role of God, chance, fate, reward, and retribution?

How have these topics been explained in traditional commentaries and translations (Christian as well as Jewish), including midrashim and patristic literature?

What is the Jewish liturgical context for each book? Where appropriate, we will also examine uses of the text in Christian liturgy. We will consider the Megillah's relevance to its associated festival, reflecting on its thematic and tonal appropriateness as well as its images or plot. We will see how it is incorporated into the religious ceremony and consider its particular cantillation and musical interpretation. That necessarily entails some explanation of the Hebraic trope system used for biblical texts, a series of traditional para-scriptural symbols that function grammatically much like punctuation marks but are also associated with musical phrases. While Song of Songs, Ecclesiastes, and the Book of Ruth share common musical patterns, the melodies for Esther are unique, as are the two distinctive musical motifs for different parts of Lamentations. These melodic shapings of the oral texts color their moods while also lifting their recitation above the base level of speech yet below the studied artifice of song.

This book does not try to posit that there was originally a meta-structure to the Megillot by attempting to find an overall coherence or logic that is belied by the likely ways in which this canon-within-the-canon developed. The Coda suggests nevertheless an unusual, unexpected common religious dimension that may link them for the modern reader, even though such a shared outlook may never have been intended or discerned by the scribes and sages who originally designated the texts for their festal observances.

Clearly the Book of Esther determines the occasion and even particular features of the festival of Purim; conversely, Lamentations constitutes the biblical commemoration of the events leading to the observance of Tisha b'Av. We might describe the Book of Esther as the cause, the feast of Purim the effect, while the destruction of the Temple is the cause of Tisha b'Av and the Book of Lamentations the effect. For both of these, there is a direct historical bond between the text and the observance, even if we doubt the positivistic factual truth of the Esther story.

By contrast, associations between the other three Megillot and their related festivals were derived homiletically from motifs common to each pairing, rather than through a direct historical relationship, albeit the associations between each text and its festival have a long past that seemingly dates back at least to the late rabbinic period (pre-tenth century).

While we lack explicit information about the genesis of the various connections, their purpose seems to be expanding the liturgical and thematic richness of each holy day through a biblical text in the Ketuvim/Writings that elaborates on the observance's keynotes. Like the extra portion of sacrificial offerings brought to the ancient Tabernacle or Temple on special ceremonial days, these readings supplement and enrich the rites.

Given the heterogeneous nature of the five scrolls, this study of the Megillot ends by arguing that one can accept the inner logic of the liturgical spiral: not exactly a cycle but more like a gyre whereby the turn of each year brings us seemingly back to the same readings but at a different spot in our own lives and the life of the world, looking at the readings from a different angle of vision, or with Heraclitean acceptance that when one steps again into the same river, it is never the same. Qohelet might be right that "there is nothing new under the sun" (1:9). Nonetheless, even the wisest sees only as much as an open door permits. This book seeks to open the door wider.

1

Ecclesiastes/Qohelet

What is the meaning of my life? What have I accomplished? What is the value of what I have done? How long will any of it survive after I am gone?

These questions are likely to gnaw at any thoughtful person, especially one who, reaching the midpoint of a normal lifespan after normal trials and labors, ponders the merit of continuing along the same path for the remainder of the journey. Why not "cash out" and find a vine or fig tree to sit under, or a hut in the wilderness, to enjoy whatever gratifications might come by each day?

Notice that the question "what is the meaning of my life?" is not the same as "what is the meaning of life?" The latter is a philosophical inquiry: given that there might have been no such thing as life in the cosmos, and given the limitations of all life forms in effecting any differences in the workings of the universe, what could be the worth or purpose of living matter?

However, "what is the meaning of my life?" is a spiritual question. It is an inquiry that, so far as science has discerned, is uniquely human. We alone reflect on the matter. No other creature seems to ponder whether its own individual personal existence has particular significance. More profoundly, we may reflect on it alone. Only in rare circumstances might someone else task us to explain the purpose of our own being. It is likely that, if we come to the question at all, it might arise for us when we stir restlessly at some 3 a.m. moment of the soul in an existential wasteland, or perhaps amid an autumnal rumination on the roads not taken and the rift between the aspirations and actualities of our life, or even as we ponder the potsherds left by the once-famous and powerful, like the imperial monument in Shelley's "Ozymandias," lying shattered as desert sands engulf it, and we wonder what if anything of our own life's efforts will outlast the days of mourning when we also pass.

If not despair, depression is likely to wind round us amid such questioning. If neither, then the path before us will require a profoundly challenging expedition. Dante, *"Nel mezzo del cammin di nostra vita"* ("Midway along the path of our life"), finds himself in a murky forest, the path lost, and ahead of him the cave that will lead him down to probe the Inferno. A Hasidic story ascribed to Rabbi Simcha Bunim of Pzhysha (d. 1827) counsels that everyone should carry two pieces of paper, each in a different pocket. Written on one is the talmudic teaching affirming the uniqueness of each person, "the world was created for me" (b. Bavli, Sanhedrin 37b), while on the other is Abraham's abasement before the God whose righteousness he is boldly confronting, "I am but dust and ashes" (Genesis 18:27). If we imagine the pockets in modern clothing, then each of us is in the middle, bounded by these two extremes, perhaps trying to maintain some equilibrium between those extremes. Ideally, we will reach into the pocket with the right message tailored to the moment. Perhaps I need to remember why I should be humble. Perhaps I need to remember why I should value myself.

Yet when we reflect, we see the challenges here to our egos and equanimity. If we are indeed but dust and ashes, then as the morning service in the Jewish prayerbook asks, "what is our life?" But then again, if the world was created for me, what have I done that is worthy of it?

Qohelet—the literary figure and the eponymous book—takes us into such ruminations from the first words of the narration, an exclamation of *"haveil havalim."* The phrase, which is an intensified form of the word *hevel*, has been translated most famously into English as "Vanity of vanities," i.e., the most vain endeavor. The root word denotes "air" or "breath," that which is without valance. While the precise nuance is difficult to capture in English ("useless," "utter futility," "waste," "mist," and "wind" are some other attempts to do so), the sense is clear. So is the mood of the speaker, Qohelet, who immediately repeats it, and yet again flings it forth even more expansively, *"ha-kol havel,"* everything is empty air. "Worthless!" is what the entire verse cries out: *haveil havalim amar Qohelet [says Qohelet] haveil havalim ha-kol haveil*. That word, *havel*, dominates the mood and language of much of this book, which contains more than half (thirty-eight) of the Tanakh's seventy-three instances of it.

But who is Qohelet anyway, and what is this profession of something that sounds very much like personal despair doing in the Bible?

"Thus says Qohelet son of David, king in Jerusalem." So begins the book. And so begins the puzzlement. For "Qohelet" (oddly, a feminine word form, although the patronym clearly states "son of") is widely understood by scholars not as a given name but rather an epithet, sobriquet, or pen-name. What that designation might imply we shall consider shortly. More significant for the work's canonical acceptance is the phrase "son of David, king in Jerusalem," for it is those words that led to the traditional ascription of the book to King Solomon, David's son by Bathsheba and inheritor of his kingdom. Solomon was otherwise proverbial even in the Tanakh for his wisdom. Consequently, this book was conveniently attributed to Solomon as a work of his old age or at least maturity (as for instance b. Gittin 68b and similarly Sanhedrin 20b posit), a sober reflection on life's lessons.

What then of the name Qohelet? The Hebrew root q-h-l signifies "assemble," thus the Septuagint's Greek title, Ecclesiastes. However, if the name implies something like "the assembler," are we to understand that to mean "the one who has assembled perspectives on life's lessons so as to gain wisdom," "the editor-collector-anthologist who assembled these diverse statements from different perspectives," or "the one who assembles the people to teach them wisdom"? All have been proposed, with good reasons; the third is the interpretation offered in the classic rabbinic Midrash Rabbah Qohelet. What is less immediately clear is why Qohelet should on the one hand choose an opaque nickname while on the other hand designating so specific a royal lineage that transparently points to Solomon.

While the midrash claims that Solomon was known for various purposes by seven different names, including Qohelet, we might suspect a dual message signified by the biblical appellation for the author, that the book is not by Solomon but, "Solomon"—in other words, a speaking persona constructed to have a lofty, privileged vantage point on power and triumphs, acquainted with the benefits of prosperity and land ownership, rich also in personal experiences of success's fickleness, and possessing the credible, earned reputation of wisdom. If not really a royal son, in other words, then an intellectual or sage with imagination enough to consider how the world might look to someone with a Solomonic perspective on attainments and disappointments. If the feminine noun ending is significant, it might be intended to place this name in the category of feminine abstract nouns (like *hokhmah*/wisdom, as the *Jewish Study Bible* suggests, or analogously the Greek *Sophia*), thus Qohelet, "The Gatherer."

The Babylonian Talmud tells us (Shabbat 30b) that during the time in the first half of the first century CE when the biblical canon was still in flux, some authorities ("the sages") wanted to exclude this text for having internally contradictory outlooks, for claiming the opposite truths of "this and that." Other talmudic passages (Megillah 7a, Yadayim 3:5, 'Eduyyot 5:3) attest to the controversy over whether it, like the other Megillot, should be regarded as sacredly inspired scripture or merely a compilation of human observations. Those incongruities are exemplified by what appears to be a radical contrast between the opening verse quoted above and the affirmation of divine justice that is pronounced in the work's last verses:

> 12:13 The final word, after all is said and done, is to revere God and keep the commandments, for this applies to everyone.
> 12:14 For God will judge every action, even the hidden, whether it be good or bad.

When the text is recited in the synagogue, verse 13 is repeated following 14 so as to end the reading with hopeful words, rather than threatening ones, the last word of the text being "*ra*," meaning bad or evil, a detail reinforcing the morose impression prevalent in the book. Between the opening and closing testimonies, the unbiased reader could not conclude that there is a clear directional arc leading from one to the other, only disparate and inconsistent sentiments. Thus a reader may be left uncertain as to whether the final commitment to theodicy were not truly a logical conclusion from all that Qohelet has said but merely a fortuitous or conventionally pious resting point for the speaker's diverse impressions.

Still, the sages concluded that the starting and ending points were nonetheless "words of Torah," that is, true religious teachings: to begin with, we find no profit in what we do beneath the sun; to end with, one should revere God and keep God's commandments, for that is every person's duty. The first idea could be considered pious if we assume that its corollary is that we should find value only in timeless rather than temporal attainments. Such an interpretation, which is asserted in the Talmud and in many midrashic commentaries in Qohelet Rabbah, would lead naturally to the text's final words, which affirm that what ultimately matters is to observe the commandments faithfully and to trust in God.

But arriving at consonance between the beginning and the end may require approaching the opening words essentially eisegetically, that is, "reading into" them a meaning that one is predisposed to find. How do we hear (keeping in mind that in Hebrew the word for "hear" can also mean "understand") the book's opening verse? Do we think that "all is worthless" implies only that all secular undertakings are empty of value, or do we think it means that nothing has lasting value?

The latter is the sense picked up by Ernest Hemingway in adopting a phrase from 1:5 as the title for his novel *The Sun Also Rises*. Not for him the optimistic conviction voiced in the midrash claiming that the correct meaning is that on the day when a great person dies, a fitting successor is born or ascends into prominence; for instance, Rebekah's birth is mentioned before Sarah's death and Joshua emerges as a leader while Moses still lives. Rather, as have many others, he finds in Qohelet's words a cycle of unending futility.

Probably the tenuous link between this text and Solomon the "son of David" was persuasive to antiquity for considering this work to be included in the sacred scriptural canon. But on what does the ascription to Solomon really rest? In the Babylonian Talmud (Bava Batra 15a) we find the puzzling claim that Hezekiah and his colleagues "wrote" Isaiah, Proverbs, Song of Songs, and Ecclesiastes, a statement that most likely means they edited or published these texts (i.e., "composed" in the sense of brought into shape), not that they were the original authors, in the way other talmudic passages certainly ascribe the present work along with Proverbs and Song of Songs to Solomon.

Indeed, Jewish tradition follows the assertion in a midrash (Song of Songs Rabbah 1:5) that Solomon wrote those three texts under divine inspiration. The midrashic exploration draws comparisons between various passages in the Psalms, which are traditionally ascribed to his father, King David, and these supposed Solomonic works. Subsequently the discussion questions the order of composition. According to Rabbi Hiyya the Great (an important third-century-CE sage), the compositional order, deduced from some numerical references in the texts, was first Proverbs, then Song of Songs, and lastly Ecclesiastes. Yet a *baraita* (a rabbinic text external to the canon) ascribes to Hiyya a different viewpoint, that all three texts were the product of inspiration late in Solomon's life, and places Ecclesiastes next after Proverbs, making Song of Songs the culminating work.

The mainstream of Jewish tradition, however, has accepted the speculation attributed to Hiyya's disciple Rabbi Jonathan ben Eleazar, naming Song of Songs as the earliest in Solomon's supposed canon, followed by Proverbs, lastly by Ecclesiastes. Revealingly, the midrash posits that "Rabbi Jonathan argues from the way of the world" (Song of Songs Rabbah 1:10). In other words, a young person presumably writes love poems, a mature one offers moralistic advice, and a venerable one speaks about the world's vanities (*haveilim*). These hypotheses show that the conventional ascription of these three works to one author, and specifically to Solomon, was already well established and apparently a matter of some literary interest. They also show that any deductions about their compositional history were based not on factual information but on hypotheses about authorial inspiration and inclinations.

If King Solomon was the author of Qohelet, the book would date from the middle of the tenth century BCE. However, the occurrence of the Persian words *pardes* (grove or garden) and *pitgam* (decree), along with some grammatical features characteristic of later Hebrew, suggests that the earliest date for our text is in the late sixth century BCE, reflecting the expansion of the Persian empire into Judah. And a quotation from the work that appears in the Dead Sea Scrolls means that it existed by the second century BCE. That is an extensive expanse of time, which can provide no useful clues about any "back story" for the book's perspectives on life's experiences. It does, however, free the text from any narrowly based speculations related to the incidents of King Solomon's reign. Unmoored from its romanticized royal attribution, it emerges as a meditative reflection that stands on its own.

It is moreover, along with (for instance) Proverbs and Job, part of an extensive body of so-called wisdom literature that flourished in Egypt, Mesopotamia, and Greece during this period. While the genre remains somewhat amorphous, it is broad enough to encompass such other biblical books as the well-constructed narrative Job and the anthology-like compilation simply called Mishlei/Proverbs. Often these writings contain pragmatic epigrammatic observations such as "A soft reply assuages anger; a sharp word provokes wrath" (Proverbs 15:1) or "One who loves money will never be rich enough" (Qohelet 5:9). Yet moreover, they also contain the sorts of existential challenging of life and theodicy that will attain cantata-like complexity in Job, succinctly and incisively pointed at by Qohelet in such passages as "Surely fruitless [*hevel*] is all that happens on earth for the righteous get what the wicked deserve and the wicked get what the righteous deserve and I say it is fruitless" (8:14). While some of the "wisdom" may express patently reverent theological affirmations of faith in divine justice, much of it, like the passage just quoted, articulates amoral reports of observed experience. In other words, wisdom may reside in seeing beyond the surface of experience in order to affirm eternal convictions of faith, but paradoxically it might just as likely consist in noting, without philosophical or religious preconceptions or predicates, what one deduces from the empirical evidence of an actual lifetime.

The contradictions that the early sages found in the text are in no way reconciled by the book's structure. Though in the form that we have received it Qohelet is divided into twelve chapters, those partitions have no clear structural function that anyone has discerned. Motifs, images, topics, and themes are interwoven throughout, as are the conflicts in the viewpoints of our single narrator. One finds sitting right next to each other such opposing judgments as "All one's days, one eats in darkness with much trouble, sickness, and anger" (5:16) and "This is what I have seen, that it is good and pleasant to eat and drink and get enjoyment from everything that one accomplishes under the sun" (5:17). Qohelet almost taunts us with blatant paradoxes again and again.

The book resists a unified and coherent vision, a syllogistic process of argumentation, or a linear development from an initial perspective to a conclusion. Rather, much like Shakespeare's Gloucester conceding "That's true too" (*King Lear*, V.2.13), Qohelet, ruminating on the experiences of a lifetime, whether as king or commoner, sees that, antithetical though they may be, "this and that" are both true. The guiding standard is empirical observation, not theological conviction. Or perhaps we should say that Qohelet's theological conviction is that observed experience, contradictory though it is, holds the truth about what life is and whatever it means.

The subjectivity of the speaker's viewpoint is never really in doubt, for the prefatory first phrase makes clear that this is one person's account: "The words of Qohelet . . . ." In other words, all that follows (except arguably a concluding passage discussed below) is the opinion of this witness to life. The narrator is the sole "character" of the text, save for the anonymous figures toward whom he vaguely gestures as "straw men" or object lessons in phrases such as "I have seen one who . . . ." These statements are sometimes explicitly phrased in the first person, such as

"I looked around and I saw" (4:1) or "I also observed this" (9:13). More often they are stated as general truths. Some of those truths are based on observation ("I have seen slaves riding on horses" [10:7]) or on personal experience ("When I longed to gain wisdom and see all that happens in the world, I slept neither day nor night" [8:16]). Some look like proverbs, such as "the wind-watcher will never sow nor the cloud-gazer reap" (11:14). Often, we recognize the touch of an epigram-maker or even a poet through the word-play in an adage best appreciated in the original language, for instance, "A good name is better than fine oil" (*tov sheym mi-shemen tov* [7:1]). Many more of them are expressed as universal generalizations, be those colored by the speaker's attitudes or presented as though objectively noted, as for example, "The wise person has eyes in his head and the fool walks in darkness, yet I know indeed that one fate awaits everyone" (2:14).

If this description makes the work sound like a disorganized collection of ramblings and musings, probably that is because it is. In truth, one can argue that this lack of organization and direction validates the speaker's integrity. The candor of Qohelet's observations, which are sometimes but not always reconciled with piety, and the absence of a clear design or motive driving his remarks establish the author's credibility as an honest witness and commonsense reporter of life's vicissitudes, puzzles, often-inscrutable injustices along with frequent affirmations of righteously logical consequences of pious and impious behavior, of wisdom and folly. If we want scriptural validation for a life's fears, doubts, and ambiguities, this text offers it in spades.

The book does not strive or pretend to develop a coherent outlook on life. Rather, like the entries in what a much later era called a "commonplace book," it is a compendium of observations and aphorisms that seem to derive their authority from being *unoriginal*. Odd as this seems in an age such as ours, in which novelty is greatly prized and artisans as well as artists advertise their "signature" contribution, be it a musical style or a cocktail recipe, uniqueness has not always had such a high value. The observations offered by Qohelet ought not strike us as innovative or singular, for a unique insight would not be universal. Qohelet's observations are truisms, even if each one of them offers merely a partial view of truth. The author's goal is not to advance some strikingly new aperçu or exceptional vision of life but to offer an incisively expressed observation that will impress the reader through a sense of recognition, not surprise.

We are not expected to admire the originality of "the assembler," rather, to think: I've seen that also. The writer aims to present, as Alexander Pope wrote in eighteenth-century England, "What oft was thought, but ne'er so well exprest" ("An Essay on Criticism," II, 97).

Qohelet's style, succinct and aphoristic, lends itself to epigrammatic statements. Some of them, being left unexplored and undeveloped, seem to hint cryptically at deeper implications lurking behind opaque metaphors. For instance, chapter 11 opens with the well-known, proverbial "Cast your bread upon the waters for after many days you will find it." The gist seems clear enough: be generous and you will be repaid. But why the strange image of throwing bread onto the water, not to mention the even stranger idea of the bread returning to the sender long after? Indeed, the Aramaic Targum explicates the passage by taking the first phrase almost literally and the second eschatologically: Give to the poor who sail on ships and you will be rewarded in "the world-to-come," a rabbinic phrase that usually means the afterlife. Going further in this direction, Rabbi Bibi as cited in Midrash Qohelet, on 11:1, asserts that "the water" means nothing other than Torah, thus the passage means, bestow charity on Torah scholars. But we might by contrast say that the imagery suggests, to begin with, a reckless abandonment of expectations for rewards; many of us have literally tossed our bread on the water, whether during the Jewish ritual of *tashlikh* on Rosh Hashanah or while feeding ducks on an outing to a lake, watching it become saturated and sinking before being gobbled up, gone for good. Finding it again, in whatever way, is a leap into the miraculous.

This is not the Torah's language of commandments (*mitzvot*). It is closer to the prophets' intense awareness of the pressing reality of our material lives. Indeed, it can even remind us of the way that prophets in an earlier era (ca. eighth century BCE) posed moral perceptions in terms of tangible goods and physical comforts, such as Micah's vision of contemporary misery ("like the leftovers after a fig harvest or the grapes have been picked" [7:1]) or the happy time he envisions when each one shall sit "under his grape vine or fig tree" (4:4), unafraid.

The crucial difference of course is that unlike the prophets, Qohelet's rich experience of material comfort is not moored to ethical and moral certainties, much less to a comforting conviction about theodicy. No wonder that Heinrich Graetz, the preeminent nineteenth-century German Jewish historian, lauded this book to Karl Marx, praising its author's commitment to a realistic sense of the world we live in rather than a hypothetical dimension somewhere beyond the physical plane. It is unarguably true that Qohelet is rooted in this world, and the wealth acquired through that is the storehouse of postulates and axioms the speaker gives over to us.

Being so connected to the material world, Qohelet moves—and moves unpredictably—between the literal and metaphorical, between the prose and the poetry of living, even while depicting in the final chapter the onset of decrepitude in old age, "when the guardians of the house shake and the strong men bend and the few remaining grinders cease working and they that peer through the windows become dim" (12:3). This allegorical depiction of failing physical faculties retains precise connections to the social world while also pointing toward disintegrating personal powers. Subsequent passages evoke a person's physical collapse while the images, whose specific denotative correspondence may be disputed (does he mean this organ or that?), attest to the beauty and preciousness of our corporeal natures: "Before the silver cord snaps and the golden bowl shatters, the pitcher is smashed at the spring and the wheel disintegrates at the well" (12:6). Choosing "the golden bowl" for the title of one of his greatest novels, and this verse for its epigraph, Henry James grasped that Qohelet's apprehension of death leads him to evoke the poignant, vulnerable loveliness of the human being as a created work, veritably an object of both art and craft.

It is also true that, not all the time but some—perhaps much—of the time, Qohelet deems the "other world" to be "doubtful." At least it appears so in regard to the customary albeit later theological construct that posits an afterworld as the location where divine justice becomes actual. That is, Qohelet overtly professes the belief that there is an *olam ha-ba*, but it is assuredly not a place for reward or punishment. "Everything that you can do, do it with all your strength because there is no action, reasoning, knowledge or wisdom in She'ol, where you are going" (9:10; he makes a similar point in 6:6).

The "other-world" place to which everyone goes after death is not a gratifying land of heart's content, a tormenting environment of divine retribution, or a realm for spiritual purification and transformation. It is not paradise, hell, or purgatory. In fact, as Qohelet imagines She'ol here and as Jewish texts of the late biblical period typically depict it (1 Samuel 28, for instance), it is an underground region analogous to the Greek Hades, or perhaps we might understand it in modern terms as a depressive condition of our post-death being, whose purpose is hard to discern except if we suppose it to be a holding zone for our bodies and souls to wait in a kind of suspended state, perhaps until some possible later time when the dead may be resurrected.

This attitude toward an afterlife suits well the book's depiction of consequences and recompenses. If "there is no eternal remembrance of the wise or the fool . . . but they die alike" (2:16) and if all of life is nothing other than "*hevel* and chasing the wind" (2:17), it seems reasonable that all alike descend to a common fate. Indeed, Qohelet speculates that both human beings and beasts will have the same destiny: "All go to the same place, all come from dust and all return to dust" (3:20). Or if we admit to uncertainty, "Who knows whether the human spirit ascends above or the spirit of animals descends to the earth?" (3:21). To a pious medieval Jewish commentator such as the major eleventh-century French rabbi known by the acronym "Rashi" (Rabbi Shlomo ben Yitzhak), the notion that there might be no distinction between human beings and beasts was simply unacceptable, therefore he argues that here Qohelet is representing a temporal perspective on the world of appearances, whereas after death human beings (unlike other creatures) are accountable before the heavenly court. By contrast, Abraham ibn Ezra, his younger contemporary in Spain, laconically notes only that Qohelet's opinion expresses the viewpoint of those who do not believe in a "world to come." (Both of these are cited in Kravitz and Orlinsky's edition and commentary, 30.)

The sense of life balanced on an edge comes through in one of the book's most famous passages, the opening of the third chapter, familiarly known through the song "Turn, Turn, Turn," asserting that "for everything there is a season," that is, an apt moment. This section is frequently quoted in funeral or memorial services as a way of encouraging the mourners to recognize that transitoriness is part of life, thus to accept that death also comes in its own time. In Hebrew, verses 4 and 5 are built on internal rhymes, assonance, and alliteration that cannot easily be replicated in English:

> 3:4 A time to weep and a time to laugh, a time to mourn and a time to dance.
> *eyt livkoht v'eyt lish-chohk eyt sifohd v'eyt r'kohd:*

> 3:5 A time to throw stones and a time to gather stones, a time to embrace and a time to refrain from embracing.

> *eyt l'hash-lich avaneem v'eyt k'nohs avaneem*
> *eyt la-chavohk v'eyt li-rachohk meychabeyk.*

In addition to making these epigrams more immediately memorable, the verbal echoes hint that each antithesis shows the opposing faces of one coin, as if only fortune or the will of an unknowable higher power determines which side lands facing up. Time spins but "chance falls alike on all" (9:11).

If that were all, or if Qohelet's vision of existence were dominated by a great wheel turned arbitrarily by the hand of fortune, we could say confidently that we understood the poem's moral vision, even if we found it wrong or rueful. However, he also offers countervailing assertions that a just God is in control of what happens to us eventually. Yet even as he does so, the speaker does not organize his testimony so that we move in a clear direction from one viewpoint to the other, for instance from the perspective that life seems incoherent and amoral to a clearly formulated affirmation of theodicy. True, that is where the book ends up, but the process of getting there is through fits and starts during which the observations of amorality and even moral injustices accumulate, interspersed with glimmers of conventional religious faith or at least belief in practical acumen tested by experience.

So, for instance, Qohelet notes, "A sinner may do evil a hundred times while punishment is delayed, though I know fully that it will go well with those who are in awe of God because they revere God" (8:12). Pausing a moment to ponder this axiom, we can notice its imbalance. We might expect the first observation ("while punishment is delayed") to be answered by a resounding affirmation that retribution will eventually be delivered. Instead, the second clause vectors in a different direction: the good will be rewarded. While the idea that the punishment is only deferred implies that it will come eventually, we may find it difficult to balance that proposition with the persistent sinner's many ("hundred") evil deeds committed in the face of divine punishment that is suspended. And though it is pointless to question why it should be suspended, that being God's will, we are certainly likely to question the justice of letting the evil-doing persist despite all the harm that does. All the more so when, just two verses later, Qohelet seems to rethink the evidence: "the righteous get what those who do evil deserve and evil-doers get what the righteous deserve—I said that this also is *hevel*" (8:14).

The shifting, ambiguous perspectives of Qohelet have proven both inviting and yet problematic for Jewish commentators through the ages. The richest commentaries are Jewish because the book has been extensively discussed in the Jewish interpretive tradition, while Christian biblical commentary has not paid it similar close attention, more often dipping into the text to extract some well-turned observational nugget or sparkling phrase, of which there are many.

The inviting quality, which comes from the enigmatic nature of many of the book's affirmations, is exemplified by Midrash Qohelet, a collection of homiletic interpretations dated from between the sixth and eighth centuries CE. To take just one instance, "All the rivers run into the sea, yet the sea is not full" (1:7) receives at least eight distinct interpretations, some given in detail with multiple examples. They include the most obvious literal explanation: rivers flow into the ocean but the ocean still can hold more. How that can be so is the topic of various analogies. Other explanations offer religious readings such as "All the dead enter She'ol but . . ." or "All Israel gathers in Jerusalem but . . . ." Yet still other readings approach the image as a metaphor of secular wisdom. For instance, one contends it means that all of a person's wisdom flows to the heart but the heart is never filled. That interpretation continues to take account of the rest of the verse, observing that the rivers (or wisdom) will flow back again to the source; in other words, whatever wisdom one imparts will come back to replenish the teacher.

Another provocative instance of the work's deep ambiguities occurs at the beginning of chapter 12, the last book, which begins with Qohelet urging, "remember your *boreh* in the days of your youth, before the bad times come." But what does *boreh* mean? The answer is complicated both by context and by Hebrew's standard lack of vowel indicators. One can justifiably agree with Rashi and many others that it means "Creator," which is the most likely seeming biblical word. A number of modern scholars opt instead for "vigor" or "well-being," perceiving here a word often used in that sense, especially in post-biblical texts such as the Talmud and also viable in context, albeit with quite a different import. To deepen the perplexity, yet another possible meaning is "pit" or "well," which can imply the grave or even the source of conception and procreation. Clearly the third option resonates with the book's passages of despondency and disgust. One can even accept them all as being pertinent, this one word containing a grim summary of life's three stages: the first-century-CE sage Akabia ben Mahalalel (according to a later talmudic authority) understood *borecha* as teaching every human being to remember that "you come from a fetid drop, are destined for a place of dust and worms and maggots, and will have to stand judgment and accounting before the Sovereign of Sovereigns, the Holy One, blessed be" (Qohelet Rabbah 12:1).

Dealing with such problematic dimensions of interpreting the text's nuances is illustrated by the approach of the major work of Jewish mysticism known as Kabbalah. The Zohar, dating probably from the thirteenth century CE, is troubled by Qohelet's *hevel*. How could wise Solomon say that all was emptiness, given that, according to Kabbalistic principles, the seven names ascribed to Solomon must correspond to the seven spheres (*sephirot*) of divine influence that animate the world physically and spiritually? Since Solomon possessed all of those names, he must have possessed all seven levels that would enable him to comprehend the divine will. Further, his three books each reflect principal components in understanding the divine, whereby Song of Songs represents love, Proverbs mercy, and Qohelet judgment. Surely he could not have simply dismissed all that exists as vain and hollow.

Rather, the Zohar claims, *hevel* here means "breath," a mixture of air and moisture. Figuratively, each of the seven spheres or foundational principles emanates a breath of influence; consequently, all that Qohelet (or Solomon, according to the Zohar) perceives happens according to whether the breath of judgment, love, or mercy predominates. Our perceptions remain subjective; only the truly wise can understand that there is one divine cohesive force, i.e., God, with deep knowledge of that which is hidden in everything and everyone, and with foreknowledge of all possibilities. God makes decisions, albeit unseen, through the various *sephirot* that are animated by the *ruakh elohim*, the breath of God that moved across the face of the waters at the beginning of creation (Genesis 1:2). Knowing the secret of what any person intends, might do, or feels inwardly, God grants or withholds favor or punishment for reasons that we are unable to penetrate by our limited human capacities. Thus the Zohar rescues the orthodoxy of Qohelet by insisting on both a restrictive definition and an esoteric explanation of the book's most crucial term.

Toward the end of the book we are likely to be surprised and perhaps not a little amused, especially if we ourselves are writers, by these admonitory words: "To say further, my child, be careful: Of making books, there is no end and too much study exhausts the flesh" (12:12). Ibn Ezra reads this as prudent advice, a warning that books are ephemeral objects and even their ideas do not last forever. Qohelet Rabbah, however, reinterprets the first word of the verse as *mehumah* ("confusion") rather than *mehemah* ("further"), thus allowing it to posit this as a warning to adhere to the accepted biblical canon of twenty-four books and not to sow confusion by admitting others, for example, the explicitly mentioned Wisdom of ben Sira (also known as Ecclesiasticus, second century BCE). Those apocryphal texts must remain outside even when, as in the case of Ecclesiasticus, they resemble the style and substance of canonical works.

We see that the dialectic within Qohelet between religious faith and experience-based skepticism or pragmatism is replicated by its commentators. To most modern scholars, as well as some earlier ones such as the twelfth-century commentator known as Rashbam (Rabbi Shlomo ben Meir), Qohelet's share of his eponymous book ends at 12:8. The remaining six verses, along with the incipit "Thus says Qohelet son of David, king in Jerusalem," they deem to be those of an editor framing the text. That would mean that Qohelet's life testimony concludes exactly where it began, the repetition in 12:8 of the book's second verse, *haveil havalim amar Qohelet haveil havalim ha-kol haveil*: sheer vapor—all of it is nothing but sheer vapor.

What follows immediately after that is a retrospective affirmation of the author's meritorious intentions, worded in the grammatical third-person, as if by another speaker or editor, or perhaps (according to a prevalent traditional view) Qohelet making a case for himself. "Let me add, Qohelet was wise and moreover taught the people knowledge while probing and compiling many adages" (12:9). If we understand the last six verses as editorial additions, then we will also perceive the work's culminating affirmations of faith in divine justice and the intrinsic value of following the commandments as also the opinion of someone other than Qohelet. Might these be an editor's conclusions, that since everything that we ourselves do in our evanescent life is often ineffectual and always transitory, therefore we can find value only through religious life and faith? Or might this be instead the final tip of the coin that, having been balanced precariously between faith and skepticism throughout, the book at last lands with the faith-side up? Either way, dissociating the perspective of these final verses from Qohelet's last *haveil havalim* means that his own conclusion takes him and us as readers precisely back to where he began, except now with accumulated evidence to brood over.

That is the viewpoint eloquently set forth in what is probably the most significant work of art based on Qohelet, the cello concerto entitled *Schelomo* (i.e., Sh'lomo, or Solomon), a "Hebraic rhapsody" composed in Geneva by the Jewish-born Swiss-American composer Ernest Bloch between late 1915 and early 1916 in the midst of World War I. He acknowledged in performance program notes being profoundly disturbed by the war as well as having been haunted for many years by the text of Ecclesiastes, which he knew better in French, German, and English than in Hebrew. Describing the cello as the voice of Solomon, "a meditative voice, tragically alone," Bloch weaves cantorially inflected melodic ruminations using Jewish and Jewish-sounding musical motifs against an orchestral texture that swirls, pulsates, or thunders. At times the cello sings in higher registers before dipping down suddenly two or three octaves to low grumbles; then again it sometimes dances, not light-heartedly but passionately; other times it protests and asserts itself defiantly. Still, the work begins as well as ends, and is pervaded throughout, with melancholy, by sadness that can still be beautiful as well as depressive, as Bloch profoundly makes real in the finale, which takes the cello down into its brooding lowest register where, exposed by a simplified orchestral texture, it seems even more alone and vulnerable than ever. The arc of the work's mood, as the composer himself expressed it, is established by the twin verses of *Qohelet* 1:2 and 12:8, which Bloch also knew in the familiar English wording, "Vanity of vanities, all is vanity." He attested that "this is my only work that culminates in a total negation—but the subject demanded it."

It certainly was not nihilism that moved the sages of old to canonize Qohelet and moreover eventually to make it a designated reading for the major fall pilgrimage festival of Sukkot, known in English as the Feast of Booths or Tabernacles. A week-long biblically mandated observance, Sukkot is referred to by many biblical and talmudic appellations, one of which is incorporated into all the liturgical references to it: *zeman simchateinu*, "the time of rejoicing" (deriving the predicate from Deuteronomy 16:14). Obviously the tradition warmly embraced those concluding verses of Qohelet because only an interpretation that sees the text as affirming God's law and justice could possibly harmonize with rejoicing. Their interpretation will not accept "a total negation." Though they may not deny the truth of *haveil havalim*, they will not grant it the final word, even from Shlomo.

What was it about this festival that led rabbis centuries ago to assign to it this work, of all the possible choices among the Prophets and Writings in the Tanakh? And what is it about the book that makes it suitable for Sukkot?

To begin with, Sukkot was one of three pilgrimage festivals when the Temple stood in Jerusalem, Passover and Shavuot/Feast of Weeks/Pentecost being the others. It celebrates the final harvest of the year. Indeed, another name for the holiday is *Chag ha-asif*, the Festival of the Ingathering. Coming two weeks after Rosh Hashanah (the New Year) and four days after Yom Kippur (the Day of Atonement), it also concludes the autumnal liturgical season, which formally ends with Shemini Atzeret, the biblical Assembly of the Eighth Day (i.e., the day after Sukkot ends). Consequently, it is observed in late September or October (depending on the Jewish calendar year), a period appropriate for one to reflect and sum up while one considers the gains as well as disappointments of the year's ingathering. Qohelet's contemplations seem especially apt during this time, matching the fruits of the harvest with a retrospective accounting of a lifetime of harvested experience and wisdom.

"Sukkot" is the plural form of "sukkah," meaning hut or shed. The word "sukkot" is frequently translated as "booths," which simply seems peculiar or misleading in our time, or "tabernacles," which sounds far more grandiose than sukkahs are intended to be. (We might keep in mind that in Genesis 23:17 Jacob builds a house for himself and *sukkot* for his animals.) The sukkah is a temporary shelter meant to evoke those the Israelites dwelt in during the Exodus (Leviticus 23:43) and subsequently the temporary shelters in which they dwelt during harvest time in the land of Israel (as implied in Deuteronomy 16:13).

Nehemiah 8:15, describing the revival of the festival after some of the exiles return to Jerusalem from Babylonia, makes clear the provisional ad hoc character of the construction devised from whatever suitably sturdy branches might be obtained locally. The Talmud devotes a tractate (essentially, a volume) to the topic of Sukkah, more than half of it dealing with the laws concerning the sukkah itself, the other part to the festival's other symbolic appurtenances, notably the Four Species, viz. a palm branch, three myrtle boughs and two willow branches (known collectively as the *lulav*, which means the palm), and an *etrog* (citron).

While the sukkah cannot be a permanent structure, the most important element attesting to its impermanence has to be the roof, assembled so that it is not a solid covering but one topped by greenery or other naturally grown vegetative matter through which the stars can be seen by night and indeed through which rain may seep. If the roof is too well-made, like that of a permanent cabin, it is invalid. The sukkah, in short, exemplifies evanescence. Here today newly constructed, it will be gone in a week. Not only that, but its transient nature means that it can be shaken by the winds of autumn; sukkahs sometimes topple in a windstorm or even, in some areas, collapse under the weight of an early October wet snow never imagined by the erstwhile Sinai-dwellers whose experiences shaped the observance. Seeping rain or chilly temperatures might drive inside the faithful observers attempting to satisfy the commandment of "dwelling" in their hut by eating a meal there. Or else the days and nights might be gorgeous, like the last blossoming of a late false summer, enticing celebrants not just to snack but dine under the minimal coverage afforded by the sukkah's roof, and even to linger and sleep there, glimpsing through the permeable covering the canopy of stars and, on the first night of Sukkot, the full moon.

In short, it suits the testimony and temperament of Qohelet. It acknowledges the transitory nature of life and our vulnerability to change, felt all the more keenly because the festival occurs at a season of change marking not only the end of the annual harvest but also the approach of winter's blasts that might carry so much, and so many, away. Autumn intimates precariousness. Has this year's harvest been good? Will it be enough to get us through autumn's rough times and the challenges of the winter months, which will bring cold, rain, and perhaps snow even to Jerusalem? We may feel uncertain, apprehensive. The sun's setting, now earlier in the day, can move us to gloomy thoughts and emotions as the darkness arriving too soon seems to herald life's inevitable end, a *memento mori* inherent in nature's design. Yet while Qohelet's morbid musings have their place here in the sukkah, so do his encouragements to enjoy life, such as "Go, eat your bread happily, with a light heart, drink your wine, for God has already approved what you have done" (9:7). Therefore Sukkot is also a time for chanting the Hallel, the psalms of praise (numbered 113 through 118), their keynote being "Give thanks to God, for God is good and God's love is everlasting" (Psalm 118:1).

If Qohelet is "the assembler" or compiler, we can find an analogy in Sukkot's other characteristic symbol, the bundled lulav and etrog, a multiplicity of four items or "species" brought together as one unified expression of divine generosity. The palm, myrtle, willow, and citron constitute Jewish tradition's interpretation of Leviticus 23:40, the commandment to gather "boughs of goodly trees, branches of palm trees, boughs of thick trees, and willows of the brook" to "rejoice before the Lord your God seven days." The method of rejoicing each weekday morning during the festival is to bring together the lulav bundle in one hand, the etrog in the other and, with arms extended, "wave" or shake toward each of the four cardinal directions as well as upward toward the sky and downward from the earth, preferably pulling the items toward oneself, while chanting prescribed Hallel verses. In this way one symbolically acknowledges divine creative energy all around as the waver mimes drawing it inward.

Characteristically, the early sages found diverse homiletic symbolism in the individual elements of the so-called Four Species, positing meanings that are still offered in our time. In one interpretation, the palm, myrtle, and willow respectively resemble the human spine, eyes, and lips, while the etrog suggests the shape and size of the heart, thus reminding us to use our faculties, indeed our entire being, in ways respectful to divine laws. Another expresses the significance of unity in diversity, for each species can represent a different sort of person, all being brought together in one assemblage, like a community that could not fulfill its function if one of the elements were missing. As *Qohelet* exemplifies, life's complex variety demands recognition.

The multiplicity of viewpoints in Qohelet seems appropriately hinted at by the diversity of traits embodied in Sukkot's physical symbols and rituals. Thus, on the Sabbath during Sukkot (or, in some practices, on Shemini Atzeret, the eighth-day observance that concludes the festival period), this is the additional text to be read. Traditional congregations will do so by chanting the book, using the same cantillation melodies as are applied to Song of Songs and Ruth. In modern times many synagogues read only a few brief selections, while traditional congregations that might recite the entire text are not likely to devote time to studying it critically. This is unfortunate. Just as Sukkot is more than only an evocation of ancient ways of living or a memorial of a deep historical past, Qohelet is more than Solomonic reflections on life.

Sukkot encourages us to contemplate fragility and impermanence, which not only characterize our literal shelters but all aspects of our lives. We have seen well-built towers, massive and tall, constructed of modern materials, crumble in dust and flames. Homes and businesses are shattered and washed away by surging flood waters or turned to ash by wild infernos; a churning tornado splinters these buildings, a spewing volcano engulfs those, an earthquake undermines a superhighway, and a hurricane devastates scores of villages. A sudden illness, an accident, a shooting, an assault by terrorists, whatever it might be, destroys livelihoods or lives.

In their destruction we sense, as Qohelet would, the vanity of our certainties. It is not only the buildings that disappear, and the people who inhabited them, but futures. Hopes and plans are obliterated. Gone will be our assumption that today we can anticipate tomorrow or even that we know what beliefs to rely on or what dangers to worry about. We desire and build, make commitments and plans, but (we may think, and perhaps shock ourselves for so thinking) it is all vanity of vanities, hollow, empty air. Also gone is the joy of living. "Every day is painful and burdened with misery; even at night there is no relief for the heart" (2:23). We know people who feel this way, burdened night and day by fear, suffering, and palpable loss, grief untouchable by any succor we can offer.

In the face of evanescent achievements or evaporated hopes and joys, we might conclude, as Qohelet often does, that the sensible approach to life is *carpe diem*, as the Roman poet Horace wrote: "seize the day." To live in and for the satisfactions of the moment is an understandable response when one contemplates the worthless evanescence of much if not all of what we do, or the failures of our worthiest ambitions. "So I saw that there is nothing better for a person than to be happy in what you do, because who knows what comes next?" (3:22). After all, "if you live many years, enjoy them, for remember that the dark days will be many and everything that follows is *haveil*" (11:8). Consequently, he observes that "it is good and pleasant to eat and drink and enjoy the pleasure from all that one does under heaven" (5:17), to wear freshly washed clothes and be anointed with fragrant oil (9:8). Despite Rashi's devout interpretation of such passages as referring to the praise of Torah study, worthy deeds, and the value of a good name, the book has a strong undercurrent of appreciation for the value of quotidian worldly pleasures. "Enjoy life with someone you love all the passing days of existence under the sun that have been given to you" (9:9).

More than a dozen times Qohelet explicitly attests, "I have seen." He values the empirical perspective of first-hand experience and personal observation. Once he has seen, he is also likely to examine, search, and finally say what he concludes "in my heart" or "to myself." Qohelet speaks honestly to us because he derives his advice more often from his own experience than from traditionally transmitted established ideas, much less from biblical precedents or commandments. The author articulates some principles of religious faith but, unlike the books of the prophets, this is not a text from which words of Torah flow.

Therein we find its daring and its value. Qohelet's doubts, skepticism, materialism, even the grudging tone of his professions of faith take us to, maybe even beyond, the bounds that people of religious faith, including members of the clergy, feel able to express even when they experience them. What honest, self-reflective person has not felt at some time in life that nothing they do really matters? Or that all of their attainments are hollow? That their greatest achievements are transitory? That they have spent their lives in vain pursuit of the wrong goals, or perhaps just as bad, in successful pursuit of the wrong goals? That the wicked flourish and the good suffer, or that the good and evil fare indiscriminately? That one's own efforts go unrewarded while others revel in undeserved success? That there is no tangible reward for virtue? That our own life feels as if it is flying by too quickly or that day after day drags on interminably? That there may be no reward or punishment either in this realm or in an afterlife because there is no afterlife, or if there is one, it is like nothingness? That if we are sensible, we ought to eat and drink and be merry while we can because when this life ends, so ends anything that can give us pleasure.

Regardless of their motives, the sages who preserved and canonized Qohelet admitted into sacred scripture a book that voices these thoughts and, by so doing, allows anyone to find a voice for their own observations, including many that a pious person might think are forbidden. Some religious people, nagged by misgivings and disillusionment in life, may feel guilty about the seemingly impoverished state of their faith; some others might struggle with feeling selfish or embarrassed for desiring above all the nourishing personal comforts of love, good food, and soothing drink. In this biblical book the reflective reader or wise counselor can find the words and viewpoints that can make it a needed guidebook for life, a handbook of living offering companionship along the way, a canonical biblical expression of everyone's spiritual insecurities and religious uncertainties.

Deriving reassurance from Qohelet's professions of trust in God may require what might be called reading against the grain of the text. We know how prevalent are the writer's expressions of skepticism and disgust, frequently interwoven with praise of materialistic comforts as the principal compensation for life's unfairness or disappointments. That, as Graetz and Bloch conclude, is the overall gist of the work's teachings. And who would call them wrong? True, Qohelet sometimes affirms belief in God's overall power and ultimate justice. However, that is the most that this speaker's acknowledgments of God allows.

We are far from the personal God we remember from the Tanakh promising, reassuring, inspiring, and comforting the patriarchs, matriarchs, and prophets. Certainly, there is no allusion to the conviction, so prevalent in other biblical books, that God has any providential concern for particular individuals or even for *am yisrael*, the "people Israel," whether scolding and goading them or sustaining and encouraging them. Isaiah's God remembers "Abraham, my friend." One cannot conceive of that from Qohelet's God. It is hard to imagine addressing Qohelet's God as *tzur yisrael eli v'go'ali*, "rock of Israel, my God and my redeemer" (Isaiah 41:8). Indeed, it is hard to imagine addressing this God at all.

Qohelet might not be the antithesis of Job but he sits radically apart from that beleaguered biblical character. For Job's miseries are monumental, arising from catastrophes that outweigh all of his previous successes; Job is the superhero of suffering, a figure who might teeter on the edge of tragedy except that his disasters are not of his own making, a man who loses all when his only fault is to believe that all he has is truly his own. His *hubris* is not that of over-reaching but over-confidence. Unlike Qohelet, he is not aware that the ground he walks on is unstable, ready in the blink of an eye to open beneath him so that he falls into an abyss. He is a special test case.

Qohelet's griefs are ours. They are the disappointments, bitterness, and feeling of futility that might affect any human being. If he looks toward the end of his life resignedly affirming a religious belief, it is not because he has confronted God and received the ultimate lesson in mortal humility but because he believes that no lesson is forthcoming, only incontrovertible facts and mysteries. He does not demand answers from God. Perhaps that is why he is spared the conclusion of Job that some of us might deem cynical, specifically, the miraculous restoration of his fortunes, as if all that went before were somehow a fantasy or nightmare from which he is awakened to find his good life restored by a *deus ex machina*, as if a new brood of children could wipe from the record the loss of all his others.

The name by which Qohelet refers to God is not the Tetragrammaton, the four-letter sacred name usually transcribed in English as YHVH (corresponding to the Hebrew letters *yud-hey-vav-hey*), which appears first in Genesis 2:4. Rather, it is Elohim, the name by which God is called in Genesis 1 and elsewhere. Many textual scholars believe these two appellations reflect different source traditions, termed Yahwist and Elohist, that were combined at some early stage in the editing of the Torah. The traditional rabbinic interpretation, however, is that YHVH expresses the aspect of God that most closely relates to human beings, as we see for example in the confrontation with Adam and Eve, the promises to Abraham, the exodus story, and the commandments to Moses. "Elohim" designates that facet of God that designs and governs the cosmos.

Regarding the proper human attitude toward both, the Tanakh often uses words from the verb root *yira* (*yud-resh-aleph*), conventionally translated as "fear," as in "fear of God." I have translated it above as "revere," one of the word's other meanings, choosing not to restrict the concept of God to a primarily punitive fear-instilling role. The two concepts are closely related because reverence may be accompanied by an apt sense of awe that can be felt as fearfulness. For instance, confronting the thundering, massive downrush of a mighty waterfall, we might well be moved with inner terror along with wonderment. So Qohelet tells the reader to be in awe of this God that does not seem engaged in intimate conversation with us (the YHVH expression of God) but can be sensed rather as God-Elohim, responsible for the confoundingly inscrutable yet incontestable laws of the universe, the God of ultimate judgment that seems distant and holds an often-impenetrable principle of justice.

Yet, the author tells us, this God is there—somehow there and decisive. God has the final word. Perhaps Qohelet, taken as a whole from the first verse to the last, validates a God for those who cannot believe what they have been told about God, or at least about life in a divinely ordered world. For that life might not make sense and it is rarely comprehensible, frequently cruel, and often unjust, and it always ends in grief because it always ends in someone's death. Still, there are, as Shakespeare also reminds us, "cakes and ale" (*Twelfth Night*, II.3.58) and, as Qohelet knows, the delight of sharing life with someone you love (9:9).

In this book God is the context and the coherence that contains it all, the deep structure that contains everything. Like the wall on which a fresco is painted, and on which it will fade, God is the deep background that holds everything that is transitory; but perhaps unlike the wall, God is invisibly active, giving judgments in ways we cannot see or comprehend.

So this representation posits that God is not simply the dispassionately systematic "prime mover" but does have an ethical dimension as well as a concern for whether we do good or ill. If Qohelet affirms God to us, it is God for a world that seems devoid of God.

2

Book of Esther

Without the Book of Esther, there is no Purim. While the other four Megillot enrich their respective holy days, they are ancillary to the day's obligatory observances; even the Ninth of Av could be commemorated without Lamentations. In contrast, Esther is the substance of Purim. The festival exists not only because of this story but because the text itself contains the statutory requirement that the day be observed by Jews in all places and times thereafter. The narrative further implies crucial features of Purim's observance by describing the communal acts of generosity with which the victorious Jews in the story celebrated their deliverance, practices that continue today. Moreover, the reading of Megillat Esther, the Scroll of Esther, is the very core, the *sine qua non*, of the day's liturgy, and of all the texts collected under the term *megillah*, this one alone is still commonly referred to simply as "the megillah."

While the originally disputed but eventual canonical acceptance of the Book of Esther validates it as divinely inspired, it is, as noted before, one of only two biblical books (along with Song of Songs) that never directly mentions God. Paradoxically, this leads to two contradictory interpretations of divine participation in the action. One, naturally, is the inference that there is none, making the entire tale one of human negotiations and strategies. The other, nudged by the seeming connection between the name "Esther" and the Hebrew word *nistar* ("concealed"), along with the providential rescue of the Jewish populace from annihilation, presumes that God is omnipresent albeit hidden throughout the story, manipulating characters and the action to work wonders unseen.

Depending on one's view of the tale, God is therefore either completely absent or completely present. In Megillat Esther, God is like Schrödinger's cat, at once there and not there.

The story begins with a louche tale of lavish and lengthy parties that Ahashverosh (or Ahashuerus, as his name is sometimes transliterated), the king of the Persians and Medes, hosts, first for his officials and then for all the residents of the capital, Shushan, regardless of rank. At the height of the intoxicated revelries, the king sends for his wife, Vashti, to display herself for the guests. When she refuses, his advisors counsel him to depose her, which he does. Subsequently, when he apparently reminisces and regrets her removal (whether through death or exile is not explicit), he is advised to hold a beauty contest to replace her. Once again he consents. A Jewish exile from Jerusalem named Mordecai places his adopted daughter, originally named Hadassah but now called by the Persian name of Esther, among the contestants, although keeping her Jewish origin a secret. During her preparation time in the spa-like environment of the harem, Mordecai paces outside, attentive to news of how she is faring. The king selects her, crowning her as queen and grandly offering yet another banquet, distributing gifts and remitting taxes. At this point the story resembles a short fairy tale with a happy ending.

At the end of the second chapter, however, the narrator inserts a brief account of Mordecai overhearing two of the king's bodyguards, named Bigthan and Teresh, conspiring to assassinate the monarch. This juncture also illustrates the text's enigmatic quality, sometimes overloading us with information such as the names of courtiers we never again hear of and other times leaving in doubt the significance of a detail that becomes substantial to the aggadic characteristics of midrash.

"In those days as Mordecai sat at the king's gate . . ." (2:21). The remark seems innocuous, albeit peculiar upon reflection. What was he doing there? In the Torah the city gate was a place for dispensing justice. Perhaps under the influence of that idea, the Aramaic translation called Targum Rishon, spinning a hypothesis from a talmudic assertion, posits that Mordecai was attending a gathering of the Sanhedrin that Esther had established for him. Thus the targum anachronistically projects into this much earlier era and in the Persian diaspora a legal institution that seems to have arisen in the much later era of the Second Temple. According to this interpretation, the guards plotted against the queen first because they resented being supplanted by Mordecai. Rabbinic tradition held that the two plotters were "Tarseans" who did not know that Mordecai, as a member of the Sanhedrin, understood seventy languages, including their own. But Adele Berlin in the *New Jewish Study Bible* (2nd ed.) asserts a different hypothesis about the gate: "More than a physical location, this is Mordecai's official position at court. Mordecai is a member of the king's 'secret police,' official spies who protected the king" (1625). To the neutral reader, it is sheer happenstance or perhaps divine will that puts Mordecai where he needs to be so as to overhear the critical information. To the Targum and the *NJSB*, he was simply doing his job, though they differ in their suppositions about that job.

Informing Esther, who reveals the plot to her husband, Mordecai saves the life of the king; the monarch executes the schemers and has the incident recorded in the royal chronicle. Though it seems to be merely a passing anecdote, this prepares for another significant turning point. It also underscores, like the peremptory dismissal and disappearance of Vashti, the underlying propinquity of sudden violence associated with the court.

We may see it also as preparing for the next development of the plot at the beginning of chapter 3, the king's sudden promotion to prime minister of a newly introduced character, Haman the Agagite, a proud and ruthlessly ambitious man. For personal and historical reasons, Haman and Mordecai are implacable enemies. When Mordecai refuses to bow to Haman and the latter discovers that his antagonist is a Jew, he has the lot (or *pur*) cast, determining that the thirteenth day of Adar (which is the twelfth month) would be the propitious one for murdering all the Jews in the empire. Easily persuading the king that "a certain people" residing throughout the lands follow their own laws rather than the king's, Haman (who also offers the king a vast sum of money) receives permission to deal with them as he chooses. In the sovereign's name he sends an edict across the country mandating the extermination of all the Jews and the looting of their property on that designated day.

Inasmuch as the edict was promulgated on the thirteenth day of the first month (3:12) and was to be executed on the thirteenth day of the twelfth month, we may puzzle over the logic of widely publicizing the intended catastrophe so far in advance. It is helpful to recall that the first month of the Jewish calendar is the month now known as Nisan, which was called "Aviv" (i.e., "Spring") in the Torah. Passover, with its great story of deliverance and freedom, begins on the fourteenth of Nisan. The ancient enmity between the ancestors of Haman and the Jews can be traced to an incident during the exodus. Thus, to take this story as historical, we can imagine on the one hand the bitterness of Passover for the Jews in Persia, especially in the year of the decree, and on the other hand the pious reader might imagine hidden in the timing of these events a divine promise of another deliverance.

No such assurance is perceived by Mordecai or the other Jews, however. In the received or Masoretic version of the book, there is *nabukhah*, "confusion" or "consternation" (3:15). We might infer that such turmoil is a natural response to a suddenly promulgated edict that upsets what had become a normal *modus vivendi* of an ethnically, religiously, and culturally diverse population. The Targum Rishon, however, dating from a much later time and different environment, posits antithetical responses giving rise to that turmoil: rejoicing among the gentiles and weeping among those of the house of Israel.

Especially notable among the lamenting Jews is Mordecai, who tears his clothing, dons sackcloth, puts ashes on his head, and makes his way through the city to the palace gates weeping and exclaiming in woe, manifesting all the traditional signs of mourning that he shares with the kingdom's other Jews, aside of course from Esther (4:1). Esther herself, ensconced in the palace, after hearing about Mordecai's behavior from her women servants and eunuchs, sends clothing for him inasmuch as no one wearing sackcloth was allowed through the palace gate. He, however, refuses to change, even in order to speak directly with her.

Much that occurs in this book centers on symbolic items of clothing or status. Who, for example, wears a crown or robes of state? Who wears sackcloth? Who has the royal signet ring? To whom does the king extend his golden scepter?

In this episode the peculiar rule about sackcloth implies that nobody in mourning may enter the precincts of the royal court, suggesting that it is a place intentionally shielded from life's unhappy realities, an implication fitting well with the many banquets that have marked the earlier chapters. Mordecai, we may imagine, faces a dilemma when offered proper garb from his daughter. He needs to speak to her as she offers the only hope of saving the Jews; but to do so apparently requires adopting a pretense of non-mourning, which he is unable or unwilling to do. Faced then with choosing between the costume of courtly manners and the costume of united Jewish grieving, he insists upon the latter. That, as much as anything he puts into words, is his message to Esther.

Her reaction to Mordecai's report, *vatithallal*, variously translated as "greatly agitated" or "deeply distressed," has an intensely visceral connotation in the Hebrew, so much that the sage Rav in the Babylonian Talmud claims that it means her menstrual period began (Megillah 15a), while in the Jerusalem Talmud it is said that she has a miscarriage (a different inference recorded also in Midrash Esther 8:3). Despite seeming antithetical, both interpretations suggest that Esther internalizes the news as having an impact on her biological and genealogical future.

The two Jewish relatives are forced to communicate with one another through an intermediary, the eunuch Hathach. This is yet another instance of the book oddly providing an identity for a minor character who appears for only one incident and who becomes virtually invisible as well as inaudible in his own right (thus, strangely "hidden" though present), since he does nothing more than transmit oral communications from the one principal character to the other. We soon forget the pragmatic construct of this go-between negotiating between court and outside as well as between male and female as we take in a conversation that seems to occur as if directly between Esther and Mordecai.

Mordecai's message to her conveys all the information we already know about Haman's plot; he even verifies his report by including a copy of the deadly decree. Her response, on the other hand, introduces a complication typical of Megillat Esther, a strange law that "all the king's servants and all people in the king's lands know, that any man or woman who approaches the king in the inner court without being summoned there will be subject to one law, to be executed, unless the king extends to that person the golden scepter" (4:11). "And I," she adds seemingly in the same breath, "have not been called to the king for thirty days."

By this last remark, is she revealing uncertainty about her own standing in regard to the king? Has she fallen out of favor? Does he presume her to be pregnant, therefore not to be summoned for intimacy? Or is that simply the nature of life with a busy, fickle, and temperamental head of state?

More important, is she offering an excuse for not helping, as it means risking her own life? That is what many readers assume, as does Mordecai. Yet opposed to this, Adele Berlin (*NJSB*, 1627), noting that Mordecai said nothing about confronting the king in the inner court, proposes that Esther is already contemplating a plan to intercede. She accedes to Mordecai's plea, offering to risk herself on the condition that all the Jews join her and her maidservants in fasting for three days. Like so much in the story, the improbability of a community sustaining a three-day fast goes unremarked, therefore the period simply passes.

Few plotlines proceed directly in the Book of Esther. Twists, interruptions, and misdirections abound. So it is as Esther's plot unfolds after the days of fasting, when the next turn will involve another feast. The Targum Rishon begins the fifth chapter by noting that it was the third day of Passover. Lingering in royal raiment in the inner courtyard, Esther catches the attention of her husband, who bids her come to him by extending the golden scepter for her to touch, a symbolic act so sexual in its signification that it seems to need no commentary. When the king, after asking what she would like, hyperbolically offers her half his kingdom, she asks only that he and Haman attend a feast that she has prepared. The narration leaps immediately to the aftermath, the king repeating his request that Esther tell him what she desires and Esther once again inviting the two guests to another dinner party the following night, at which she promises she will reveal what she wants.

    Hebrew biblical texts are almost always laconic when we want them to provide explanations. That is certainly true of the Book of Esther. Why would the king not ask why his wife includes his principal minister when she invites him to dinner in her private quarters, and not once but twice? Indeed, what is Esther's purpose in not revealing what she knows at the first dinner but requiring a second one before she speaks her mind? As for the first puzzlement, Ahashverosh is certainly easily suggestible, whimsical, and even gullible throughout the story, disturbing traits in the monarch of a huge empire but simply one of the givens of the plot, and perhaps not out of keeping with the capriciousness of some real historical personage. Esther's behavior is more clearly strategic. We might suppose that she, after all, does not really know Haman; she knows nothing of the way he and the king interact; and she might expect her adversary to behave guardedly during the first unexpected banquet. It is at the second, when he and the king are likely more relaxed, that she can catch both of them unawares.

The second half of chapters 5 and 6 together constitute a brilliant example of dramatic crosscutting (or, the religiously devout might say, divine irony at work). Haman, gleefully going home after the feast, sees Mordecai seated at the palace gate, indifferent to the chief councilor. At home Haman, though boasting of being honored by the queen, complains that all is spoiled for him by seeing "Mordecai the Jew" sitting there. His wife Zeresh and his friends advise him to erect a gallows or stake (the exact translation is disputed) fifty cubits high and in the morning convince the king to have Mordecai executed there, thus allowing Haman to enjoy fully the next night's banquet. As Timothy K. Beal rhetorically asks, "Can advice ever displease anyone in this story?"(76). Consequently, Haman has the fatal instrument erected and goes to bed happy.

It is worth noting that a cubit was equal to about half a yard. While the general idea must be that the execution would be a widely visible public spectacle, either a gallows or stake seventy-five feet high is completely implausible as well as impractical. Take the idea literally and we are horrified. Take the idea literally and we laugh. The height of the instrument of execution is as exaggerated as Haman's furious resentment. The book oscillates between farce and social satire. Hyperbole is the rule in *Esther*.

Meanwhile, the king, who has been unable to sleep, requests that the royal chronicle be brought and read to him. The talmudic sage Raba offers the interpretation that he is disturbed by the fact that Esther invited Haman to the dinner because they might be conspiring against him, consequently he asks for these annals to be read in hope of revealing someone whom he could trust to expose any conspiracy—perhaps someone whom he had not rewarded for a previous good deed. Taken on its own, apart from aggadic speculation, this episode teeters between apprehensiveness and comedy. Apprehensiveness may be marked by the fact that "sleep eluded the king," who may be troubled for reasons of which he is not even conscious, according to Raba's suggestion. "Uneasy lies the head that wears a crown," as Shakespeare's Henry IV laments (*Henry IV, Pt 2*, III.1.1735). Comedy is at least suggested by his choice of material whether we imagine he selects it for solace or as a sleep aid, namely, the historical chronicle of his own reign.

Yet it is timely because the written record reminds the king of the planned attempt on his life that Mordecai thwarted. What, he asks, had been done for Mordecai as a reward? Again, the blandness of the question might distract us from seeing humor in the oblivious monarch apparently not recalling whether or not he had rewarded the man who saved him from an assassination plot, an incident that could not have happened terribly long before and that resulted in the execution of the two plotters. Told that nothing had been done, he asks who is in the court. It seems a strange question, though there is a point to it. Haman in fact is in the court, approaching with the intent of persuading Ahashverosh to hang Mordecai, the king's just-remembered savior, on the gallows newly constructed. Therefore Haman conveniently arrives right on time to take the brunt of a joke in which the king seemingly inadvertently uses his prime minister to honor the man the same minister sought to slay. We shall examine that mordant joke subsequently.

At the end of the episode Haman's wife and "all his friends," the very people who had counseled him the night before to have Mordecai hanged, warn Haman that if Mordecai, "before whom you have begun to fall," is indeed of Jewish ancestry, "you will surely fall to ruination through him" (6:13). In this frame of mind Haman is escorted to the second, fateful banquet given by Esther, which will indeed end with his complete undoing and that of his adherents. He goes to this dinner not realizing that he is headed toward his death. Once again we are left wondering whether the story shows us that fortune is fickle or that "the guardian of Israel neither slumbers nor sleeps" (Psalm 121:4).

As the account rapidly unfolds, Ahashverosh under the influence of Mordecai and Esther authorizes the Jews throughout the kingdom to defend themselves against the slaughter intended for them on the thirteenth day of Adar. In the walled fortress of Shushan, five hundred foes in addition to the ten sons of Haman are slain; the latter, by Esther's request, are displayed on stakes or gallows. On the next day, the assault continues in the capital, with another three hundred killed. Throughout the provinces, acting on the thirteenth of Adar only, the Jews kill seventy-five thousand enemies, without looting and without mention of any Jewish deaths. The day following the battles is a time for the victorious Jews to rejoice and feast. The contrast between the circuitous path taken by the human drama that has been interacted in intimate scenes involving five principal characters and the swift, complete reversal in the large-scale historical narrative of the Persian Jews' fate could hardly be greater. The book's narrative voice seems to express wonderment at the transformation of Adar "from grief to joy and from mourning to holiday" (9:22).

The communal observance of *Ta'anit Esther* or the Fast of Esther, which seems to have originated in the eighth or ninth century CE, honors the fast that Esther imposed upon herself and the entire endangered Jewish community (4:16) before she approaches the king. However, one notable difference is that the biblical Esther commands a full three-day fast. This seems to be another hyperbolic moment in the narrative, rather than indicating the more plausible sunrise-to-sundown fasting period that marks the more modern *Ta'anit Esther*. Those Jews who observe the fast today do so just before Purim, generally on the 13th of Adar (unless that date conflicts with the Sabbath), as it is the date on which Haman and the Jews' other enemies were set to slaughter them. Being a post-talmudic addition to the holiday, this fast is observed less widely and less stringently than the fasts of Tisha b'Av and Yom Kippur.

We recall that according to the biblical text, Esther's fast was instituted right after the publication of the royal decree against the Jews that was declared "on the thirteenth day of the first month," Nisan. As Esther, Mordecai, and the entire Jewish community would be fasting during the first three days of Passover, this remarkable trespass of the Torah was doubtless meant to dramatize the urgency of the situation.

Throughout most of the Jewish world today, 14 Adar is observed as the festive day of Purim. In Jerusalem (and theoretically other cities like Jericho that were walled when Joshua and the Israelites entered Canaan), 15 Adar is celebrated instead as Purim, often specifically called Shushan Purim because it commemorates the day when the Jews of Shushan could cease their combat. Along with the other forms of rejoicing, people voluntarily follow the practice prescribed by Mordecai of contributing to the poor and sending gifts (plural, therefore usually two kinds or flavors of pastry) to family and friends (9:22–23), known respectively in Hebrew as *matanot la-evyonim* and *shalach manot* (in Ashkenazic and Yiddish pronunciation, *shalachmanos*).

When and where the book was written is also open to uncertainty. Esther 9:20 states that "Mordecai recorded [*vayichtov*] these events." The Talmud supposes that the text was edited from Mordecai's account by "the men of the great assembly" [*anshei knesset hagedolah*], a quasi-legendary assembly of 120 scholars, prophets, and leaders bridging the period from the end of the First Temple to some indefinite time in the late Second Temple era. The talmudic view accords somewhat with the general consensus of scholars today, which is that our Masoretic Esther text reflects familiarity with the Persian empire and its administration in the time of Xerxes I (485–465 BCE) but actually originates from a later period. Linguistic evidence, such as the many Persian names and loan-words along with Aramaic, combined with the absence of Greek, suggests that it was transcribed or edited between the reign of Xerxes I and the conquest by

Alexander the Great (333 BCE), which introduced Hellenic cultural elements to the region.

It is the one book of the Tanakh for which there are no remnants among the Dead Sea Scrolls. The canonical status of Esther was the subject of some dispute, as we see in the Talmud, which also comments on numerous passages, notably but not exclusively in b. Megillah. It is discussed as well in midrashim, especially Esther Rabbah; there are also the two Aramaic translations (*targumim*) that function as interpretations of the Hebrew text. Furthermore, we have a version of the book transmitted by Josephus in his Greek *Antiquities of the Jews*; while recounting the story as historical, Josephus relies heavily on the Septuagint, albeit with distinctive touches that (yet again) provoke inconclusive scholarly speculation about possible source materials and transmissions.

Important Jewish captives were taken to Persia after the fall of Jerusalem. To the extent that the Book of Esther represents the Jewish impression of Persia, it shows us an opulent court that lives lavishly and a kingdom autocratically run by the rather willful and extravagant sovereign, who also depends on an extensive set of advisors and administrators. In addition there is an extensive imperial administration with postal and courier networks and a large bureaucracy throughout the kingdom. Some of those who are associated with the royal household have personal secrets; many have their own goals. Time and again the story employs courtiers, servants, and messengers to play significant roles. There is an elaborate royal household in which few have access to the king; alongside that is a separate women's area, including the harem and queen's quarters, which are also restricted. When Mordecai needs to convey vital news to Esther in chapter 4 and she replies to him, the communications take place through the eunuch Hatach, one of several named court officials (like Memucan in chapter 1 and Hegai in chapter 2) who appear briefly in the text and then are never again mentioned. All of this seems realistic.

Yet at the same time the account, laden with plot implausibilities, depends upon an omniscient albeit highly selective narrator. We are told what transpires privately in conversations that take place within disparate groups of people, such as the king and his servants, Haman and his wife, or Mordecai and Esther; sometimes the narrator supplies motives for actions but often we are left wondering what, for example, Esther thinks about her role, a lack that the targumim and midrashim often remedy.

A measure of the book's artful construction in the Masoretic text is the delayed introduction of the title character, and indeed of the only two

Jewish figures in the work, as well as the even more delayed introduction of the villain. The entire first chapter and opening verses of the second are taken up by the episode of Ahashverosh's deposition of Vashti his queen and the preparations to choose her replacement. Only in 2:5 is Mordecai introduced, followed two verses later by Esther, who first seems mentioned as if in passing. Haman, essential as he is to the story, arrives on the scene only in the opening verse of the third chapter, following Esther's ascent as queen and another seemingly unrelated plot twist involving the conspiracy against the king.

The more closely we read the Book of Esther, the more examples we are likely to find of sophisticated, purposeful construction in the story. For instance, either the title character or Mordecai could be the "hero" of the tale. They operate in tandem, even at the conclusion of the plot. He first sends out letters to the Jewish communities throughout the land commanding the observance of a festival with appropriate gifts to the poor. Subsequently, Esther (grandly referred to as "Queen Esther, daughter of Abihail") follows with her own letter to validate, as with a seal of approval, all that he mandated. Are they a team or is she determined to assert her own authority? He is publicly known as a Jew from early in the story, one who operates in the world at large, though at the margin of palace culture, where he is not a stranger but not an intimate, either. Esther, whose background is hidden for a time and whose name may be related to the Hebrew verbal root for "hidden," functions in the palace realm exclusively, the domain appropriate to a Persian queen or for that matter a married Jewish woman in a traditional environment. Having been elevated to royalty, she has as direct access to the king as anyone can; Mordecai, though meritorious and loyal, must exercise his influence indirectly through her and through other figures on the social borderline, the palace eunuchs. Neither one alone would be sufficient to accomplish the historic task.

Yet one trait that they have in common is that they use their wits. Mordecai is inconspicuously attentive and alert; he passes relevant information about the plot against the king as well as the plot against the Jews to the people who can make the most effective use of this secret intelligence. While Esther acts under Mordecai's prompting, he gives her no instruction as to how she should accomplish the task. All that she does in regard to the king and Haman seems to come from her own faculties, skillfully employed; she devises a remarkable and daring strategy to trap the villain, not only saving the Jewish people this one time but eliminating their sworn enemy along with his family and allies.

When Mordecai is introduced, he is identified as an *"ish yehudi,"* a Judean man, in other words, a Jew, from the tribe of Benjamin, one of the exiles from Jerusalem driven out by the Babylonian King Nebuchadnezzar. The grammar of this passage being obscure, it is not clear whether we are to understand that Mordecai was of that generation and therefore ancient at the time of the story or whether he is a descendent. He has taken adoptive responsibility for raising his orphaned cousin, Hadassah, meaning "myrtle" in Hebrew; her name is also given as Esther, which is clearly Persian, suggesting that she dwells in two social realms, one public and the other covert, for her Hebrew name is never mentioned again, though her Jewish patronymic ("daughter of Abihail") is appended to her Persian name "Esther" in both 2:15 and 9:29.

Much later in the book it becomes clear that there is a sizable Jewish community in the capital of Shushan as well as in provinces throughout Persia. They will be endangered and join Esther's fast, and they will rise up in arms in sufficient numbers to kill not only 810 enemies in Shushan but even (9:16) "seventy-five thousand" in the rest of the land. Setting aside the obvious exaggeration, these numbers suppose a Jewish community of substantial size. However, no other Jewish characters appear or are named in the work, a fact that is striking given the number of Persian counselors and palace functionaries, such as various eunuchs both good and malicious, and even bit players such as Haman's wife and their ten sons, who are all named even though the sons' names are given only to record their deaths. The impression of the Jews is of a minority people who, with rare exceptions such as the two protagonists, remain in the background of this society. They are not a subject of conversation or controversy until someone makes them that; but when that happens, their numbers and social position leave them vulnerable. Their improbable military triumph over a multitude of foes helps explain why this story became dear to Jewish communities in many places and times.

And it is in many regards a communal story, notwithstanding the fact that the dénouement depends on decisions made under duress by particular individuals. The balance between personal and public consequences in the narrative is an exquisite one. For instance, Esther keenly feels (as how could she not) the mortal danger she faces if she oversteps the rigorous protocol of the Persian court by approaching the sovereign unbidden. Yet she also recognizes an obligation to her people. Not only that but she implies that the obligation must be reciprocal: she will risk her life on their behalf, but they must also incur the burden of preparatory fasting, not in place of her but along with her. Perhaps it is easy to overlook another instance of communal identity coming forth in a moment of crisis, one that is even more dramatically selfless when we reflect on it. That is, of course, Mordecai pleading with Esther to take the initiative that may save the Jews. Caught up in the action, we might forget that thus far only one character in the story is identified publicly as a Jew: Mordecai himself, who we learn in 3:5 had made his Jewish identity known. Yet he does not appeal to his adopted daughter by saying that *his* life was in danger. Rather, he appeals to her sense of the Jewish people.

For a figure who disappears quickly from the scene, Vashti—Ahashverosh's displaced queen—has a grand dramatic effect in chapter 1, precipitates the action of the story, and stimulates a great deal of subsequent commentary, even though she simply vanishes and is never again mentioned in the book after 2:17. In modern times her significance may be even greater than in the past because we perceive her behavior through modern eyes. We may well view her as an independent woman who knows her own mind, feels secure in her social position, and has a strong enough sense of herself to refuse heeding the whimsical beck and call of her husband. Given the consequence, we can also see what her imprudence (the king and councilors would call it impudence) costs her greatly. There is, however, a remarkable difference between the traditional Jewish views of Vashti and modern interpretations, either Jewish or otherwise.

A classic Jewish interpretive tradition posits that Vashti was the one surviving child of Belshazzar, the son of Nebuchadnezzar, destroyer of Jerusalem. There is no evidence at all for that idea in the Book of Esther, though the claim appears in both the Talmud and midrash collections, where the connection is either assumed or inferred on the basis of highly conjectural interpretations that seem intended to provide a text source to justify what was traditionally accepted. For example, the third-century Babylonian sage Samuel finds in the prophecy of Jeremiah 49:38, "I will destroy king and princes," references to the downfall of Vashti and the seven princes of Media and Persia. Regarding the prophecy of Isaiah that "I will cut off from Babylon . . . offshoot and offspring" (Isaiah 14:22), his contemporary, the Babylonian sage Rav, similarly interprets the former to mean Belshazzar and the latter Vashti (Midrash Esther Prologue 12). In the Talmud, R. Yonatan, speculating on the same passage, interprets "offshoot" as "kingdom" but also posits that "offspring" refers to Vashti (b. Megillah 10b).

We might suppose that to the early rabbis and sages, who were not ascetics but certainly not hedonists either, two traits that link these various figures to one another is haughty and reckless pride combined with self-indulgent banqueting and carousing that lead to unrestrained behavior. Those are traits that we find in the biblical accounts of Nebuchadnezzar, Belshazzar, Ahashverosh, and Vashti as well, who is hosting her own feast while her husband entertains in his part of the palace, and who dismisses out of hand an order to appear before the man who is both the king and her husband.

For the early talmudic-era commentators as well as for the Jewish commentators over the ages who have largely followed their line of imaginative reconstructing of ancient history, Vashti's disappearance from the book is more significant than a character merely exiting off-stage. It is the fulfillment of prophecies and marks the end of the dynasties responsible for the destruction of the Temple and Jerusalem. Therefore to them, Vashti is not merely shunted off to some remote town or sent into foreign exile where she can live out the rest of her life in obscurity. She is presumed to be killed, albeit behind the scenes.

Certainly, those who perceive the outcome this way also know enough of the behavior of real-life tyrants to perceive that this would be the most likely fate of someone who defied the expressed command of a willful autocrat. Nor has she defied him in private, she has done so in a way that challenges him before the public and the nobility, thereby exposing him to embarrassment before all who must respect him.

Furthermore, she refuses his order while engaged in her own soirée in the king's palace (not, one talmudic sage notes, discreetly "in the women's quarters"). Vashti the supposed daughter of Belshazzar and granddaughter of Nebuchadnezzar, thus the descendent of two biblically notorious royal heathen libertines, is behaving with what the Babylonian Talmud calls *pritzuta*, licentiousness (Megillah 12b). It is not clear exactly what they are imagining but it is clear that, according to the rabbinic standards of decency that disapprove of immoderate behavior, Vashti is a wild woman.

Yet she is not so wild as to accede to a summons from her husband that Jewish tradition regards as even more licentious, that she satisfy his pride by making a command appearance nude except for her crown. Here we have a typical midrashic interpretive method, reading the text in a hyper-literal way: if the king specifies that she attends his banquet "wearing a royal crown to display her beauty to the people," it means that is all that she is supposed to wear. The idea seems scandalous even today; it is surely intended to signify a king and a culture that are both intoxicated and corrupt. When one sage questions why, if Vashti is so dissolute, she would refuse even such an order, the talmudic answers are that she was temporarily suffering from disfiguring afflictions, not that she considered it improper.

Vashti's simple refusal (1:12) becomes, in talmudic midrash, a brazen direct insult to the king's lineage. Again, the origin of this interpretive strand is not known; perhaps to the rabbinic interpreters the text's reference to "the Queen Vashti" implies some arrogant pride in her. Apparently there was a legend or tradition claiming that Ahashverosh or his father had been a servant of Belshazzar. So they say that in her reply she sneeringly called the king, "my father's steward" (or in another version, "son of my father's steward") and mockingly persisted, "My father drank wine in the presence of thousands without getting drunk, yet this man has gotten himself totally besotted with his wine."

A modern reader coming to the text without the mediation of this weighty tradition is likely to see the whole Vashti episode as broadly farcical, like a situation comedy squabble that escalates preposterously; one expects it to end with a slammed door or a hurled shoe. The rabbinic view, however, looks more like one of the especially volatile scenes in *Who's Afraid of Virginia Woolf?* except that this version finishes with the wife murdered offstage. Characteristically, the text of *Esther*, like a Jastrow rabbit-or-duck illusion, vacillates between radically different possible interpretations.

Thus as well, modern perspectives on Vashti's story are likely to be much more sympathetic to her, appreciative of her feisty independence. Despite her not being the female protagonist of the book, Vashti turns out to be a popular character for girls and young women to portray in modern Purim plays. It is always interesting to see who will choose to depict Vashti and who will portray Esther!

Of course we now see clearly from a modern point of view the sexual dynamics at work in this section of the book. A powerful man married to a beautiful woman wants to display her on command as an enviable trophy in front of the men who work for him, no matter the humiliating manner of the show. He and she are each giving their own party, he for the men, she for the women, when he sends servants to summon her. She refuses. Setting aside midrashim to look only at the biblical text, we see that it ascribes nothing to the manner of the rebuff; it merely says, "But Queen Vashti refused to go as the king ordered by way of the eunuchs" (1:12), which sends the king into a rage. His will has been thwarted, always infuriating to an autocrat; he also has been defeated by a woman, and specifically by his wife. The other men quickly sense the implication: what is at stake is the power to control. He has been humiliated, virtually emasculated, by an embarrassing message conveyed by a eunuch.

In a gesture toward verisimilitude, the text lists by name seven "sages" (*khokhamim*) to whom the king turns for advice about dealing with this act of rebellion. Typical of this book, however, the term "sages" proves ironic because their response, being exaggerated and ridiculous, is anything but sage, while it is nonetheless ultimately essential for our story. The words of only one of these councilors appear in the text. Midrashim taking the tale as historical posit that all gave their advice; only this one response is recorded because that was the advice the king took. The speaker is Memucan, who is never again mentioned, albeit a talmudic commentator hypothesizes (Megillah 12b) that this is another name for Haman. Memucan happens to be the last-named in the list, though he is the first one who appears to respond. The alacrity of his reply leads one midrashist to observe that "an ignorant person always pushes himself to the front" (Esther Rabbah 4:6).

We might add that an ignorant person is also likely to talk at length without stopping. In a book in which a prolonged speech tends to take two or three verses, Memucan's screed is seven verses, in which he enumerates every possible problem that could arise from Vashti's refusal, amounting to a panoramic depiction of male fears about female autonomy. As if deducing from the excesses of his speech that he must have more personal reasons than he admits, Esther Rabbah 4:6 also cites various phrases from it to infer that Memucan had been insulted and beaten by Vashti, or that his wife had not been invited to her party, or that he wanted to replace her with his own daughter. Whether or not his motivations are so particular, his protests are not directed exclusively or even primarily toward removing Vashti but even more to enforcing wives' subordination to their husbands. Her offence, he insists, is not solely *lèse-majesté* but an offence "against all the officials and all the peoples living in the lands of King Ahashverosh" (1:16). As it becomes known publicly, it will motivate all wives to be contemptuous of their husbands. Indeed, he continues, even today the women of Persia and Media who have heard of the queen's behavior will treat royal officials with scorn, to which there will be no end. It is he who proposes that she be exiled forever from the king's presence, cast aside, and her queenly status given to another who more deserves it (thus suggesting a midrash that says he has a daughter of his own in mind to fill that spot). This example, he argues, will teach wives of all ranks that they must show their husbands respect.

Part of Memucan's proposal is that Vashti's banishment be written into law, which apparently meant that dispatches announcing it would be sent throughout the empire, in the script of every province and the language of each community (1:22). According to this edict, every man should rule in his home and speak his people's language. The Hebrew verb used here for "rule" has the same root (s-r-r) as the title of the royal officials. We can sense here a patriarchy that is entrenched yet brimming with insecurity about its control, needing to assert domination at all levels.

The absurdity of this hyper-vigilance along with the impossibility of making it work emerges through the insightful scorn of midrashic commentary. If, Rav Huna says, a husband wants to eat lentils and a wife wants to eat beans, does he think he can force her to eat lentils instead? Rav Pinchas pursues the matter further. If a Median man marries a Persian woman or a Persian man marries a Median, can they force their wives to speak the husband's language that presumably they do not know? (Esther Rabbah 4:12). The talmudic authorities imply these would be preposterous efforts, suggesting somewhat more flexible attitudes than we might expect toward gender roles and multicultural living.

In the way of the tyrant, Ahashverosh (who immediately takes favorably to Memucan's plan) attempts to force obedience to his over-reaching command even when doing so denies individual choice and ignores practical commonsense experience. It might not be possible to identify a consistent, coherent political outlook in Esther. However, as a satire of power undermining itself by overconfidence, this text can be trenchant.

Although most often referred to in Jewish practice as a *megillah*, "scroll," it is also called a *sefer* ("book") in the Talmud as well as an *iggeret*, "letter," the latter term reflecting the text's claim that Mordecai sent letters to the Jews throughout the kingdom instructing them about the events and the ensuing festivities, thereby inaugurating the holiday of Purim. Where possible, Esther is still read from its own scroll, containing no other text, though it may have ornaments and even illustrations, making it unique in

Jewish scribal practice regarding biblical texts intended to be declaimed during public worship. The notion that the story came originally in the form of a letter is acknowledged still today by a widely observed practice of letting the scroll fold upon itself segment by segment, accordion-style, as one reads, simulating a long letter. Even in Mishnaic times it was read at both the evening and morning synagogue services; in places where Hebrew was not widely known, it was read in the vernacular; and it could also be recited at home, especially in the evening.

The singular character of Esther extends as well to the musical traditions for chanting the text. For one, the *nusach* of this book is unique, different even from the other megillot. At least in Ashkenazic practice (that is, among Jews originating in northern, central, and eastern Europe) it is dramatic and flamboyant rather than being lyrically flowing or serviceably clarifying the text's phraseology. It also is sometimes intended as a subtle interpretation of the story. For example, according to midrash, the goblets and utensils that the king uses in the palace for the lavish feasts include those that Nebuchadnezzar looted from the Jerusalem Temple. Consequently, some cantors or skilled synagogal readers substitute the *nusach* of Eykhah/Lamentations when reciting those five lines, as well as certain others that speak of mourning and lamenting, a practice that of course works most effectively in communities knowledgeable enough to recognize the difference and appreciate the allusion. For those listeners, the melodic shift signifies how easily Purim's raucous energy can give way to disaster, how we may teeter heedlessly at the edge of danger, how even amid merriment Jewish people sense the echoes of a painful past.

One verse (7:9) highlights an especially dramatic and suspenseful turning point with two cantillation marks that appear only here and in one verse of the Torah, nowhere else in the entire Tanakh. At another spot (9:7) the difficult and unfamiliar names of the villain Haman's ten sons, who are all executed at the same time, are customarily chanted by the reader on one note and in one breath, turning this grotesque moment into a highly anticipated performance rather like a stage trick appropriate to Purim's carnival atmosphere. Several other verses are sometimes distinguished by local musical variants. Uniquely, the recitation of this megillah is also preceded and followed by a series of special blessings traditionally chanted according to singular melodies.

Another way in which this book is distinctive is found in the making of parodies and imitations written to memorialize personal or communal deliverances from danger or destruction. These local or special Purims (as they are known), of which there have been more than two dozen recorded in Jewish history primarily from the Middle Ages into the nineteenth century, take place on the anniversary date of the relief itself rather than at Purim, which is also celebrated at its proper time. As with Purim, a scroll (with phrasing recalling that of the original) is read recounting the events and decreeing the commemoration to later generations; appropriate festivities with food gifts and donations to the needy ensue, as the survivors generally mandate in the scroll itself, much like the Book of Esther. Of course, nowhere has the rescued Jewish family or community been given permission or sought it to avenge themselves violently on the foes who attempted to destroy them.

Purim's atmosphere is analogous to Mardi Gras, Carnival time, or Halloween, all of which are festive celebrations with religious connections but involving masquerades and sometimes alcoholic drinks. Among Purim's many traditions that developed over time, the Purim play, called in Yiddish a *Purimspiel*, is one of the most popular. Sometimes it is a shortened version of the biblical story presented by religious school students, frequently incorporating a pageant in which the children vie for having the best costume representing one of the principal characters. Often on Purim all the congregants, including the rabbi, will arrive in costume, with masks or makeup pertinent to whomever they are depicting, whether a persona in the story of Esther or not. It might be that the scroll's themes of hiddenness and inversions of fortunes motivate Purim's worldwide embrace of costumes and disguises as part of the synagogal experience. The Purimspiel or megillah reading might incorporate a burlesque version of the story outline filled with topical references and parodies of well-known songs whose lyrics are adapted to be more or less appropriate. Some modern songs have been written for Purim, though they are generally intended for sing-along entertainment rather than contributions to liturgical music.

Another practice is drowning out the name of Haman at each of the fifty mentions of it during the reading, using noisemakers (either special ones or improvised household items). As this requires close attention, a copy of the text for each individual is needed or an M.C. who will signal when to raise a din and, just as important, when to stop so that the narrative can continue. Ismar Elbogen, a great historian of Jewish liturgy, was premature when he wrote in 1913, "The noisy disturbances have been eliminated in every civilized country."[1] His view undoubtedly represents a time and outlook when many Jews strove for cultural acceptance and social respectability that prioritized decorous behavior. He was also writing prior to the enormous upheavals of the Jewish world in the twentieth century that produced so many Hamans and required so many acts of individual and collective courage and daring from women and men to save the Jewish people.

As feasting and sending gifts are among the observances commanded throughout all generations by Mordecai and Esther (9:22), special foods appropriate to be given as gifts are associated with Purim, a practice more generally observed than the preceding fast. Triangular filled cookies called hamantaschen are especially popular among Jews from Ashkenazic backgrounds. Literally the name means "Haman's pockets," though it is likely that the name and the delicacy originated in the German-Yiddish word for poppy seeds, *mohn*, which is a traditional filling ingredient, preceded by the Hebrew definite article "*ha*." Sephardic Jews are more likely to make curls of fried dough dipped in honey that are said to represent Haman's ears. Gobbling down some treat that represents a part of the villain is a sweet revenge.

If we accept as a working hypothesis that the book's portrait of Ahashverosh is based on Xerxes, we can say that it reflects what is reported of Xerxes' behavior in Herodotus's *History*, Book Seven. There we see a monarch who is willful, unpredictable, short-tempered, heavily dependent on advisors and easily swayed by them, though also one who rewards loyalty. He was, we note as well, assassinated by members of his palace inner circle, a fact maybe recalled fictionally in Esther when Mordecai discovers and exposes the plot by the two palace guards to kill the king (2:21–23). The historian also depicts an extensive Persian and Median empire with an elaborate system for transmitting communiqués and edicts throughout its provinces, thus harmonizing with an important plotline in our story, the sending of messages and proclamations to all parts of the nation and in every language spoken in each region.

Notwithstanding the hints of historicity in Esther, there are also improbabilities at every turn, not to mention the fact that none of the main features of the narrative can be supported by any external source. Among its implausible claims, in addition to the enormous tally of hostile

---

1. Ismar Elbogen, *Jewish Liturgy: A Comprehensive History*, translated by Raymond P. Scheindlin (Philadelphia: JPS, 1993), 110.

Persians and Medians killed apparently without loss of Jewish life, the story claims that many people "became Jews" (*mityahadim*) because of the fearsome power of the Jews, and especially of Mordecai (8:17; 9:3–4). Here is a shocking reversal of expectations and fortunes: the Jews now have power over those who thought to have power over the Jews. This fantasy is the perhaps-wishful thinking of an exiled minority cognizant of its own vulnerability, living generally tolerated but nonetheless precariously among its conquerors, imagining turning the tables, extracting revenge so complete that those who once held sway over the Jews now want to become Jewish themselves.

The claim is remarkable for various reasons, not the least being that it indicates that "Jewish" means something different from, and in addition to, "Judean," which is one of the simplest meanings of "Yehudi." When Mordecai is first introduced at the beginning of chapter 2, verse 2, the sentence begins, "*ish yehudi haya*," "a Jewish man there was." Even before his name is given, his primary identity is stated in terms of his place of origin as well as, apparently, his ethno-religious culture. We quickly learn that his family, of the tribe of Benjamin, had been exiled from Jerusalem (that is, in Judea) after the Babylonian conquest. In designating him "*ish yehudi*," the text establishes a distinctive motif that is continually associated with him and him alone. The book states clearly the obvious genealogical fact that Esther is Jewish; however, she is never "Esther the Jew." By contrast, in addition to the numerous references to Mordecai being a Jew and to his significant place among the Jews of the kingdom, six times he is specifically referred to by the narrator and others as *Mordecai ha-yehudi*, "Mordecai the Jew."

But if Persians are converting by becoming *yehudim*, regardless of whether that is fact or fiction, *yehudi* must mean something different from "Judean" or member of a tribal group descended from Jacob/Yaakov. It might mean that they say or do something to affiliate themselves with the people called Jews, who have their own practices and beliefs in addition to their family history. Not only is Jewish identity separable from national identity and place of origin. To the writer(s), redactor(s), and readers of this story, *mityahadim* must have had some meaning; in other words, converting—becoming Jewish—must have been effected through some sort of ritual or act of public affiliation that they could suppose these intimidated Persians seized upon. Perhaps it was less affiliation with than rejection of: in the Talmud Bavli, Megillah 13a, Rabbi Yonatan asserts that Mordecai from the tribe of Benjamin is a *yehudi* because anyone who forsakes idolatry (*avodah zara* in Hebrew, "alien worship") is called a Jew (*yehudi*).

Whatever the rite of conversion involved, if it was indeed conversion rather than embracing something like "fellow traveler" status or simply formally rejecting idolatrous worship, it appears to be a remarkably expeditious experience totally remote from the demanding course of learning and practice expected under all modern forms of rabbinic Judaism. We can only speculate about what it might have entailed. Nonetheless, in this text we can perceive a sense of Jewishness that resembles modern notions in all of its various dimensions along with its ambiguities. Is one a *yehudi* by virtue of genealogy, cultural heritage, nationality, communal identification, beliefs, or practices? The answers are all seemingly yes.

The absence of any mention of priests and prophets in this text, especially during the shaping of the holiday of Purim, is notable. What might be called Jewish secular authorities decree the festival and its obligations in concert with "the consent of the governed." The Jewish people take on the observance of Purim for themselves and for their "seed," as well as for all who join with them, that is, those who become part of the Jewish community. They decide how the day will be observed. Moreover, this is not a remembrance to be observed only during their own generation: "nor shall the memorial of the events perish from their seed" (9:27–28). A rabbinic commentary from the eighth or ninth century CE (Midrash Mishlei 9) interprets that verse to mean that even in messianic times when all other holiday observances end, Purim will still be celebrated. While the original sense of that interpretation seems to be simply a literal understanding of the biblical phrasing, we can take a further step and say that Purim means we rejoice that all of our foes have been vanquished so that we may abandon ourselves to gladness with all our people along with, as the text posits, those who have been drawn to us.

Megillat Esther, we might also say, is informed by knowledge of Persian history but not limited by it. Here, art takes precedence. Or perhaps it is art in the service of a heroic narrative of Jewish survival. And how is that survival achieved? In essence, the book provides a veritable manual of all the possible ways, including armed resistance. Notably, their strategies attest to successfully negotiating dual loyalties to the sovereign ruler of the country they live in and implicitly therefore to the nation itself, as well as to the Jewish people, in part through self-interest but in part also to the communal bond. The two Jewish champions, though part of a marginal minority, at times submerge their Jewish identity without forgetting or forsaking it. They rise to positions of prominence through their faithful reliability and discretion, to which Esther also adds physical beauty and grace.

Esther's physical charms are abetted by an unsought ally from another potentially marginal group. That is the official in charge of the harem, Hegai. Esther "pleased him and received kindness from him" (2:9), as a result of which he promptly gave her cosmetics, rations, and the seven maidservants that she was due from the king's palace and promoted them all to a privileged place within the women's quarters.

We might wonder why he favors her in this way. However, since the text does not say and provides no hints (nor do the rabbinic commentaries), any speculation about his "motives" unreasonably supposes that this is a historical story about real people. Rather, the more relevant question should be, why does the text see fit to take this direction? If it merely said that of all the women presented to him, the king was most taken with Esther, we could simply accept that. When she is introduced in the story (2:7), she is described as pretty and comely in appearance (or perhaps, depending on how we translate, with a nice figure). That alone would seem to be an enticing enough description for Vashti's replacement. Why does the story emphasize her special treatment?

One possible reason of course is an appearance of verisimilitude. Given that the royal casting call was for "all the fair young virgins" throughout the land, why was this one chosen to be queen? One plausible answer is that she had the advantage of inside help. Another possible explanation for the Hegai episode lies in the interesting reciprocity between her "pleasing him" and him favoring her. The Hebrew suggests that her manner was pleasing or engaging. Not just her physical appearance but her personality is in her favor, winning her an ally who is placed highly enough to do her good. He cannot sway Ahashverosh directly but he can provide her with all that she needs to present herself persuasively to the king. Might this mean that, although young, she is perceptive enough to be politic in her interaction with the person in charge? Or does it simply mean that she is amiably engaging toward people regardless of their station? Yet a third possibility is that, although Esther is keeping her Jewish identity a secret as directed by Mordecai, she and this other character living on the borderline of this society (she as an orphaned Jew in an ambiguous familial relationship with Mordecai, Hegai existing between the realm of men and that of women as well as between officialdom and servitude) respond to one another with an instinctive bond of camaraderie?

While "Esther" and "Mordecai" become quintessential Jewish names, they appear here in a Jewish context for the first time. (When George Eliot, in her 1876 novel *Daniel Deronda* created a passionate Zionist Jewish character, she named him Mordecai.) Esther's name is likely derived from the Persian word for "star," though some speculate it is related to the goddess Ishtar; his may be related to the god Marduka. Esther has a Hebrew name, Hadassah ("myrtle"), used only when she is first introduced into the narrative. Ezra and Nehemiah include a "Mordecai" among the names of those who returned to Jerusalem when King Cyrus permitted the exiles to go back. The book's temporal and syntactic ambiguity leave in doubt whether Mordecai was among those Jerusalemites taken into captivity by Nebuchadnezzar or, as seems more plausible, the great-grandson of an exile from the tribe of Benjamin. Esther, as his uncle's daughter, is perhaps somewhat younger but could be of his generation. Both, therefore, are authentic Judeans by descent; both are exiles whose families came from the Jewish capital and can be imagined as coming from high social status inasmuch as they were taken into captivity by the Babylonians. The Talmud (Megillah 13b) and targumim claim that he was a member of the Sanhedrin and therefore knew seventy languages, as required, fitting preparation for a life of public service in a polyglot empire. And both are named in ways that suggest their dual identity as Jews and as residents of Persia who are somewhat integrated into the culture of the land to which they or their ancestors were taken.

Mordecai, in "adopting" Esther "as his own daughter," has taken on responsibility for her welfare. He watches out for her, advises her, and when necessary urges her to action. But the nature of their relationship is distinctly odd. She is undeniably attractive according to everything the text tells us about her; Mordecai also seems to have no other family; and under *halachah* (Jewish law) they could have married. Yet instead, she goes to the harem along with Persia and Media's other beautiful young virgins who might be chosen as queen in place of Vashti. To our eyes it seems that he is virtually prostituting his adopted child, though we ought not ignore the fact that this resembles the way that royalty for centuries used their children for advantageous alliances. What could be more advantageous for members of a minority group in exile than marriage with the sovereign ruler?

The Talmud is reluctant to accept this odd arrangement at face value. Playing on the succinct statement that Mordecai "took her *l'bat*" (took her for his daughter), one sage in Megillah 13a ventures to read this as "*l'bayit*," literally, for his house, which is one way of saying that he took her to be his wife. Even more daring is a talmudic gloss on the comment that Esther followed Mordecai's guidance "just as when she was brought up by him" (2:20). This interpretation glosses the passage as meaning that "she rose from Ahashverosh's lap, bathed, and sat on Mordecai's lap" (Megillah 13b), which seems like a thinly disguised suggestion that she had sexual relations with both men, a plausible inference if one assumes that they were both her husbands.

Mordecai's role is so significant that we may wonder why the book was not named for him rather than Esther. He plays an active role in some of the most crucial events, though discreetly behind the scenes. At turning points, Mordecai turns up. He more than she is the influential figure, virtually an *eminence gris*, during the climactic rebellion against anti-Semitic forces in chapters 8 and 9. It is Mordecai who dictates the public decree allowing the Jews to defend themselves and he whose triumphant departure from the palace in a crown and magnificent robes of state sets forth a grand celebration among the Shushan Jews. Even the book's coda, the three verses constituting chapter 10, is little more than a celebration of Mordecai the Jew's prominence as "second to King Ahashverosh" (*mishneh melekh achashverosh*), his considerable popularity among the Jews, and a tribute to him, in the book's final phrases, as a great benefactor of "his people . . . and his kin."

This encomium is notable for three elements. One is that it is likely to remind us of the paradigmatic story of Joseph, who rose to prominence in Egypt as a valued counselor to the Pharaoh as well as a savior of his family and thereby of the Jewish people. The second is an interesting reference to Mordecai's deeds being recorded in a text we do not possess but one whose title seems plausible enough, The Chronicle of the Kings of Media and Persia, thereby laying a claim for the historicity of the tale. The third, notwithstanding Mordecai's significant role in the kingdom as a whole, is the exclusive emphasis on his prominence among his fellow Jews (*l'amo*), both as a successful public figure and as a unifier, for the final phrase literally says, "speaking peace to all his seed" (*u-dover shalom l'kol-zar'o*).

The concluding word is somewhat surprising, given that there is no mention of Mordecai marrying, much less having offspring, the usual biblical meaning of "seed" (*z-r-y*). Though we have somewhat of a genealogy for his ancestors in 2:5–6, the text says nothing about descendants. However, this wording carries through a verbal motif introduced by Haman's wife in referring to Mordecai as being "from the seed of the Jews" (6:13) and repeated twice near the end, when Purim's commemoration becomes a commitment for the Jews "and their seed" (9:27) as well as for future generations, that the remembrance shall not pass "from their seed" (9:28). These passages emphasize the preservation of the people along with the memory and rites of Jewish historical experience. The dual possible meanings are neatly reflected in the two Aramaic Targums of Esther. In the first, Mordecai proclaims peace "to all the descendants of the house of Jacob" (i.e., the Jewish people) while in the second it is "his descendants."

Looking closely at the Book of Esther is always likely to reveal a countercurrent of some sort. The concluding praise of Mordecai actually says that he was popular with "the great number of his people" (10:3). Not all? According to the Talmud, some fellow members of the Sanhedrin disapproved of his actions (Megillah 16b); the Targum Rishon restricts his popularity even more remarkably: "accepted by most of his brethren from the tribe of Benjamin."[2] These commentaries seem responsive to political realities that still hold true, for no leader is accepted wholeheartedly by all.

Yet again, *Esther* keeps us off balance. Why is the title character herself, Queen Esther, not even mentioned in this conclusion? In a manner different from Vashti, she disappears from the story, which concludes with a focus on two prominent men, the king and Mordecai. We may well feel that she has been sidelined from her own story, a woman once again cast into the shadows as if she is insignificant. Perhaps an odd detail suggests an attempt to counterbalance her marginalization. As the culminating events finish with a Jewish victory, Mordecai sent letters to the Jewish communities throughout the kingdom enjoining on them the celebration of the days of Purim through all generations (9:20). Yet following this account, which includes a summary of the plot against the Jews and the events that followed saving them, we read that "Queen Esther, the daughter of Abihail, and Mordecai the Jew wrote emphatically" confirming the

---

2. Bernard Grossfeld, *The Two Targums of Esther*, translated with apparatus and notes (Collegeville, MN: Liturgical, 1991), 90.

observances of Purim, which were fulfilled according to the instructions of "Mordecai the Jew and Queen Esther" and as the people also had obligated themselves. Apparently notwithstanding Mordecai's prominence, a decree countersigned by the queen that ratifies what he has mandated as well as what the people were committed to elevates the obligation of Purim to a higher legal status. Just when we think that Esther is nothing more than a figurehead, it turns out that she has some actual authority.

Perhaps it is the palpable sense of precariousness, even danger, in which Jews have lived in so many places over so many centuries that accounts for Purim's giddiness as well as the Book of Esther careening from laughable improbability to keen danger and from foolish bumbling to cartoonish brutality. While there are traditionalists who believe that every word of it conveys historical facts (perhaps feeling that truth is stranger than fiction), those who approach Esther as a literary work will recognize that whoever was responsible for the original material and its editing produced a narrative showing considerable dramatic skill and tonal range, along with creative defiance of the norms of probability. In all sorts of ways, Megillat Esther is an outrageous tale; the carnival-like atmosphere of Purim celebrations throughout Jewish history, even in staid traditional synagogues, reflects the story's dizzying, unlikely turns of fortunes.

The word "intoxicating" comes to mind appropriately regarding this tale that begins with an ongoing festival at which royal wine is lavishly poured at will for everyone, and leading up to the first fateful crisis when the king is "merry with wine" (1:10). Purim is the one time of the year when rabbinic tradition encourages drunkenness. According to the Talmud (b. Megillah 7b), one should drink so much that one cannot distinguish between "blessed be Mordecai" and "cursed be Haman." The rare encouragement of intoxication has been significantly curtailed in modern times for various good reasons. The wit of the talmudic saying derives from the fact that according to *gematria*, a form of interpretation based on the numerical equivalents of the Hebrew letters, both phrases have the same numerical value. The deeper meaning is that the two phrases are in essence the same. There is no practical difference between "bless our champion" and "curse our foe." They represent the two sides of the central experience of living on the edge of danger.

Countering the hero Mordecai is the villain of the story, Haman, who also comes from a nation other than Persia or Media and whose foreignness, like that of Mordecai, is emphasized both when he is introduced into the story and five subsequent times. He is not just Haman but "Haman the son of Hammedatha the Agagite." Hammedatha is not otherwise mentioned in the Tanakh. However, Agag was king of the Amalekites, who were Israel's especially hated enemy, stemming from an episode in Exodus 17 when Amalek and his army attacked the Israelite stragglers in the wilderness. The experience was so bitter that in Deuteronomy 25:17–19 Moses commands, "Blot out the remembrance of Amalek from under heaven; do not forget." Paradoxical as this message is ("do not forget to blot out"), the name "Amalek" becomes over time, like the name "Haman," a synonym for "enemy of the Jews."

Agag is mentioned once in Numbers 24:7 as a powerful king; but he, or a king of the same name, figures more prominently in 1 Samuel 15. There, after Agag was defeated and captured by Saul, his life was spared, contrary to God's instructions conveyed through the prophet Samuel. Samuel himself, however, executed Agag and dismembered his corpse. Linking Haman with Agag the Amalekite from the beginning succinctly establishes a deeply rooted, generations-old hostility between him and Mordecai the Jew, who is from the tribe of Benjamin, as was King Saul. This connection might also explain a comment by Haman's wife and his advisers, who tell him that if his enemy Mordecai is in fact "of Jewish seed" (*mi-zerah ha-yehudim*), Haman will surely fall because of him (6:13). This warning resonates much more meaningfully if we recognize that a historical conflict underlies it. The cycle of that conflict will be completed when, after Haman's execution, the king bestows on Mordecai the ring of royal office that he had once given to the villain and gives the house of "Haman the enemy of the Jews" to Esther, who promptly transfers it to Mordecai. In this instance "house" probably means not only the physical domicile but all of his property.

This link between Haman and Amalek also accounts for the long-standing Purim custom of "blotting out" the name of Haman each time it is mentioned in the public reading of the Megillah, usually by raucous noises and boos; some write his name with chalk on the soles of their shoes, stamping or scraping when he is mentioned in order to eradicate the name. Of course, listeners need to know or be alerted every time the vicious one's name comes, which is in keeping with the ironic tension of remembering in order to obliterate. It is also the dramatic antithesis of the rabbinic prohibition against erasing God's name. Judaism has no "Devil" or "Satan" in the sense that Christianity interprets that persona but it does typify some nations such as Edom and figures such as Amalek and Haman as multigenerational antagonists of God and Israel.

Fitting his role, Haman gives voice not only to his particular antipathy toward Mordecai, who is like him a foreigner in this culture, consequently a challenging model of how to adapt to it without completely yielding to it. When Mordecai refuses to kneel and bow to Haman after the king appoints the latter prime minister, the offended official turns his anger not only against this one man but against all Jews. Haman the Agagite (i.e., not a Persian or Mede) approaches the king in the guise of a super-patriot who is offended by a people (*am* in Hebrew) who will not adapt themselves fully to the laws of the land and the king. As Haman explains to the king, this *am*, "scattered and dispersed among the peoples of all the provinces," keep their own laws while not obeying the king's. Haman's argument suggests that the Jews were integrated throughout all the regions of the empire, not physically segregated but (if we believe him) not totally assimilated.

Haman, unquestionably the villain of the piece, is perfectly suited to the tone of Megillat Esther, for he is a tragicomic villain. While he intends to do real harm, his deep malice and implacable rage continually result in his own frustration as well as public humiliation or worse, leading up to his death, hanged and displayed on the very gallows that he had prepared for Mordecai. In a light-hearted anticipation of the end, the king, meaning to honor Mordecai though not yet naming him, obliviously asks Haman to advise how a person the king wishes to honor should be treated. Haman, ignorantly supposing he is that man, advises an elaborate ritualistic parade with the favored man mounted on horseback led through the streets, only to be told that his arch-enemy is the man being honored and he is obligated to be the one leading the horse. It is broadly, absurdly farcical. A Talmudic midrash (Megillah 16a, repeated in Targum Rishon) posits that his daughter, in a travesty moment arising from her own misunderstanding of who is riding the king's horse and who is leading it, dumps the contents of her chamber-pot on his head. It seems that it's not only the proverbial egg that the scoundrel has on his face! He is wicked and could be feared; yet he is constantly foiled by his over-reaching and reduced to a preposterous figure of ridicule. A modern reader might think of Charlie Chaplin's satirical undercutting of fascist leaders in his 1940 film *The Great Dictator*.

However, the moment of his ultimate undoing is an episode of drawing-room comedy suddenly gone lethal: pleading for his life to

Esther (who has just unraveled his plot and revealed herself as Jewish), he veritably throws himself on her just as the infuriated Ahashverosh, who has conveniently stepped into the garden for a moment of fresh air, returns, takes in the scene, and accuses the terrified counselor of assaulting the queen even in the house and presence of the king. For an instant it all seems a laughable way of humiliating an evildoer, who might in a true comedy slink away in disgrace . . . but then Ahashverosh sends him to summary execution.

The entire scene, from the exposure of Haman's intrigue to his hanging, takes place within just four verses. The vicious plotter whose scheming has dominated the story from his first appearance in chapter 3 to very near the end of chapter 7 is dispatched in a brief phrase. After a long build-up, it is a head-spinning reversal even for those who have read or heard the story many times. At any moment the lot may be cast again and "luck" changes, like the medieval wheel of fortune revolving.

The Akkadian-Persian loan word "*pur*" means "lot," as in casting the lot so as to make a decision; *purim* is the Hebrew plural. Specifically in our story it refers to the lot being cast for Haman to decide the propitious date for annihilating the Jews (3:7 and 3:13). Casting lots was a practice widespread in the ancient world, similar to rolling a die in a game. In a book that does not specifically mention God, this method of determining future acts seems to make chance or fate, rather than divine providence or justice, decisive.

That supposition is undermined of course by the actual turn of events. We might compare this story with the episode in Numbers 22–24, in which Balak hires the pagan soothsayer Balaam to curse the Israelites but is foiled when God inspires Balaam instead to praise and bless them, in words that have long been incorporated in daily Jewish worship, "How goodly are your tents, O Jacob, your dwelling places, Israel" (Numbers 24:5). As Thomas à Kempis attests, perhaps recalling Proverbs 19:21, "Man proposes; God disposes." Haman's day of wrath is turned back against him and his followers.

Though God is neither invoked nor even directly referred to in the book, it appears to many readers that something like divine protection is nevertheless at work. It does not act through overt miracles but through the confluence of propitious circumstances and human agency. The Jews would not be saved merely because Esther, the chosen queen, was Jewish. She needed to act bravely herself. However, had she not become queen, she would have had no way to intervene. Mordecai's proven loyalty would not have been enough by itself to save even him, much less his people, from the intended destruction; he would have been killed, even as the patriotic German Jews who had fought for Kaiser and country in World War I would fall victim to the Nazis despite their service and military medals. But through the chain of circumstances that he helped create, he was properly situated to appeal to the queen.

Jewish mystics have been intrigued by the verbal connection between Purim and Yom ha-Kippurim, literally "The Day of Atonements," another name (Exodus 30:10) for Yom Kippur, the Day of Atonement. We perceive the relationship more strongly in Hebrew, where the initial syllable in "Kippurim" can be read as the Hebrew prefix "*ki-*," meaning "like" (i.e., the day like Purim). Assuming that there are no coincidences in verbal similarities, they ponder what the deep relationship might be between Purim, the most carnal and carnivalesque of Jewish festivals, and Yom ha-Kippurim, the most spiritual and abstemious. One place in which they find it is the casting of lots, by which the high priest on the Day of Atonement selects one of the two sacrificial goats of identical value to be cast out into the wilderness "for Azazel" (or in some English translations, "as a scapegoat") while the other is sacrificed to God (Leviticus 16:6–10). Casting lots is cited in the Tanakh only in this rite and in Esther. Azazel being nowhere else mentioned in the Bible and that goat's fate being rather obscure, this is one of the most mysterious rituals in the Tanakh. Nevertheless, the import is clear: the fate of each depends on the proverbial roll of the die, at best a "judgment call" that has nothing to do with intrinsic worth. One might term it chance.

Or one could instead say that it is the divine will being actualized in ways beyond our control or understanding. Purim's invitation to intoxication, if we are motivated by gratitude and appreciation of the divine, takes us to such a plane. We do not perceive God at work in the story but experience the miraculous effect of God working unseen to save the Jewish people. Such a sublime state might be approximated on Yom Kippur. This is a day when we read the account of that sacrificial ritual, a day in which we abstain from food and drink and sex and many other forms of physical pleasure or luxury, a day during which we acknowledge that the fate of every living creature is fully in God's control, indeed a day on which some follow a special tradition of praying while wearing the white shroud (not just ordinary white clothing) that will be their burial garment. On such a day we may have a loftier, more profound experience of the divine at work in, as well as beyond, our lives, in ways seen and unseen. We recognize that our being present and alive at that moment is neither a given nor a guarantee; it is not something that we have even earned or deserve on account of our good deeds or our personal efforts at remaining well. Reflecting on this one who died young in an accident and that one struck down by disease in apparently healthy middle age and yet another whose heart failed while they were biking to keep healthy and yet another who lives into old age despite chronic mental or physical griefs, this one on whom fortune never smiles while their sibling's every word and deed turn into gold, we can be pardoned for imagining the casting of lots as the rule of life and death on Yom ha-Kippurim, a day like Purim. At the same time our lips recite affirmations that all occurs according to God's will. While divine will is certainly a different concept from chance, both are equally inscrutable to a mortal mind.

If we then turn to the passage in 4:13–14 where Mordecai urges Esther to intercede with the king, we see there another moment when everything seems to turn on a decision that could go one way or the other. Mordecai tries skillfully yet discreetly to tilt the odds, sending word that if she fails to act, the Jews will find relief and deliverance *mi-maqom akher*, "from another place" (4:14). This phrase has been much discussed as the book's one possible allusion to God inasmuch as "*ha-maqom*" (the place) is a rabbinic term for God, notably in the midrashic Genesis Rabbah. The Targum Rishon makes this religious interpretation explicit: the Jews will be saved "on account of the merits of the Patriarchs of the World and the Lord of the Universe will deliver them";[3] Targum Sheni characteristically insists explicitly on the working of divine providence by adding, "as He produces redemption for them constantly."[4] The Masoretic text, however, leaves the "source" ambiguous. Will help come from the Maker of Heaven and Earth or from some human stratagem?

But Esther, knowing the danger to herself if she oversteps the boundary of royal decorum in approaching the king, must make a choice, recognizing that as Mordecai prompts her, there is danger on the other side of the decision as well. That is, if she fails to act, she will lose her own community, cutting herself off in the process from "your father's house"

---

3. Grossfeld, *Two Targums of Esther*, 60.
4. Grossfeld, *Two Targums of Esther*, 158.

(*bet avicha*). What Mordecai's understatement does not mention is that he, her adoptive father, seems to be the only other living member of her family. At stake is the life of her people; more particularly the life of her parent is also at stake, along with any hope of the familial continuity of her father's "house." Esther's momentous response, "If I perish, I perish" (4:16) is *prima facie* an acceptance of the possibility that she will infringe the king's law and be executed; or else that she will fail to alter the edict and, having identified herself as a Jew, die with her people.

To the rabbinic interpreters of the talmudic and midrashic times, who are less interested in Esther as an example of heroic defiance and more interested in her as a Jewish woman who is married to a gentile in a gentile environment, Esther embodies another dimension of risk and loss. She has told Mordecai that "I will go to the king, though it is against the law" (4:16). Since this interpretive tradition infers that Mordecai is also her husband, Rabbi Abba understands her to mean that previously she was intimate with the king under compulsion, when he summoned her; but now in going voluntarily (as it were) to him, she will be regarded as adulterous and forbidden to Mordecai as a wife, thus cut off from him and from her familial lineage. It is an ironic twist to her intervention, albeit scarcely voluntary, through which she will attempt to rescue her people.

The book is marked otherwise by strange, implausible, and historically unattested laws and procedures that seem to exist only to serve the plot. To begin with, there is the beauty contest constructed to choose a new queen, a totally improbable premise at a time when royal marriages were negotiated for diplomatic and strategic value, not romance or physical attraction. Later, a significant moment of drama occurs because of an alleged law mandating death for anyone presuming to approach the king in the palace's inner courtyard without being summoned by him (4:11), a stricture that Esther will risk violating but one that has no known basis in actual Persian law. Even more bizarre is the claim that a royal edict sealed with the king's signet may not be revoked even by the same king (8:8), though he may issue a countervailing one to offset the effect of the first. This last complication, resulting in the anti-Semites first being given permission to destroy the Jews and then the Jews being granted permission to defend themselves, not only results in a brief civil war resulting in tens of thousands of Persian and Median deaths; it also recalls the motif of casting lots, first one side having the advantage, then the other. Taken as a whole the improbabilities situate the text in a border realm between history and fable, hinting at historical veracity ("for a decree that is written in the king's name and sealed...") but driven instead by opportunities to elaborate the plot engagingly.

What anyone makes of Megillat Esther depends greatly on how much of a biblical traditionalist the reader is. For those, whether Jewish or not, who consider the Bible factual, the Book of Esther is a guide to history. When the text refers to Persia's "127 provinces," they infer that this is correct information about the country's administrative regions. When it describes a celebratory feast for the kingdom's elite that lasts for 180 days, followed by a week-long banquet for all of Shushan, the capital city, they presume it faithfully attests to the lavish self-indulgences of the monarch. When it recounts how the Jewish Esther became queen of this foreign empire and, at the instigation of her kinsman Mordecai, not only saved her people from slaughter and allowed them to massacre vast numbers of their Persian foes, literally inclined readers are certain the book recounts real events, indeed a momentous experience in the historical persecution of Jews. Further, when the Jews celebrating their victory "committed themselves to do what they had commenced doing" (9:23), referring *prima facie* to the sending of gifts and charity, the Babylonian sage Rava (b. Shabbat 88a) argues that this means they recommitted themselves to the covenant made at Sinai, a diaspora community linking itself consciously to its ancient ancestors' act of faith. Many ages later the fourteenth-century Catalonian Jewish philosopher and rabbi Hasdai Crescas read the passage similarly. Thus the book was interpreted for centuries to harmonize the text at hand with the reader's religious convictions, which is how it is still understood by many, especially within traditionally minded communities.

For others, this is a brilliantly outrageous, anecdote-filled short story crammed with historical impossibilities that range from the hilarious to the heroic, a pastiche of serious and comic dramatic scenes cobbling together elements of spy and mystery narratives, including hidden identities and marvelous coincidences, with an entertaining variety of burlesque episodes. Its long and winding path to a conclusion demonstrates why a rambling tale that an English speaker might call a shaggy-dog story is referred to in Yiddish as a *gantse megillah*, a whole megillah. To these readers, the book's historicity crumbles from the slightest weight of verifiable fact (such as Persia's actual number of provinces, recorded in ancient documents as no more than thirty-two) or even plausibility (for instance, the preposterous supposition that a successful emperor would give a party that kept him, all of his nobles, and senior administrators dissolutely carousing in the capital for half a year).

For such readers, especially in the Jewish community, this is a rollicking adventure story with broadly delineated characters and daring adventures in a glamorous Eastern palace filled in equal measure with feasts and intrigue. It features not one but two resourceful Jewish heroes, the first a clever and righteous man and the other a beautiful and brave young woman. A hidden identity is revealed at the climactic moment; there are startling reversals of fortune. The king is powerful, willful yet gullible, while the villain is devious but easily outwitted by the two intelligent Jews. An elaborate scheme to destroy the Jewish people turns into a total victory for them and destruction of their foes. So it is a tale made for celebrating with food and drinks, a historical story that Jewish children and parents can embrace alike as a lighthearted fantasy, a tale of anti-Semitism resoundingly defeated. As a modern joke offers in summarizing Jewish history, "They tried to kill us, they failed, let's eat."

How is it that this book warrants such different readings? To start, we might consider the distinction between facts and truth. Facts are provable, subject to the hard light of empirical verification and documentary evidence. To some Bible readers, "Holy Scripture" is self-proving: I know because the Bible tells me so. Granted, among those are people, including very sophisticated people, who will point to traditional commentaries and interpretations to support their claims, but this simply interposes another layer of acceptance because the authorities they cite are those for whom the scriptural record stands beyond questioning. Notable rabbinic commentators like Rashi did not seek to test the historicity of the texts on which they commentated. Rather, taking the texts at their word as historical, they sought to explicate or expound on their meanings and sometimes even to explain away any apparent anomalies or contradictions with whatever they knew of the historical records. The fact that no accounts outside the Tanakh itself support a particular biblical story is to them irrelevant at best. If the Bible says it happened, it happened. Thus, when passages in Esther allude to past historical events following the destruction of the First Temple but offer a chronology that cannot possibly be correct, or use allegedly historical names that cannot be aligned with actual Persian records, or refer to practices that are belied by what history or logic tell us, the true believer will take the biblical story as the correct one, all the others being compromised in some way or improperly redacted.

For example, at a critical juncture the Jewish Mordecai refuses to kneel and bow to Haman, who has been granted a high governmental position and a royal warrant mandating he be shown such deference. The Masoretic text implies that Mordecai identified himself as a Jew to the other courtiers to justify his behavior. However, this refusal to kneel to a human figure of authority is sufficiently at variance with biblical Jewish precedents that other sources are moved to explain his behavior. The Talmud (Megillah 19a) says that Mordecai did not bow because Haman was making himself like a god. The Aramaic Targum Rishon and Midrash Esther Rabbah 6:2 assert by way of explanation that Haman wore the image of an idol on his chest, thereby demanding reverence to the idol, while a later Targum presents Mordecai as arguing that he cannot bow because Haman is a scion of an age-old enemy of the Jews. In other words, the Masoretic text and rabbinic commentaries offer divergent culturally and historically shaped interpretations of this brief yet dramatic and crucial but enigmatic incident in order to validate its historical verity.

There is however a level of truth that might not be verifiable but nonetheless commands assent because it tells us something that other sorts of experiences validate. In the biblical accounts of Esther and Mordecai we encounter depictions of circumstances we know well from history. These are Jews living in non-Jewish and potentially hostile environments who may keep their Jewish origins hidden for their own safety or to allow them to advance in their society. One might not be able to say that they practice Judaism (or, if one prefers, Israelite religion) where they are living because there might be nothing specifically Jewish in the normal conduct of their lives, though their principal foe ascribes religious as well as cultural independence to their Jewish identity, a "difference" that allegedly makes them untrustworthy and inassimilable. We might see them instead mainly as members of the Jewish people who have managed to "pass" as adherents of the social majority.

There comes a time, however, when their Jewishness is either uncovered by others or must be disclosed by them because their Jewish beliefs conflict with some new development or because of an existential threat to Jews at large. At that point they are forced to choose whether to keep themselves safe by continuing to shield their background or instead to reveal themselves as Jews in order to act on behalf of the people they claim as their own people. We see that it also shows the precarious situation of the Jew who rises to a place of influence and prestige in an alien and perhaps antagonistic culture, at risk of becoming a target because of being Jewish and being revealed as such. That is a situation that we recognize as true, validated in many times and places.

The Book of Esther therefore as we can perhaps see more clearly in the twenty-first century is partly a story of how women have sometimes gained, wielded, and then lost power and even their lives in patriarchal societies. It is also a paradigmatic story about how Jews living in the diaspora negotiate their identity, vulnerability, and power. For modern Zionist Jews, noticing the possibility that this book might date from an era in which the Second Temple existed, this is also a cautionary tale of how precarious Jewish existence, let alone cultural integrity, could be in the diaspora. Further, it has been seen and applied as not only about Jews in such a circumstance but about any minority or subjugated group struggling for security or precariously navigating the upper reaches of society.

Our perspectives on sexual dynamics and abuses of power are not the same as those of antiquity. We may look at the story of Esther and perceive personages or types we recognize. The book may give us instruments for discerning situations of our age and experiences, much as our knowledge of the world allows us to notice aspects of the text that might otherwise go unnoticed. We see Vashtis and Esthers of our own time—wives and consorts, sisters and daughters who are subjugated by autocrats and oligarchs, or abused and manipulated by spouses or partners or male relatives—and we may want to read the text accordingly. Yet to do so, driven by the force of the narrative, is to forget that really there is no Vashti and no Esther, rather "Vashti" and "Esther," not actual people experiencing these events and feeling them as human beings might but instead literary characters, whose reactions and motives are shaped within the boundaries of the book's language. A human social question for us today might be, what should a woman today in Esther's circumstance do? A literary question surely must be, what is possible for the character Esther to do within the narrative constraints of her literary world?

As is true in sexual politics, so too in geopolitics. The hyperbolic dramas of Megillat Esther would seem so broad that one could not imagine taking them as models for direct action. Certainly no Jewish community, even those that celebrated their own Purim analogues, ever visited violence on the majority population that had endangered them. However, on Purim in 1994 an American-born right-wing extremist

Israeli man invaded a mosque in the Cave of Machpelah, the burial site of biblical patriarchs and matriarchs, where he killed twenty-nine Muslim worshipers and wounded over a hundred others before being killed himself by survivors. His inspiration for the massacre seems to have been a warped interpretation of the Megillah's ninth chapter celebrating the victories of the Jews over their foes. In 2024, as Purim occurred in the midst of the devastating Gaza war that followed Hamas's horrific October 7, 2023 assaults in Israel, the progressive American Jewish organization The Shalom Center published a "Chapter 9 Project" web-based compilation of revisionings by rabbis, writers, and activists offering their own peaceful community-building alternative versions of the biblical story's violent conclusion.

Juxtaposing the Book of Esther with the incontrovertible historicity of Eykhah/Lamentations, we are immediately struck by the differences in the ways that liturgical dramaturgy copes with the events on which the texts are based. For Tisha b'Av immerses us totally in the mood of catastrophic communal defeat, persisting in holding tenaciously to that outlook even in our own time, while Purim giddily reels away from thoughts of real danger, instead seizing the hint of farcical reversal in every risky moment and celebrating a triumph ascribed mainly to a moment in the life of the book's female protagonist.

It is easy to understand why Esther is popular in Jewish lore: she heroically saves her people, liberating them from persecution. She also proves a model to non-Jewish audiences. Aptly, two classical musical oratorios, one by Alessandro Stradella (ca. 1670) and the other by Carl Maria Ditters von Dittersdorf (1773), specifically characterize her as a liberator of the Jewish people, each calling her (respectively) *"liberatrice dell' popolo ebrae"* and *"La liberatrice del popoplo giudaico nella Persia."* She is one of very few women mentioned by name in the Bible who do something significant other than bear children. Indeed, there is no mention in her book and little in the commentaries of her having any progeny; however, according to a rabbinic midrash she is the mother of Darius, who was consequently "pure from his mother's side but impure from his father's" (Midrash Esther 8:3).

Moreover, her courage is on a scale that we can imagine reaching for ourselves. Mordecai fatefully says to her, "Who knows but that it was for a moment such as this that you were placed in this situation." What is asked of her is one crucial intervention, not a lifelong struggle. Most of us will likely feel unable to take on a challenging lifetime of risky commitments. But to rise to one trial in a critical moment affecting both oneself and one's entire nation is something that many more of us could imagine, or at least fantasize about. She has met her moment of testing and passed it superbly.

Unlike the Book of Ruth, which ends with a genealogy that points the story toward a larger place in Jewish history, the Book of Esther concludes with a "happily ever after" gesture suggesting that Mordecai made an indelible mark in Persia and especially the Persian Jewish community. Of his descendants, and even more remarkably Esther's, the text offers not a word. Perhaps this fact as much as any other hints at the tale's fictional, not historical essence.

One of the many unusual features of this book is that there are substantial differences between the Hebrew version, known as the Masoretic text (so-called for the Jewish editors in late antiquity who stabilized the textual *masorah* or "tradition"), and the two Greek versions, the most significant of which is the Septuagint. (A shorter and apparently later one, called the "Alpha-text," is relevant only to scholars.) For Jewish and Protestant readers, the Septuagint might be of historical and scholarly interest but is not otherwise significant because their biblical texts of Esther follow the Masoretic version. However, Roman Catholic and Eastern Orthodox Christians use the Septuagint, which presents a radically different view of the book. Therefore, some brief commentary about that version is important.

As transmitted in the Masoretic Hebrew text, Esther is remarkably devoid of any explicit religious references (save for one arguable implication, discussed below). No one prays, not even when Mordecai and Esther are in greatest distress and would seem most in need of appealing for divine help. Nor does anyone offer hymns or prayers of thanksgiving when the Jews ultimately are victorious. Esther, her servants, and the Jewish people fast for three days, yet the purpose of that fast is never ascribed to (for instance) seeking divine compassion but could instead just as well be an act of personal discipline to danger. Just as striking is the absence of any reference to Jewish practices and ritual observances, such as dietary restrictions of *kashrut* that Esther might have followed amid the gustatory riches of palace life and its banquets, although rabbinic commentaries on the story have asserted that Esther adopted an exclusively vegetarian or vegan diet in the palace, subsisting on nuts, seeds, legumes, and fruit. Similarly, the text avoids specifying that when she cohabits with the Persian monarch who has married her, they are sexual partners as well, though again the early rabbinic and later medieval commentators go to considerable lengths to explain and justify her "passive" or involuntary acceptance of her marital duty. Additionally, the behavior of the Jewish characters in the time of crisis, such as covering the head with ashes, wearing sackcloth, and fasting, are mourning and penitential rites found in other cultures, not conduct exclusive or obligatory to Jews.

These omissions from the text, however, are filled in the later Greek Septuagint (abbreviated LXX, probably deriving from Alexandria in the second century BCE) by a half dozen extended passages along with several other additions or changes. They include an opening section of seventeen lines introducing Mordecai along with an allegorical premonitory dream of his that does not figure in the Masoretic version but may suggest a stylistic link to the Books of Ezekiel and Daniel. This and the other additions transform the tone of the text from the seriocomic balance of the Hebrew into a religiously reverent and earnest drama in which the Jewish characters' trust in God is never in doubt. They express their faith, for instance, in lengthy petitionary prayers, declaring their fidelity to the God of Israel, the Torah, and traditional Jewish observances as well as their abhorrence of the heathenish practices of (as Esther says there) "the uncircumcised" (LXX, 8:15). Her terminology obliquely alludes to the uncomfortable narrative element in which this Jewish woman is married outside her faith and people to a gentile, the king named in this version as Artaxerxes, who historically was a son of the Xerxes whom some have identified with the Hebrew book's Ahashverosh. (Indeed, the two Aramaic Targums call the king Xerxes.) Esther even dramatically proclaims to God that she detests her pagan crown "as much as a menstrual rag" (LXX, 8:16) and avers that she wears the royal headdress only in public. Both Esther and Mordecai in this Greek version ask for divine assistance, explicitly recalling biblical instances of divine favor toward Israel. This they never do in the Hebrew version, relying there on their own resources.

As one might expect, scholars have engaged in considerable speculation about the relationships between these versions, particularly on the subject of which of them represents the original or more authentic text. It seems proper to say "more authentic" because it is possible that there was an earlier, so-called *Urtext*, that was somewhat differently transmitted by the Masoretic and the Alpha renditions.

Nevertheless, since we do not know how or if that hypothetical *Urtext* text might have changed in the chain of transmission, it seems most plausible that the Masoretic Hebrew version is either the original or at least closest to the original. It is hard to fathom that the narrative originally contained fervent prayers and devout professions of adherence to Jewish traditions that some exceedingly pious Jewish editors stripped away so as not to profane religion by incorporating such material amid the story's sometimes bawdy, vulgar behavior. One can more easily imagine that a later generation, especially one living in the Hellenic diaspora, would keenly perceive the lack of these religious elements in a raucous, tonally unpredictable short story and attempt to mend the record by imposing both orthodoxy and orthopraxy on the protagonists, as far as seemed possible given the plot.

This book has proven relatively attractive to creative artists, even apart from the vast number of Purimspiels and other parodic or burlesque presentations that take place during the festival itself, those being highly derivative and purposely silly works that by and large do not claim and rarely approach artistry. Given that the festival is supposed to be distinguished by merriment not associated with other Jewish holidays, the Purim play generally only hints at the tones of lurking catastrophe that we can perceive in the text, and if it does so, the violence is cartoon-like. By contrast, the works of genuine art that represent Esther focus on its inherent scenes of drama and danger, frequently relying heavily on midrashic additions or theological framing that come from the Septuagint rather than the Masoretic version.

    Characters and dramatic scenes from Esther appear occasionally in visual art, especially works with biblical themes popular across Europe in the seventeenth century. These include Artemisia Gentileschi's tumultuous *Esther Before Ahasuerus* in the Metropolitan Museum of Art as well as paintings by Rembrandt and his students. Among the latter are *The Banquet of Esther* (1645) by the Dutch painter Jan Victors (1616–76) and Arent or Aert de Gelder, Rembrandt's last pupil, who depicted *King Ahasuerus Condemning Haman* (1680) and two paintings of Esther with Mordecai.

    Despite having a compelling, extravagant, and colorful story that seems made for opera, the Book of Esther has received only a few musical treatments, the best known and most often performed and recorded being Handel's oratorio of the same name. Said to be the first English oratorio ("or Sacred Drama," as the title page explains), with a libretto based on a translation of the eponymous play by Racine premiered in 1689 as a moralistic entertainment for a girls' school, Handel's *Esther* was originally performed in 1718, revised and expanded for a 1720 performance and then again for 1732, a process common for the composer. Following Racine, Handel's libretto (usually ascribed to Samuel Humphreys), rather than deriving directly from the biblical text itself, affirms the workings of divine providence with a consistency that will surprise those familiar only with the standard Jewish Masoretic biblical text. Racine also revised his play for a musical adaptation by Jean-Baptiste Moreau, which was performed by the girls of Mme. De Maintenon's St. Cyr school. Alessandro Stradella's oratorio *Ester* has also been recorded but not, as yet, Marc-Antoine Charpentier's roughly contemporaneous *Historia Esther* (1677). Élisabeth Jacquet de la Guerre's solo cantata, *Esther*, published in 1708 was the first in her series of *Cantates Biblique* and is built on three arias, two of them succinctly recounting in outline the well-known defeat of Haman's plans, the third (addressed presumably to the "Sun King," Louis XIV) urging the monarch to seek out truth actively rather than relying on brave individuals to disclose it.

Unfortunately, three twentieth-century works by Jewish composers have not been recorded or widely performed. Darius Milhaud's opera *Esther de Carpentras* is a version based on a Purim play with the action transposed to the Middle Ages in Milhaud's home region of Provence; though composed in the 1920s, it was presciently premiered by the Paris Opéra-Comique in 1938. A 1956 *Esther* by the composer Jan Meyerowitz, born in Germany but subsequently an émigré to the United States, is set to a libretto by the African American poet Langston Hughes, with whom he collaborated on other projects; around the same time Meyerowitz also composed a Symphony *"Midrash Esther"* that has been recorded but is said to contain no musical material from the opera.

More recently, the Moravian-born American Hugo Weisgall's final opera, his 1993 *Esther*, on a text by the experienced librettist Charles Kondek, was rapturously received when it was first performed that year by the New York City Opera Company with Lauren Flanigan in the title role; in 2009 the same company revived it with Flanigan reprising the part, again to outstanding reviews. Weisgall, a prolific composer who also had a doctorate in German literature, was thoroughly familiar with Jewish, especially cantorial, traditions; in addition, he had served in the U.S. Army in World War II and visited Terezin at the end of the war, all experiences that shaped his treatment of the story and music. Developments of various subsidiary characters from Megillat Esther along with explorations of their motives and psychology turn this work into a midrash on the text rather than simply a dramatization of it. For example, Esther's initial unwillingness to approach the king on the Jews' behalf is treated here as reluctance to disrupt the privileges of regal life that she has grown to enjoy. Regrettably, while some short scenes have been recorded, the opera has languished, probably for economic reasons: mastery of the composer's dense harmonic language requires longer rehearsal time than more directly melodic scores and it demands, along with a large orchestra, a sizable cast as well as a double chorus, as the composer literally gives voice to some characters whom the biblical text merely mentions.

In their various ways, these theatrical musical settings destabilize our impressions of the remarkably varied tonalities in this biblical book. When read in private or experienced publicly through synagogue services and religious school plays, the tale of Esther is filled with irony, humor, and hyperbole. Represented through high art, it becomes a saga brimming with danger, melodrama, and high sentiments. A Jekyll and Hyde book, it engages us through bold, unmistakable farce while alarming us through equally unmistakable menace and multiple varieties of violence, implicit and explicit, potential or actual. It does not easily settle. Familiar as we think it will be each year, Esther has a seemingly endless capacity to surprise.

3

Song of Songs/Shir ha-Shirim

> "Let him give me of the kisses of his mouth—
> For your love delights more than wine."

What an opening for a biblical book—or for any book! No wonder that Song of Songs has been a favorite since ancient times or that its inclusion in the Tanakh as a sacred work was once controversial. Nor that the embedded story has enticed speculations about its facts. Nor that mystics find it a treasury of spiritual insights.

If someone is familiar with the religious interpretations of Shir ha-Shirim—in other words, the justifications for it to be included in the biblical canon—the experience of reading it can be somewhat akin to listening through headphones to a foreign-language play in which one ear gets the original text and the other a simultaneous translation, or perhaps even more similar to Jastrow's rabbit-duck drawing, in which the viewer sometimes sees one image, sometimes the other, while straining to hold the two together. Is this a secular, even erotic series of love poems, or a religious poem lightly garbed in earthy profane scenes? On top of the highly energized yet delicate surfaces of the texts, comprising eight poems or chapters totaling just 117 verses in the original, stands an imposing edifice of spiritual and theological interpretations constantly threatening to crush the literal meanings with weight beyond what they can bear or to topple over because the structure is too lofty and complex for the actions and images on which it is built. Yet the edifice holds, and Song of Songs stands across these many centuries as simultaneously inventive, imaginative, fragrant, and unforgettable love poetry as well as a profound mystical expression of the spiritual devotee's visionary communion with transcendent holiness.

The phrase "song of songs" has at least three meanings. It can be a superlative like "king of kings," thus, the song that is beyond all other songs. It can also mean a song made of songs, that is, a poetry book that is itself one long composition comprising individual songs, not an anthology but what we might call a song cycle, works meant to be sung together in sequence because they carry a story or explore a relationship, such as we find in the Renaissance sonnet sequences by Sidney, Shakespeare, and many others or nineteenth-century masterpieces for voice and piano by composers such as Schubert and Schumann. Lastly, it might even be thought of as a song about songs, a poem of being in love with poetry.

Were these poems originally only spoken? Were they perhaps also sung? Were they even accompanied instrumentally, on a lyre, for example, a kithara, or psaltery? All these possibilities are open for speculation; neither internal evidence nor tradition points us to definite answers. We can be sure that eventually by the time of the Second Temple various verses from the book had found their way into common secular musical use because Rabbi Akiva, the great late-first- to early-second-century mystic and romantic, taught, "whoever sings Song of Songs in taverns or treats it like popular songs has no share in the world to come [i.e., the afterlife]" (Tosefta Sanhedrin 12:5).

The Christian biblical canon tends to call our book of poems Song of Solomon, based on the reading of the incipit, *Shir ha-shirim asher li'shlomo*, "song of songs of [or by] Solomon." This ascription links the Song with the two other biblical volumes traditionally attributed to the king according to the Talmud, that is, Proverbs and Ecclesiastes. According to 1 Kings 4:32, King Solomon, who is also explicitly mentioned in Shir ha-Shirim, composed 1,005 poems. One sage of the Talmudic era, Rabbi Hiyya Rabba, claims that these three works were products of the monarch's spiritually inspired old age, concluding with Shir, while another, Rabbi Yonatan, maintains that they were composed at different stages in his life, Shir expressing the feelings of the young lover. These divergent hypotheses obviously imply that they are exactly this, theories, without factual support. More than that, they mark the two principal ways of reading this book across the centuries. To Rabbi Yonatan, the lyrics voice the romantic and erotic emotions of youth, artful outpourings from a man who became legendary for many reasons, notably having countless wives and concubines. Rabbi Hiyya, however, believes they are the final inspired insights of the proverbially wise visionary who also brought to fruition the building of God's Temple in Jerusalem, crowning his life's work with stones and words, an edifice and a text, both structures to facilitate the union of the human with the divine. (Lovers of literature will appreciate that the words have endured over these many centuries, though the Temple did not.) Thus, in the two rabbinic origin stories we see the tension between the profane and the sacred views of Song of Songs.

The narrative details, so far as we can discern, make the ascription of the cycle to Solomon improbable, despite or because of his later history of acquiring wives and concubines. So too do the numerous borrowings from diverse languages, suggesting that the compositions derive from a wide period of Israel's history. Of course, as an old movie line says, "When the legend becomes fact, print the legend." Some of the poetry might be by Solomon; it is also possible that Solomon possessed, collected, or perhaps even commissioned a group of these poems, treating them as thematically unified and making them into a scroll that would eventually become a book of the Tanakh. It is also possible that later poets or editors contributed to what had been a core group of early poems. The structure of the book and even the unity of the eight individual chapters are debatable: early editors of the Hebrew biblical texts, the so-called Masoretes, identified their own different units of division, while in the late twentieth century, the translator and poet Marcia Falk composed her version of the song as thirty-one lyrics, essentially deconstructing the poems and providing a separate table aligning her poems to the corresponding chapters and lines of the original works.

Because of the ways that Jewish thinkers have interpreted the love language of Shir religiously, images and even verses from the book have permeated Jewish liturgy as well as secular literature. For Jewish liturgical use as a festival text, it would ordinarily be recited in the synagogue in the morning service on an intermediary sabbath during the week or eight days of Passover, using the same *nusach* (melodic mode) as Ecclesiastes and Ruth, the other two special readings designated for the three Sh'losh Regalim/pilgrimage festivals. In some practices, the recitation takes place during an afternoon service or is divided between the seventh and eighth days of the festival. Many people will also include verses during their

Passover seder. In modern times, Arthur Waskow offers another connection between Shir and Passover. He interprets *haroset*, the sweetly spiced fruit and nut mixture that appears on the ceremonial Passover seder plate in every Jewish culture, as an allusion to this book, which he says provides the menu of ingredients *haroset* uses. To Ellen Bernstein, the poem offers "a holy ecology" that she unfolds through her full translation and commentary emphasizing the work's rich relationships with nature, emotions, and ecological wholeness.

Additionally, because of the traditional spiritual interpretations of the poems, images and quotations from *Shir* have been used in liturgies for several other Jewish holidays. Particular verses, such as "I am my beloved's and my beloved is mine" (6:3), are frequently quoted in wedding ceremonies or other celebrations in order to praise love's dual nature, sacred as well as erotic. Most importantly, beyond its reading on Passover, Song of Songs (or at least selections from it) is often recited on Friday afternoon as the Sabbath approaches because one of the dominant images of Shabbat is that of the beloved bride as a queen being welcomed by her "groom," the people Israel. In this way, the images of the Song of Songs resound in Judaism's mystical teachings about the spiritual as well as physical lovers' union that occurs on Shabbat. As the great medieval Jewish commentator Abraham ibn Ezra observed, for a reader familiar with the imagery of the Jewish prophets (notably, Hosea, Isaiah, Jeremiah, and Ezekiel), the account of a passionate albeit sometimes challenged relationship between a lover and the beloved or between a bride and her spouse will recall prophetic uses of these analogies for Israel's relationship with God, no doubt contributing to the sages' religious and spiritual readings of Shir ha-Shirim.

A modern reader approaching the text with preconceptions about the ancient biblical world is likely surprised to realize that the boldly sensual language of the opening lines, in which the speaker pleads for the kisses of the lover's mouth, are addressed to a man, presumably by a female speaker. (An even greater surprise awaits the reader who consults the classic compilation of rabbinic interpretations called Midrash Rabbah on this verse, only to discover lengthy commentary bearing no discernible connection to the words of the poem.) Destabilizing the reader is one of the book's effects. Given the conventions, or lack thereof, of early texts, particularly the absence of such clues as quotation marks and parentheses, it is difficult for us to discern and adjust to abrupt shifts in points of view and terms of address.

Further, readers encountering the poems only in English translation can miss complexities or ambiguities because English, unlike Hebrew and many other languages, does not inflect second-person pronouns according to gender or number. In English, "you" refers to singular as well as plural, masculine as well as feminine. Without help, one may be unsure about who is being addressed. For example, 1:1 speaks of the beloved in the third person ("Let him kiss me . . ."), but 1:2 shifts abruptly to second person ("For your love . . ."). Among possible solutions, we might suppose the first line to be internal monologue, a thought held in the speaker's mind, a desire felt and imagined but not orally expressed. Some modern translators attempt to smooth the reading experience, resolving the disparity by silently changing the first verb to an imperative direct address to the man, "Kiss me . . . ." This oddly reduces the passage's erotic charge by holding nothing back: the thought is more tantalizing if the speaker refrains from saying it while anticipating the kisses.

Sensuality suffuses the verbal nuances of this moment. After all, what is the difference between "let him kiss me" and "let him give me of the kisses of his mouth"? In the second, more literal version, the preposition implies that his mouth has not just kisses but a plentiful abundance of them. Further, the apparently superfluous word *pi'hu*, "of his mouth," calls attention to the physicality of the fleshly contact. We know that a kiss comes from the mouth, but the original text makes us sense that mouth vividly, in a way that the speaker perhaps is not yet ready to say directly but nevertheless anticipates with thrilling longing.

The poem quickly immerses us in her sensual arousal, along with her conviction that other young women also desire him. "Your oils give forth sweet aromas, your name is like precious oil, and so the maidens are in love with you" (1:3). Not only his physical scent but his name itself arouses desire. Her words brim with passion and urgency, even given Hebrew's lack of emphatic markers such as exclamation marks: "Draw me after you, let us run . . . . Let us delight and rejoice in your love, savoring it more than wine—like heady wine they love you" (1:4).

However, amid this fervor intrudes a disorienting phrase, "*heviani ha-melech hadarav* / the king has brought me to his chamber." King? Chamber? What have we missed? Has the text been jumbled? Or are we confused because we now must oscillate between the poem as narrative and the poem as metaphor? That is, if we are reading a story within the poetry, then we may construct a dramatic scenario based on these three words. Here is one possibility. The female speaker has been lured, summoned, carried away, induced, or seduced into the private quarters of the king (Solomon, perhaps) and calls to her lover to rescue her, taking her with him to enjoy their love. Or, for another angle of approach, we might rather suppose that the lover himself is "the king/*ha-melech*," either because he really is the king or because he is the sovereign of her emotions. However, if this apparent interjection is metaphoric, and keeping in mind that allegory is a form of metaphor, then she is exclaiming over entering into the innermost dimension of intimate union with her lover, a privileged familiarity with the one so desired by the other maidens.

Here we recognize the tension or seeming contradiction between the paths of reading this book. The text is a poem made from a series of poems; and while that does not make it unique, for we could describe Eykhah/Lamentations in the same way, the narrative as well as the emotional range of Shir open complexities and ambiguities of meanings again and again. One path takes us on an episodic journey through an intense, emotionally fraught, erotically charged, and socially challenged love affair between a young woman and a man, each of whom is sometimes the speaker, sometimes the one spoken to; at times we cannot be certain which of them is the speaker and which the addressee, unless a Hebrew grammatical form indicates gender. Their meetings are often clandestine and nocturnal; the woman has brothers, "my mother's sons," who are protective, maybe to an abusive point; they regard her as too young, vulnerable, and impulsive, needing to be controlled. Municipal guards supposedly keeping order at night can be dangerous. Other young women, "daughters of Jerusalem," are her companions, though she is not close to any one of them in particular; she senses that they may denigrate her dark complexion. She knows that she has taken risks in love, that she has "not guarded my own vineyard" (1:6). Despite the obstacles and hazards, the lovers persevere, enjoying both their own relationship and the sensory pleasures of nature's vernal fertility, with all its sights, sounds, and fragrances.

This path invites literary interpretations of familiar sorts, for we are aware of the author's stylistic mastery; the poem's striking images and significant recurring themes; and along with these, we encounter vivid representations of dramatic situations and emotional relationships. A close reading of the text, looking at what Jewish interpretive practices call *p'shat* (the direct contextual meaning), still requires grappling with puzzlements and complexities. This exegetical approach deals with, for instance, the switch in pronouns in the first two verses as mentioned above. It would consider the implications of the phrase "my mother's sons" for the familial dynamics affecting the female speaker, as it might imply that the brothers' father is not hers.

It would grapple also with the provocative phrase "*sh'khorah ani v'navah*" (1: 5), which the King James version of 1612 famously translated as, "I am black, but comely." In this instance, the conjunctive prefix *v* (in Hebrew, the letter *vav*) can indeed mean "but." However, more often, it means "and," as in, "I am black and beautiful." How one interprets that one-letter conjunction significantly shapes one's reading of the character and her circumstance. Furthermore, we see how one's own culture may determine that understanding. For readers of Jacobean England in the late Renaissance, raised on centuries of European literature and art glorifying pale complexions and golden hair, not only for women but even in paintings depicting biblical characters such as Jesus, "but comely" was the likeliest favorable complement to "black." But what of, say, a ninth-century-BCE writer whose ambit was the land of Israel on the western edge of Asia and just east of Africa, who might have known little of fair-skinned, fair-haired people, much less perceiving them as beauty's ideal? For that matter, what might have been the literal and cultural meaning of *shakhor* (black) in the biblical era? Did it denote a very dark complexion, a ruddy one, a dusky Mediterranean one? Did it imply something about one's ethnic or geographic origin, social status, or (as seems to be the case here) the amount of outdoor labor one did, or was it simply an aesthetic criterion? She also says she is *navah*, which can mean pretty, pleasant, or desirable. Is she remarking on her appearance, her personality, or her effect on others? All of these questions and more would engage the exegete.

The other path takes us beyond the surface of the text into realms of metaphorical, symbolic, or allegorical meaning. As also happened during late Antiquity and the early medieval eras in Classical, Christian, and Muslim textual interpretations, Jewish scholars developed a fourfold model of analysis. The Hebrew acronym for this method, PaRDeS (garden), derives from the names of each approach to interpretation. The primary meaning and most accessible level, as we have seen, is the *p'shat*. The three other approaches explore the allegorical (*remez*); homiletic, especially ethical or moral (*drash*); and mystical (*sod*) dimensions. Even though the texts preceded the methodology by many centuries, one could theorize that the meanings, which resided in the texts from the start, could have been perceived by sophisticated readers or auditors and are merely made overt later through techniques such as PaRDeS. Michael Fishbane's magisterial commentary significantly highlights this fourfold exegetical approach by providing four levels of running interpretations, drawn from innumerable sources.

Entering the "garden" of interpreting Shir ha-Shirim and seeing beyond the sorts of questions addressed through the explicitly contextual *p'shat* readings outlined above, we perceive the text rather differently: as an intellectual and spiritual testimony. Readers who see insights into profound philosophical and religious truths in the words of Shir can appreciate the often-quoted testimony of Rabbi Akiva, "the whole world is not as precious as the day that the Song of Songs was given to Israel; for all the Writings are holy, but the Song of Songs is the Holy of Holies" (Mishna Yedaim 3:5). Understanding Song of Songs as the Holiest of Holies means that the yearnings of the lovers and their clandestine meetings express such deep experiences as the philosopher's quest for enlightenment, the righteous person's hunger for true goodness in the face of worldly disdain, and the religious devotee's secret yearning to be united with God—that is, to be one with the One. Thus, the book's other characters represent not only players in a dramatic romance narrative like *Romeo and Juliet*; they are the social, moral, or spiritual forces that challenge, complicate, and strive to block the movement toward perfect unity between the seeker and the ideal. Through the centuries since Akiva (and no doubt long before him), philosophers, rabbis, and sages of different eras, places, and beliefs have found insights cloaked in Song of Songs that they unfold through their searching, discovering hidden and stunning revelations of great meaning, unclothing truths.

A significant talmudic teaching, asserted in response to an interpretation that argued a purely metaphorical reading of a biblical passage, holds that the Torah never loses its plain meaning, its *p'shat* sense (b. Shabbat 63a). That is, no matter how creatively and perceptively one might gloss a text, no matter how compelling or profound a metaphorical or allegorical or metaphysical reading might be, the work is still grounded by the simple, literal sense of the words as we can understand them within their relevant context. Its *p'shat* is like the primary sound, beyond which some listeners might perceive reverberations or overtones at different pitches and intensities, the other PaRDeS levels, while even those who do not perceive these other levels will nonetheless derive value from their attention to the primary meanings of the words. In light of this idea, it makes sense to look first at the human narrative and drama of Shir ha-Shirim, while also considering the stylistic nuances of its poetry, engaging with the beautiful, impassioned love lyrics that continue to captivate readers of all backgrounds and interests, before exploring the second path of reading, a more esoteric way that has engrossed theologians, philosophers, composers of sacred music, and mystical seekers, through whose insights Shir has become a major text of biblical spirituality.

The woman in the poem—the "dark lady," to borrow a term later associated with the woman in Shakespeare's sonnets—asserts to the "daughters of Jerusalem" that her dark-hued beauty is like "the tents of Kedar, like the tapestries of Solomon" (1:6). Kedar, whose name means "dark," is mentioned in Genesis and 1 Chronicles as a son of Ishmael, thus connecting him with Arab lineage, and linking him as well with the eponymous northern Arabian nomadic tribe. The king's ornamental draperies, perhaps the ones in his chamber, contrasting with the rustic tents (likely made of animal skin) suggest the dual physical qualities that comprise her self-definition: dusky and *navah*.

But why is she dark enough to seem anomalous in her own Semitic culture, so much that the other women stare disdainfully at her? "The sun has looked down on me," she explains. She got suntanned because her brothers punished her with outdoor labor. "My mother's sons were angry with me," she complains, and "made me guard the vineyards." Wittily but perhaps bitterly, she seemingly turns the literal vineyard into a metaphor for her physical welfare: "My own vineyard I did not guard" (1:7).

This somewhat cryptic episode of family drama is left unexplained here. We do not know why they were angry, or whether her "vineyard" is meant literally or figuratively, nor whether her unguarded vineyard refers only to her darkened face. Such disjunctions in the narrative contribute to interpreters' inclinations to seek meanings beyond the text's surface.

In the next passage she abruptly turns from explaining herself to the other young women, now directly addressing the man she loves; it is, so to speak, a film director's jump cut to a flirtatious dialogue between two lovers in some undefined private space. "Tell me, my soul's beloved, where you pasture your sheep, where you rest them at noon, so that I do not stray alongside your friends' flocks" (1:7). He responds at once, just as playfully, "If you do not know, most beautiful of women, follow the sheep's tracks and graze your kids near the shepherds' tents" (1:8). First, vineyards; then, grazing sheep: we have entered the faux-naïf realm of pastoral poetry, in which the poet—often a lover—pretends a rustic role to signify honest intentions and simple personal desires, ironically donning a falsely low social standing as a way of rejecting sophisticated urban or courtly pretentiousness and ambition.

This passage also underscores the book's literary artifice by making clear that it embraces a dialogue between characters. While the previous passage could be interpreted as one individual's confessional outpouring, introducing a second speaker's voice and viewpoint reminds us that the text is being shaped by an artistic consciousness that is not simply the same as one of the protagonists but comprehends both of them along with their social contexts. This work is a collection of sophisticated, nuanced individual lyric poems that form a loose narrative, like scenes in an episodic drama, with the overarching storyline heightening their individual significance. The poems themselves are redolent of literary techniques and genres, suffused with the energy of desire, longing, and devotion. Throughout, the attentive reader or listener, particularly one who is engaged with the Hebrew text, will appreciate the finely crafted artistry that shows an author well acquainted with poetry's craft.

For example, as if responding to the young woman's self-description as *sh'khorah . . . v'navah*, her lover celebrates her beauty ekphrastically, sometimes in metaphors that may seem odd to us ("like a mare of Pharaoh's chariot horses" [1:9]) or strikingly familiar ("your neck encircled with jewels" [1:10]), affirming her in her own terms: *na'vu*. Nonetheless, he imagines ornamenting her beauty further with golden circlets to accompany her silver spangles. Pharaoh's magnificent horses retained their near-legendary status in biblical times, and this simile suggests that the man esteems her not for delicacy or shyness but more for her daring energy and power.

She proudly declares that this power is sensual, even sexual: "While the king was on his couch, / My nard gave forth its fragrance" (1:12). The intense, heady, musky aroma of nard (one of the ingredients of the ancient Temple incense) suggests her erotic desire that moves toward fulfillment in the lines that follow. "A sachet of myrrh is my beloved to me nestled between my breasts. A sprig of henna is my beloved to me, from the vineyards of Ein-Gedi" (1:13–14). Reclining on their couch, the lovers engage in a sensuous duet, each in turn lauding the other's beauty. That couch becomes a veritable marital arbor, a love nest, a sheltering home with beams of cedar and rafters of cypress, the two trees that in Jewish tradition are planted for the birth of a son and daughter (respectively), to be made into a huppah (wedding canopy) at their marriage. When the first chapter ends at that point, the effect for the modern reader is like a movie fade-out just as the intimate encounter between a romantic couple approaches sexual fulfillment.

Chapter 2 opens with the two lovers in the full celebratory flush of delight. "I am a rose of Sharon, a lily of the valleys" (2:1), she begins in what seems like the inevitable English terminology given us by King James's translators, though lexical commentaries dispute what flowers are actually meant by the *havatzelet* of the coastal Sharon plains and the *shoshanim* of the valleys. Botanical metaphors dominating this first series of exchanged compliments between the lovers connect Shir ha-Shirim with spring as well as with a vast body of love poetry across countless languages and centuries. As they trade encomia, they match imagery, at once displaying their fine blending of imagination while also suggesting the literary craftsmanship guiding the composition Since she proclaims herself "a lily of the valley," to her lover she is "like a lily among the thorns" compared to other women (2:2). Are they speaking directly to one another, or do these lines express what they would say for themselves? Either is possible.

For her part, she proclaims (to the reader and perhaps, in the poem's apparent storyline, to her friends) he is "like a fruit tree among the forest's trees" compared to other young men, providing her with delightful shade and fruit sweet to her mouth (2:3). We can recognize the cultural conventions (woman as flower, man as tree; she a nonpareil, he a shelter for her) and yet can perhaps be surprised again by her sensual delight of his taste in her mouth. (The *tappuah*, incidentally, seemed to be assuredly an apple tree to most later interpreters but almost certainly was not, though whether it was originally an apricot or some other species of fruit we can no longer determine. But sweet it was.) These are two young people fervently, passionately taken with one another's physical beauty. As readers, we are likely impressed and charmed by their eloquence, wit, imagination, and adventurousness as well. The characters themselves, however, seem not to love one another for the qualities of their minds but because they are each naturally gorgeous.

The next passage, also directed toward auditors, expands on the notion of love being intoxicating. Again, the lines are allusive enough that we are not sure whether they are purely metaphorical or at least partly refer to an actual scene. "He brought me to the wine hall [*beit ha-yayin*] and his banner over me was love" (2:4). To some translators, this new place, which in Hebrew is a "wine house" or "place for drinking wine," is a tavern; to others, a banquet house. Those familiar with Chinese or Japanese art and literature will perceive an analogy with the tea house. But the phrase might instead be a metaphorical way of expressing her intoxication through love. Similarly, "his banner" (*degli*) might suggest a flag of conquest, maybe a phallic erection, or (another way of taking the word *alai*) a sheltering cover or canopy.

"*Samkhuni ba'ashishot rap'duni batapukhim ki-kholat ahava ani* / Strengthen me with sweetmeats, revive me with ripe fruits, for I am weak from love" (2:5). The Hebrew line wafts musically (*ooh, ah*) on broad *u* and *a* vowels. Presumably addressed to her female companions, these words express love's debilitating, destabilizing effect on her before she returns to the physical enactment: "his left hand under my head, his right arm embraced me" (2:6). Oscillation between the outer and inner experiences of passion effectively suggests the swirl of a lover's emotions and senses, along with a compulsion to talk about her experience to her peers. "I entreat you, maidens of Jerusalem, by gazelles or by deer of the fields, do not stir or waken love before its time" (2:7). This line, with its oath or pledge sworn "by gazelles or by deer," aptly keeps us in nature's realm, invoking the potency of wild animals conventionally associated with sexuality. Love's vital energy, she cautions, can be intoxicatingly dangerous, not to be aroused until the time is ripe, either (the meaning is ambiguous here) for the one who desires love or for the progress of love itself.

The first seven lines constitute one complete poetic element. The chapter's next movement—what we might think of as the next stanza of the poem—returns us to the places where the lovers meet and to the urgent immediacy of passion. "The voice of my beloved—behold, he comes!—striding over mountains, leaping over hills" (2:8). Now the lover himself is compared to a gazelle or stag, boldly chancing the boundary between natural freedom and the social constraints that enclose her, for "there he stands behind our wall, peering through the window, peeping through the lattices" (2:9). He comes beckoning her to new enticements of the new year, in words that have become among the most famous in all literature.

> So my beloved spoke, saying to me, "Come, my dear, my lovely one, come away!
> See, the winter is past, the rains are over and gone.
> The flowers appear in the land.
> The time of pruning [singing?] is here;
> The song of the turtledove is heard in our land." (2:11–12)

Although the noun *hazameir* ambiguously may mean either pruning or singing (another appropriately vernal impulse), the passage unambiguously invites the woman to plunge into nature's wealth of sensory experiences, be they the murmurs of doves, the promising sensuality hinted at by the emerging green figs, or the scent of blossoming vines. His imploring and melodious *kumi lakh rayati yafati ul'chi lakh* / "Arise, my beloved, my beauty, and come away" (2:14) invites her to immerse herself in all the pleasures of the physical world, which she herself also embodies: "Let me see your face, let me hear your voice, for your voice is sweet, your face lovely to behold" (2:14). The anaphoric structure (face-voice/voice-face) suggests how fully she embodies beauty.

But to where do they go? The beginning of verse 14 seems to recall passages from Exodus and Jeremiah in which a cleft or cranny in the rocks is a hiding place, here a refuge he strives to induce his "dove" to emerge from, hidden and sheltered as she is, so that he may see and hear her. Are we to imagine her as timid, shy, coy, reluctant, reserved, or self-protective? As expressive as she is to her female companions and therefore to the reader about her passionate feelings, is she more withdrawn with him as their relationship surges ahead? Or is this part of the dynamics of their courtship? At the least, her apparent withdrawal, or elusiveness, appears to stimulate his ardor.

The imagery of the dove among the rocks likely disorients us, at least briefly. Even more will we be set awry by the ensuing image, one that might seem like a fragment out of place. "Catch us the foxes, the little foxes that spoil the vineyards, for our vineyard is in bloom" (2:15). While clear enough literally, this passage makes us wonder how to integrate it into the book's narrative and thematic material. We know that in the "story," the woman tends the family vineyard, which could certainly be endangered by marauding foxes. However, this reference seems a non sequitur here, as it is both preceded by the passage just discussed and followed immediately by her declaration, "*dodi li va'ani lo* / My beloved—to me, and I—to him" (2:16), or as more conventionally translated, "My beloved is mine and I am his." We might recall her earlier lament that she had not guarded her own vineyard, an equivocal remark that might be taken literally or might be understood as a metaphor for personal incautiousness. Consequently, we can imagine line 15 as a ripple of concern, reminding us of the disturbances that can damage a relationship (their "vineyard" of ardor) even at its moment of flowering. Snaring those gnawing little pests, be they doubts or rumors or impediments of other sorts, is necessary so that the vineyard can survive, its blooms given the chance to turn into ripe fruit. She continues, "I am his who pastures among the lilies [*haro'eh bashoshanim*]." The poem returns us to the delicate, suggestive nuances of pastoral love poetry, in which the shepherd lover seeks nourishment for his flock of sheep in the field and for his erotic yearning in the person of his beloved.

Getting the right nuance in English for the phrase "*dodi li va'ani lo*" is difficult, and the difficulty is not merely a translator's quibble. A literal rendering might be, "my beloved is to me and I am to him," a construction that is simply unidiomatic in English. The neat, familiar "my beloved is mine" does not have that problem but it suggests possessiveness—in this case, shared possessiveness, to be sure. However, "to me" hints at something different: a relationship. They do not so much "belong" to one another as they are mutually committed toward each other.

But these lovers must keep their tryst discreet, so with dawn he must depart. The second chapter ends therefore with her urgently sending him away. "Before the breath of day and the fleeting shadows, go, my beloved, swift as a gazelle or young stag, to the jagged hills" (2:17). The concluding image, *al-harei bateir*, is another phrase whose exact meaning baffles commentators, who have tried various translations, though the general significance remains as clear as Juliet's plea to Romeo after their night of passion: morning is coming and you must not be found here, so head for the hills.

Naturally, at the beginning of chapter 3, she misses him. "Nights on my couch, I longed for the one I love—I longed but did not find" (3:1). She is, however, an active lover herself, not a passive one waiting for her suitor to arrive (unless we believe, as Marcia Falk suggests, that what follows is a dream or fantasy). "I have to get up and search through the town, through its streets, its squares; I need to seek out the one I love." After a brief, inconsequential encounter with the night watchmen, who cannot direct her to "the one I love," she finds her beloved, to whom she tightly clings, bringing him to her mother's house, "to the room of the one who bore me" (3:4).

This oddly doubled way of specifying the location's connection with her mother is perhaps meant to connect the lovers' reunion with sexual fulfillment. That connects with her subsequent address to the "maidens of Jerusalem," repeating the earlier one in which they were cautioned, "by gazelles or by deer of the fields," not to awaken love before its time, but now (3:5) with a crucial difference in the lovers' situation. At this juncture the couple's urgency is heightened; their erotic union may be more complete, or at least she recognizes her sexual passion as intense enough that it did or could drive her into the streets at night, boldly confronting the watchmen on their rounds, entreating them for the whereabouts of her lover, whom she identifies not by name but only as "the one I love." She expresses the scenario as real enough that we can be satisfied leaving it hovering between reality and dream, or between reality and Freudian manifestation of desire.

The first part of this eleven-verse chapter begins with the young woman's longing and progresses to the fulfillment of her yearnings. The second part, seemingly a celebration of King Solomon's wedding, appears to be a disorienting and radical shift in perspective and content. If, however, we imagine the lovers' union in the preceding lines as prelude to the consummation of love through marriage, the chapter seems more clearly unified, despite the shift in point of view and tone. For now the viewpoint shifts to that of an observer astonished by the fragrance of the woman who approaches like an exotic, nearly intangible mystery. Rather than a typical ekphrastic delineation of her visible beauty (her eyes, her hair, her complexion), this annunciation of her arrival impressionistically evokes the sensual aroma of sweet and spicy perfumes that adorn her so richly that a physical form is scarcely imagined. "Who is she, arising from the desert like columns of smoke, fragrantly clad with myrrh and frankincense, with all the merchant's powders?" (3:6). The woman's approach is treated as an almost magical manifestation, beyond the literal or realistic.

Suddenly—*hinei*, Behold!—there is Solomon's bed, surrounded by sixty of Israel's choicest warriors, all trained soldiers, each with a sword on his thigh to guard against dangers by night (3:7). As Fishbane notes (95), later rabbinic texts see the marital night as needing special protection against vulnerability. We might also recall, as evidence for this widespread anxiety, the conclusion of Shakespeare's *Midsummer Night's Dream*, in which a protective spell is chanted for Theseus and Hippolyta for their wedding night. Not only is it a bed; it is a splendid palanquin, a canopied bed ornately made from cedar of Lebanon, its posts silver and pillows decorated with gold, fitted with purple cushions, and bedding made with love by the daughters of Jerusalem (3:10). It is, in short, a fairytale love nest.

This chapter concludes by shifting gaze once more. Now addressing the "daughters of Zion," the speaker (perhaps the young woman, perhaps simply a narrator) urges them to go forth to see King Solomon bedecked in the crown given him by his mother on his wedding day, the day his heart rejoices. From the magnificence of the marital bed, the king emerges as a figure to be admired, glorious in his joy.

If we ask, why Solomon and how this reference relates to the narrative, we see there are different sorts of answers. To some, the king is the third party in a love triangle with a young woman passionately in love with the man who figures in the previous poems; but the grand Solomon somehow woos and wins her to his chamber in this passage. Others, believing that Solomon really is the male figure in the cycle, interpret the "other man" as the king in pastoral guise, sometimes either disguised or playfully pretending to be a simple herdsman. Still others see the encounter with the king as perhaps the woman's fantasy or else her projection of her true love as a figure of royal magnificence. Interpretive ambivalence underlies the entire episode. Is the oddly specific reference to each soldier having a sword "on his thigh" intended merely to indicate that they are protective figures rather than threatening ones with unsheathed weapons in their hands, or does the physical image heighten the atmosphere of sexuality? Is there a narrative to be followed here, or does the text move in non-linear fashion between a world of familiar social interactions and an imaginary psycho-dramatic dimension expressing desires, anxieties, and fantasies? We cannot be sure.

Nevertheless, following the logic of a narrative including a seeming wedding in chapter 3, the next chapter is voiced as the exuberant bridegroom's ecstatic praise of his bride's beauty following its full revelation on the wedding night, concluding with her equally robust, urgent beckoning of him to enter into "his garden" to enjoy its delicious fruits (4:16). The entire sixteen-verse poem, including the woman's response, is a unified and sensual, even erotic, blazon—a detailed, image-filled evocation, rife with hyperbole, of her physical charms. His encomia embrace sensory experience of all kinds, most notably visual and olfactory; her physical appearance and aromas in particular arouse his desire and praises. Fittingly, much of the imagery derives from elements of the natural world. His evocations of her scent (myrrh and aloe and cedar, nard and saffron and cinnamon) sound like a modern oenophile's description of a superb wine's bouquet.

And yet, for all its wealth of specific details, the poem is more affective than descriptive: the words emphasize her impression on the speaker, rather than, say, the precise physical appearance of her features. His descriptions of her, all addressed to his beloved rather than imparted boastfully to the reader, seem intended both to honor and arouse her by calling attention to the effect her body has on his desire. We grasp that he admires and hungers sexually for her. But when he tells her that her limbs are "a pomegranate orchard / *pardes rimonim*" (4:14), we cannot know exactly what she looks like or what this almost synesthetic metaphor really denotes, i.e., in what way he thinks she is like this orchard. Similarly, when he tells her that her "two breasts are like two fawns, a gazelle's twins, grazing among the lilies" (4: 5), her beauty is more implied than depicted, and we might believe that this representation is driven less by precision of visual imagery than by mellifluousness of sound: *sh'nei shadayikh kish'nei afarim t'omei tz'viah haro'im b'shoshanim*. This meltingly gorgeous verse, spoken by lover to beloved, is surely as seductive in sound as in content and is meant to be so. We can easily imagine it as a line from one of those tavern songs to which Rabbi Akiva furiously objected, and there are numerous other similarly lyrical, sensual verses in the poem.

In 4:8, the speaker addresses the young woman as *kallah*/bride, a sudden change from *rayati*/beloved. So, too, in both 4:9 and 4:10 she is *akhoti kallah*, sister bride, suggesting the closeness of a kindred spirit. That they are at one in desire and in fully embracing sexuality is made clear in the final verse, in which the woman calls upon the winds to "blow upon my garden" to waft its perfume to her beloved, inducing him to come "and savor [*v'yokhal*] the delicious fruit" of the garden (4:16). Their mutuality also emerges through her references to the garden first as "my garden" and subsequently, when she urges him to enter it, also "his garden." Earlier, he proclaimed that "you have captured my heart" (4:9). Each feels that part of them has become part of the other. Yet rather than being diminished by this, each lover is augmented by it. She is, to him as well as to her garden and to their garden of love, *b'eir mayyim khayyim* / a well of living water (4:15), or, we could say, fresh and life-giving water.

The next chapter begins where the previous one ended, this time with the bridegroom celebrating his thorough enjoyment of his *akhoti kallah* as she and he both desired. Her sexuality is now part of him, for in satisfying desire, "I have gathered my myrrh and spice, eaten my honey with the honeycomb, drunk my wine and my milk" (5:1). The repeated first-person pronouns point to his personal gratification along with his unique possession of her sensuality. Giddy from his own experience, he extends a universal call: "Eat, lovers, drink! Get drunk on love!"

Because of their theme, tone, and structure, chapters 4 and 5 may be paired with one another and regarded as the central hinge of the poem. Not only are they preceded and followed by three chapters. Each has sixteen verses. In chapter 4, the first fifteen verses are spoken by the male figure, the last one by the female; chapter 5 begins with one verse from the male speaker answering the female one, as just noted, and continues with fifteen by the female. What at first might appear like a capricious jump from one viewpoint to another looks on closer inspection to be artistic craftsmanship. So, in chapter 5, the man's impulsive urging in the first verse, "Get drunk on love," seems answered in the final line by the woman's ecstatic appreciation of her lover, "His mouth is like sweet wine and all of him is delightful" (5:16).

Between these verses, a small drama engrosses us, much as it engrosses the young female speaker. The passage beginning at 5:2 prods each of us to engage once again with the abiding question, which Song of Songs am I reading? A series of events unfolds with such vivid language and concise episodes that we rush through it, eager to reach the denouement, knowing what is happening along the way, yet unsure about how to understand the account. In brief, the woman explains that she was asleep and yet not fully at rest when she hears her lover knocking to be admitted to her chamber, pleading with her to let him in, his hair soaked by the morning dew. She doesn't answer him, because (she says) she had already removed her robe and washed her feet; but when he departs, she is at once regretful and rushes off to find him. Again she meets the night watch, but now they strike and bruise her, even stripping her cloak from her. She pleads for help from her friends, the *b'not yerushalayim*, to tell her beloved, "I am faint with love." But, they ask, how is he better than any other? At that, she replies with a seven-verse encomium of his physical magnificence feature by feature, complementing his praise of her beauty in chapter 4, culminating in what seems like her exhausted collapse in sensual experience and desire, proclaiming "all of him is delightful." In the opening verse of chapter 6 the friends help her resume the search, which reaches its successful conclusion in the next two verses as she reveals that he has gone to browse in his spice garden and pick lilies. Reunited with him, she emphatically declares, *ani l'dodi v'dodi li*, "I am to my beloved and my beloved is to me," a sentiment that is clearly mutual.

What happens, or seems to happen, during the night is clear enough. But has it happened? Is there a narrative or emotional rationale for this episode that seems like a digression from the lovers' outpourings of praise and commitment to one another? Why have the city watchmen, who seemed neutral if not benign in 3:3, turned hostile and aggressive? Is it an incident in the "real" life of our protagonists? Is it instead her dream or even a fantasy that for a while takes a nightmarish turn? As befits a nighttime experience of one who claims to have been asleep but acknowledges that her heart was wakeful, i.e., that she was emotionally astir, the episode occupies a borderland between reality and imagination, between tangible experience and dreaming. Perhaps her longing for her beloved leads to his imagined presence, while her pragmatic awareness finds reasons not to arise from bed so as to open the door to this fantasy of desire, a lover whose wet hair is soaked with dew.

She explains her unwillingness to let him in with practical excuses that in this circumstance verge on the comical, protesting that it is inconvenient because she had already undressed and even washed her feet, so she did not want to put on her robe again or sully her pristine feet. We do not know, however, whether her reaction is her rationalizing to herself, explaining her behavior to her friends, justifying her actions to us, or even turning him away with these words. All are possible readings. We can nonetheless notice that she does not explain the rejection by claiming modesty or propriety. Instead, if she is calling out to him, she lets him know tantalizingly that she is naked and clean. But whether discouraged by her retort or her silence, he departs too quickly, though not before his hand (depending how one translates) tries the latch or breaches the hole of the door.

Now, overwhelmed by desire for her beloved, "in turmoil inside for him" (5: 4) she rises to admit him, her hands and fingers exuding fragrant myrrh, coating the latched door bolt. Dew, myrrh—moisture drips from both lovers in this night of sexual longing, only for them to be frustrated in the moment by ill timing or inconvenient prudence. She opens the door for her lover but finds he has gone away, yet she has been more than aroused by his words; "my whole being was dizzy because of what he said" (5:6). She seeks for him; she calls for him; but to no avail.

As she searches, the town watchmen find her, but now their encounter is hostile. If we interpret this entire episode as a dream, then their chastisements of her, including stripping her of a protective garment (variously translated as a veil or mantle), signify judgments of her transgressive emotions. If we interpret the passage as a real event, her impassioned solo nighttime quest for her man meets with physical chastisements and shaming from the public guardians of civic order. Here is a poem thoroughly suffused with images of nature, both flora and fauna, and along with them, the vibrant physicality of romantic desire and sexual love, celebrated more richly in this work than anywhere else in the Tanakh. It is furthermore a poem limited in its social sphere, populated principally by the two lovers, along with sporadic references to the young woman's friends (the "daughters of Jerusalem"), and occasionally to her family (mother and brothers) who appear on the margins of the text; and it is narrow in its implied geography comprised mainly of gardens and bedchambers. It is moreover centered on a love affair that might be transgressive and is certainly bold, public, and unfettered. Suddenly, the intrusion by agents of the state jarringly reminds us of a larger social realm, one over which a king might exercise authority.

But this intervention by the watchmen does not really deter her. She beseeches her women friends that, should they find her beloved, they must tell him that "I am sick with love" (5:8). Nor is she fazed when the other women ask what distinguishes her lover, that is, what sets him above others, that she should pursue him with such determination. She is in fact ready to recount his physical beauty in terms as lavish, detailed, and sometimes mysterious as his praises of her, filled with similes and metaphors through which he emerges as a paragon of nature's magnificence, just as he had verbally depicted her. His complexion is clear and robust; his hair is raven-black and curly; his eyes are like doves bathed in milk; his lips, wet with myrrh, emit rich aromas and his mouth is sweet wine; his thighs are like marble pillars set on gold pedestals and his belly a throne of ivory adorned with sapphires; he is like the cedars of Lebanon. She concludes this formal evocation of masculine perfection by proclaiming the fullness of their relationship: "This is my beloved and this is my friend" / *zeh dodi v'zeh rei'i* (5:16).

Understandably, they are eager to see him for themselves. As chapter 6 begins, they twice implore her to say where he has gone, offering to help her look for him. Though she has just pleaded for help as she urgently searches for him, she knows his favorite spot, which is his garden of delights, endowed with beds of spices and blossoming lilies ready for plucking (6:2).

He resumes his extravagant praise of her in 6:4; and if we want to think of this poem as the work of King Solomon, his new paean to her loveliness is especially apt because he compares her to Tirzah and Jerusalem, the capital cities of (respectively) the Northern and Southern Kingdoms, switching from the more intimate natural metaphors to the more imposing and regal scale of regional metropolises. He also praises her with a phrase that remains cryptic across the centuries, *ayummah ka-nidgalot*, a much-debated term that seem to mean something like, "as awesome as vast multitudes." This is one of the poem's sections that especially lends itself to geopolitical and religious interpretations, perceiving it as (for example) God's appreciation of Israel.

From the grandeur of cities the speaker returns to more intimate comparisons of the beloved, repeating, albeit with variations, his earlier celebrations of her physical beauty, begging her to turn her eyes from him because they overpower him (6:5), a trope we can find repeated across centuries of love poems. With her gorgeous hair ("like a herd of goats descending from Gilead"), perfect teeth, and vibrant complexion "like an open ripe pomegranate," she surpasses sixty queens and eighty concubines (references again suggesting a regal milieu), and young women beyond number, earning the praise of them all (6:8–9). If the pomegranate simile seems discordant to a modern reader, we should recall the many Western poems that have lauded a woman's beauty with comparisons to roses or lilies.

At 6:10 perhaps another voice enters in her praise, or maybe the enraptured lover has become giddily disoriented, for this verse (which concludes one of the chapter's traditional divisions) begins with the wondering exclamation, *mi-zot*, "who is she," placing her splendor now in cosmological terms. She is radiant like the dawn, gorgeous as the moon, brilliant as the sun, magnificent as the heavenly hosts. From the geographical through the earthly to the celestial, all of which we have traversed in just ten verses, this young woman's physical beauty is without equal.

The chapter closes with two lines, each containing another of the poem's disorienting shifts; the topic or situation suddenly changes, and we cannot even be sure who the speaker is. "I went down to the orchard of nut trees to look for signs of spring, to see if the vines had budded, if the pomegranate trees were blooming" (6:11). Many translations, perhaps influenced by the poem's patterns of alternating speakers and the young woman's earlier situation tending the vineyard, take this to be her line. The imagery, however, also fits with the man's descriptions of his beloved as a garden and features of her beauty as like a pomegranate. In this case, we are left to ponder whether the garden is a garden or whether it is his metaphoric way of testing whether she is ready, or "ripe," for lovemaking.

Yet more deeply perplexing is the next verse, one so cryptic that Marcia Falk did not translate it, explaining (reasonably enough) that "its meaning is not decipherable."[1] Seemingly, the young man speaks, and his first four musically assonant words seem easy enough to translate literally, though one might ponder whether "*nafshi*" means soul or selfhood or whole being: *Lo yadati* (literally, "I did not know") *nafshi samatni* ("my soul placed me"). However, the grammatical connection between these two phrases has to be inferred. Although I did not comprehend it? Before I knew it? I was beyond understanding what was happening? Then, we have the deeper puzzle of the concluding phrase, *markevot ammi-nadiv*, "placed me [in] the chariots of *ammi-nadiv*." We can try a partial translation of the passage, such as, "Though I could not understand how, my soul transported me to the chariots of *ammi-nadiv*," a reading that offers grammatical and syntactic coherence without really explaining what the image means. For some, the puzzling final word is a proper name, Amminadiv, a possibility albeit one that clarifies nothing. Others, through some lexical gyrations, deduce that it signifies one distinguished among the people, in other words, an important person with especially grandiose chariots. We might hazard that the verse seems to mean the speaker, presumably the man, had an emotionally and spiritually transporting experience that was as if he had been carried away in magnificent vehicles. While we can thereby make some sense of the passage, we can also grasp how Shir sometimes feels intoxicating as we lose our certain grasp on the literal. The chapter consequently concludes with a pair of enigmatic verses that might be understood in just that way, as analogies to the speaker's restless quest for sensual fulfillment and the feeling that love, or at least the urgency of desire, has left him disoriented and unmoored.

Chapter 7 begins with yet another jolting displacement in our viewpoint, but one that is somehow moderated by the speakers' confident rhythmic and grammatical assertiveness along with the musicality of the language. The force of this verse is best appreciated if we group its phrases into modern poetic lines.

Shuvi, shuvi ha-shulamit.   Return, return, Shulamite.

---

1. Marcia Falk, *Song of Songs: A New Translation and Commentary* (New York: HarperCollins, 1990), xix.

Shuvi, shuvi v'nekhezeh-bach.	Return, return, and we will watch you.
Mah-techezu ba-shulamit	Why should you watch the Shulamite
Ki'm'cholat hamakhana'im.	as in the Makhana'im dance?

Again, there are puzzlements to ponder as we work through the literal sense. Who is speaking these phrases? We can imagine the first pair as a choral voice, perhaps answered by another semi-choir or group, maybe even by the young woman herself, now seeming to chastise the would-be onlookers, criticizing what we might call today "the male gaze." The crowd beckons, "Come back and dance," or perhaps "dance again for us," while the answering voice challenges or objects, "what right do you have to be an audience for this dancing?" These are not the words of the lover but other admirers of the young woman, who for the first and only time in the poem is referred to as the "Shulamite," a word that appears nowhere else in the Bible. Though it has become an epithet often used by commentators to refer to the poem's young woman, and a popular female name in modern Hebrew, neither its meaning nor its etymology is clear, despite both having received extensive analysis. It might derive from "Yerushalayim," meaning that she is a Jerusalemite, though that hardly seems a notable distinction. Its cognates imply peace, wholeness, and completeness; it also connects with the name of Solomon (in Hebrew, *Sh'lomo*), all of which might be pertinent. Some go so far as to emend the name to Shunem or Shunam, a place name occurring several times in the Tanakh, notably in the story of Elisha (2 Kings 4), including numerous references to Abishag the Shunammite (*ha-shunamit*) in the story of King David (1 Kings 1–2), thereby associating this poem with another biblical erotic episode.

Perplexing as well is the reference to the "*Makhana'im* dance." Makhana'im is a biblical place name ("God's camp," bestowed by Jacob in Genesis 32:3 after seeing angels there). Plausibly, the usage in the poem could refer to a folk dance that was associated with that area. But many commentators, noting the plural *-im* suffix, think that it is a kind of dance involving two groups, perhaps in rows or circles, or (less believably in choreographic terms) a dance between two "camps" and even two armies. The prepositional prefix *ki-*, implying "as," is also hard to resolve but might imply that they watch her as if she were dancing for display. Yet again we find that we can discern the gist of the meaning without being totally certain of what is said, or by whom, or exactly how to visualize the scene.

What follows leaves little unsaid or unimagined. Verse 2 responds to the question, "Why should you watch?" The response might come from the chorus of the previous verse, though it sounds more like the admiring descriptions of the smitten lover. Appropriately for this celebration of her dancing—or rather, her appearance when she dances—the speaker affirms, "How beautiful are your sandaled feet as they move, daughter of nobility!" It is immediately clear that the interest is not choreographic, for his gaze moves upward to her "shapely thighs, like jewels a master has crafted," thence to her navel ("like an orb-shaped bowl"), her belly, "a mound of wheat rimmed with lilies," and her breasts, "twin fawns of a gazelle" (7:3–4). The passage is suffused with images of eroticism and fecundity. While the description eventually continues to her facial features and her richly dark hair ("ensnaring a king" [7:6]), his grandiose full-length portrait of her finds its way once again to her breasts, now desirable like grape clusters, her breath fragrant like apples, and her mouth, with the savor of fine wine. The full sensuality of his descriptions become even more intense through these olfactory and even gustatory evocations of the scents and tastes of her body in his mouth. "Let me climb the palm, grasp its branches," he implores, as if desperate to wrap himself around her. In a last, confusing phrase (which once again commentators struggle over), he seems to imagine their kisses being like gulping a heady wine that causes drinkers to mumble in their sleep (7:9).

She reacts with delight and fervor, "I am for my beloved, and his desire is for me" (7:10), before answering his plea with her own invitation, *L'kha dodi*, "Come, my beloved," later the key phrase of a mystical kabbalistic hymn welcoming the Sabbath as queen and bride. Notwithstanding some lexical ambiguity about whether she is inviting him to go with her to villages or to the henna bushes, she beckons him to the vineyards and orchards to see whether spring has ripened and the time is right for love, if (as he himself had earlier proposed) the vines and flowers and pomegranates are in bloom, for "there will I give my love to you" (7:13). The concluding verse of this chapter makes explicit her promise of sexual fulfillment, noting the scent of the proverbially aphrodisiacal mandrakes (*duda'im*, echoing the word of endearment, *dodi*) and the ready and waiting bounty of fruits available for enjoyment, both the familiar and the new, "that I have kept, *dodi*, for you" (7:14). No less than he, she embraces the erotic implications of a natural world, human as well as vegetative, richly endowed and ready for pleasure.

At the start of the eighth and final chapter, the young woman acknowledges once again a social context in which they live, reminding us that their relationship, or at least its physicality, must still be clandestine. "If only you were my brother," she sighs, "I could kiss you when we met in public and no one would think ill of me for it" (8:1). Even more boldly, "I would bring you home to my mother's house to quench you with spiced wine, and juice from my pomegranates" (8:2). The last phrase evocatively recalls his references to her body as like the pomegranate, highlighted here by the possessive suffix for "my" that transforms the phrase into an unmistakable double-entendre. We sense that she is offering not just a beverage for him to taste but the savor of her own body's sexuality.

Thus her thoughts may stir a remembrance of their lovemaking (echoing 2:6), or perhaps a desire for the future, inasmuch as the tense is ambiguous, or perhaps capture a glimpse of their private moment now: "His left hand beneath my head, his right stroking me" (8:3). As if recognizing how she is carried away with desire, she again cautions the *b'not yerushalayim* against rousing love impulsively.

Suddenly, the poem's flow is interrupted again, this time by an apparition or vision reported by an unidentifiable astonished observer (or, as some speculate, the other maidens). "Who is that arising out of the desert, clinging to her beloved?" The rhetorical question, which also appears in 3:6 and 6:10, registers how the viewer is touched by wonderment, underscored for us by the singular word (*mitrappeqet*) describing her "clinging" physical attachment to him. It is but a brief moment, nonetheless as memorable as an intimate scene glimpsed through a briefly opened door.

The woman who just a few verses earlier wished that her beloved could be her brother now speaks of having sexually aroused him under the apricot tree where he had been conceived (8:5). As earlier (2:3), while some translate the term as apple, the *tappuach* or apricot represents his sexuality. Some commentators also assume that the speaker of this passage recalling the seduction under the fruit tree is the man; however, the grammar clearly indicates that it is he who is being addressed. In the poem's patterns of correspondences, the young woman is as likely to be assertive about her desires as the man is, and their sites of lovemaking match each other's. In this instance, her ardent need to clasp and be clasped, to be so allied by kinship that they could touch and kiss publicly, to cleave together, extends to hunger for a biological union that goes back to his own conception.

It is an apt introduction to one of the best known, profound, and unforgettable passages not only in this poem but in all literature. Only by approaching this verse in context can we appreciate its fully earned force, recognizing it as an understanding of love lit by the white flame of the lovers' passion, an insight that the young woman has approached each time she had adjured her contemporaries not to awaken love before being ready for its power.

> Imprint me as a seal upon your heart
> Like a seal upon your arm,
> For love is strong as death,
> jealousy fierce as Sheol;
> Its sparks are a blaze,
> A raging conflagration. (8:6)

Craving for physical and emotional union reaches an even deeper level of intensity with her desire to be like a seal stamped on his visible physical body (here, on his arm) and even deep inside him, on his heart, marking that indelibly with a sign of mutual commitment.

Love's fire, she declares, is tenacious. "Swelling seas cannot extinguish it; rivers cannot carry it away." Yet even as it cannot be put out artificially, it cannot be merely acquired. "Were a man to offer all the wealth he possesses for love, he would be ridiculed with scorn" (8:7). These phrases seem to mark the culmination of her reflection on love, concluding with a nod to society's outlook on an emotion that she experiences viscerally.

As if offering a contrary social outlook, the next section abruptly shifts its perspective, introducing what seems to be a new choral voice. This is however another notoriously problematic passage. The Blochs' edition, for instance, notes, "There is hardly any consensus even on essential questions";[2] and Falk, calling it "one of the more enigmatic" sections, observes that "it is difficult to say who is speaking, and to whom," noting also that its imagery is also "strange."[3] While concurring, we can try to make sense of this section in its context.

It begins with a statement posed perhaps by the brothers of the young woman. "We have a little sister whose breasts have not yet developed. What shall we do for her when the day comes that she has suitors?" We can imagine them pondering a familial issue in pragmatic terms

---

2. Ariel and Chana Bloch, *Song of Songs* (New York: Modern Library, 2006), 214.
3. Falk, *Song of Songs*, 194.

that seem a world away from the dimension of passionate love in which the young woman and man of this poem speak. Still, they also express themselves poetically, using metaphors, though centuries of readers have found their images and intentions particularly opaque. "If she is a wall, we will build on it a turret of silver; if a door, we will reinforce it with cedar" (8:9). Even resorting to linguistic analogues from elsewhere in the Tanakh, commentators have been unable to solve conclusively whether (among other perplexities) these assertions are synonymous or antithetical, and whether they refer somehow to ornamenting her appearance or to defending her chastity. Regardless of whichever we choose, the implications are essentially the same. The speakers—be they protective, paternalistic, or domineering—believe that while their sister has not yet reached sexual maturity and therefore marriageable age, she soon will; and they believe just as strongly that they are responsible for presenting her well as a potential wife.

She forthrightly rejects their patronizing concern, though it is unclear whether her response is a private aside or an open retort to them. "I am a wall and my breasts are like towers," she asserts, as if to say that they do not recognize how their sister has grown, or perhaps that they do not realize how her body has awakened because of her lover. "That is how I have become in his eyes, as one who attains peace / *k'motzeit shalom*" (8:10). She is the wall and she possesses her towers herself. She has found not only love but, through it, self-confidence.

Once again, in the lines that follow, the tone and point of view shift suddenly, and again we cannot be sure who the speaker is, or even whether the speaker is male or female, questions much debated in the commentaries. The poem returns to the vineyard motif, this time through what resembles a parable. "Solomon had a vineyard in Baal-Hamon" (8:11). We presume that is King Solomon; but no one knows whether Baal-Hamon (a name that appears nowhere else) was a real place with a real vineyard or a fictive name literally meaning "master of bountiful wealth." The more important point to the story is what follows in this verse, though yet again the commentaries and translations vary tremendously as they grapple with the challenge of making sense of the literal meaning of the text. According to some readings of the passage, Solomon must hire watchmen (*not'rim*) to protect the vineyard because its fruit was valued at "a thousand silver pieces" (*elef kesef*). According to others, notably more recent scholars, the *not'rim* would each tend a plot in the vineyard, sell the produce for a thousand silver pieces, and earn two hundred for the work (8:12).

The point of the parable emerges with the speaker's contrasting jibe, "I have my very own vineyard just for me" (*karmi sheli lifnai*), so you can keep your thousand and the watchmen their two hundred. Plausibly, the speaker might be alluding not just to Solomon's vast wealth but more significantly to his vast acquisition of women: according to 1 Kings 11:3, seven hundred wives and three hundred concubines, in other words, a thousand of them. In the poem's economic reckoning, the lover's singular "vineyard" all to himself is incomparably preferable to Solomon's costly "bountiful wealth" (*hamon*). We might also discern here a continuation of the woman's assertion that anyone who tried to buy love with all his riches would be ridiculed.

From the vineyard the poem turns back at last to the garden and presumably to our young lovers, who so often have met there. "You who dwell in the garden, friends are listening for you—let me hear you" (8:13). Among the many puzzlements in Song of Songs we must also include this reference to the friends (*chaverim*). Who are they? Where are they? What is the point of referring to them here? One explanation is that they represent the community of their peers, all of whom are eager for her company; but he most of all desires to be close enough to hear her, probably remembering all that they have said to one another.

However, if there are others around, their still-covert relationship is in danger of discovery, which is perhaps what motivates her concluding plea to him, echoing her words in 2:17. "Flee, my beloved, run like a gazelle or a bounding deer, to the hills of spices" (8:14). That, surprisingly, is where the poem ends, though of course not without interpretive controversy. Many translators, wanting the lovers to dash off boldly into the sunrise together, interpret the opening imperative verb *b'rach* accordingly, as if it meant "let us go" or "come with me," rather than "escape." Instead, her final words send him away, though her use of images we have long associated with their romance implies that it is a temporary breach stemming from the exigency of the moment, not a permanent dismissal. Their love remains incompletely fulfilled, their longing still heightened by the pain of separation, somewhat like Keats perceived the avid tension between the young lovers depicted on a Grecian urn, yearning toward one another without physically embracing.

A modern reader, even one inspired by the grand, passionate, erotic intensity of Shir, might notice that the two lovers never say the sorts of things about one another that one finds today's engaged couples conventionally offering when they explain to family and friends why they are attracted to each other. She does not claim to love him because he has a good sense of humor and likes animals and children, nor does he say he loves her because she is very intelligent and a good listener. No, these two cannot stop looking lustily at one another; they cannot keep their hands or lips from one another. Their desires are carnal and visceral. Certainly their love is an *amour fou*, a mad passion.

We might feel upon reflection that the book's view of love, and therefore its representations of the beloved, while perhaps as deep as the Grand Canyon, is also narrow. Undoubtedly it is also heterosexual, though at any given point the Hebrew could allow the speaker to be male, female, or undetermined. Yet to deny the reality or power of such fervor would be to deny the depth as well as the varieties of love. Their passionate physical relationship is unlike anything else in the Tanakh. Isaac loved Rebecca and Jacob loved Rachel, but the lovers in Shir ha-Shirim are aflame with hunger for one another. How many of us would not wish to be admired and desired, or to admire and desire, the way these lovers do, at least at some time in our life?

Reading Shir ha-Shirim thus far, we have looked closely at the *p'shat* meanings of the text, appreciating its drama and beauty that speak to us with expressive intensity even when some literal interpretations may be uncertain and the narrative seems to hover indefinitely between reality and fantasy, or between actuality and a dream. The book's resonant evocation of love and desire articulated through the diverse elements of the natural world seems to imprint itself on the language of poetry even into our own time. This is how the poem made its way into tavern songs and centuries of love lyrics as well as readers' imaginations, vibrant in sights and sounds, redolent of scents, suffused with longing, sexual desire, and love as intense physically as emotionally.

That is, of course, not why the poem was embraced by the ancient Jewish sages and synagogue teachers or by the Christian church and her liturgists across the centuries. It is not even—or at least not completely—what countless composers of sacred music have found in the poem, whether classical composers like Lassus, Palestrina, and William Billings or modern composers like David Lang and the liturgist Shefa Gold. For them, the poem is an account of a sacred relationship between God and us as a people or between our spiritual and physical aspects, capable of being understood (as noted earlier) in different allegorical or metaphorical ways.

Michael Fishbane's commentary offers a capacious, engrossing traversal of readings reflecting all these approaches to the text. While we cannot fully traverse the text again through all of its possible spiritual levels, it is important to sample how readers have understood the poem as a religious and mystical testimony, bringing it into liturgies and teachings that helped preserve this ancient text for world literature. For had the text not been incorporated into the biblical corpus but regarded solely as secular love poetry, thus uncanonized, it might have slipped into the margins of literary history, explored mainly by scholars, written about or gestured toward more than actually read, like the lyrics of Sappho or Anacreon.

In the extensive midrash collection called Shir ha-Shirim Rabbah, one of the verses on which Rabbi Meir and Rabbi Yehuda disagree is the homiletic interpretation of "While the king was on his couch, / My nard gave forth its fragrance" (1:12). Meir, presumably focusing on nard's pungency, glosses its meaning as, "When the King of Kings, blessed be, was feasting above, Israel gave forth a vile odor and said regarding the Golden Calf (Ex. 32:4), 'This is your God, Israel.'" Yehuda remonstrates with him, saying, "Shir ha-Shirim is never to be interpreted negatively, only favorably, because it was only given to praise Israel. Rather, it means that while the King of Kings, blessed be, was feasting above, Israel gave forth a sweet aroma, saying, 'All that God has said, we will do and we will learn' (Ex. 24:7)." Despite their disagreement, the rabbis share significant assumptions. One is that the surface or *p'shat* of the poem's text covers a more profound layer of meaning. Another is that every detail, even a scent, can and should be interpreted through Torah, which gives that detail its real significance. A third assumption, which is basic to the *d'rash* or midrashic approach, is that the poem is really about the historic relationship between God and Israel, who are portrayed in it as respectively the male and female lovers. Consequently, the fourth assumption is that in this text we see the intense devotion between the two, notwithstanding occasional obstacles. While Shir ha-Shirim Rabbah dates from the seventh or eighth century CE, it builds on many earlier sources and, as Akiba's defense of the text shows, must reflect long-standing ideas about it.

Midrash constitutes a genre of Jewish literature that continues today; it is commonly found in numerous classic compendia developed over several centuries. Each detail of the poem's text becomes a seemingly inexhaustible starting point for the rabbis' interpretive ingenuity. Through their alternative interpretations, potential meanings are not narrowed until one finds the correct explication but multiplied until the possible inferences are exhausted. Their intention is not to explain the text but, first, to derive a teaching from it that can be applied to the Torah and, second, to show that every element of the poem has a sacred meaning, that it is scripturally authentic and a handbook to Israel's political and religious life. Probably the most frequently encountered transitional phrase in midrash compilations is *davar acher*, meaning "something else," which introduces a different interpretation that stands alongside the previous one, neither more nor less authoritative but simply an additional idea. The quoted rabbis, whether cited by name or anonymously, feel no need to construct a coherent, systematic, single narrative for their interpretations; rather, they explicate each moment or image in light of some seemingly applicable biblical reference point.

So, for example, glossing the "black and lovely" phrase (1:5), one interpreter says that it teaches, I am black in my own actions but lovely through those of my forebears; another proposes, I am black when I recognize my failings but lovely in the view of God. From there, many biblical examples are offered of contrasting negative and positive moments of the Jewish people's failures or successes in obedience to God. One sage offers, "I am black six days of the week and lovely on Shabbat; black through the year, lovely on Yom Kippur; black regarding the Ten Tribes but lovely in Judah and Benjamin," while another adds, "Black in this world, lovely in the world-to-come" (Shir ha-Shirim Rabbah 1:5:2).

According to midrashim, descriptions exuding sensuality when taken in a literal sense have a more profound signifying level that provides religious insight. The young woman's two perfectly formed breasts represent the two essential elements of Jewish teachings, the Written Torah and the Oral Torah. Her comparison of her beloved to a gazelle stimulates readings such as, "Just like a gazelle, the Holy One, blessed be, leapt from Egypt to Sinai, from Sinai to the sea," or (according to a different interpretation) "from this synagogue to that synagogue, from this study hall to that study hall, so as to bless Israel" (m. Shir 2:9). Her statement that her lover was behind the wall, peering through the lattice, is interpreted as meaning that God was behind the walls of these holy spaces and gazing at the community of Israel through the spread fingers (the lattice, so to speak) of the *kohanim* (priests), their hands raised to bless the congregation. When she ecstatically praises his hands as golden rods, midrash takes that to be the two tablets of the covenant; his belly, which she calls "a throne of ivory," is glossed as Leviticus, the middle book of the Torah, analogous to the human midsection.

The midrashic approach often embraces wordplay that suits its intention of constructing a different order of meaning. One example construes a counter-reading of the oft-repeated phrase *b'not yerushalayim*, "daughters [or maidens] of Jerusalem." According to the midrash (1:5), "the rabbis" (i.e., presumably a consensus) taught that this should be understood not as *b'not*, "daughters," but *bonot*, "builders," interpreted variously as the Great Sanhedrin, which was responsible for teaching and governing, or all those who will make Jerusalem a grand city drawing people from every part of the world. This play on *b'not* is wittily a feminine version of exactly the same pun that appears several times in the Talmud using the masculine forms. As this example demonstrates, midrash is not focused on explicating a text to clarify its meaning but rather, finding a homiletic purpose, however that might be derived.

Thus, at the end of the poem, when the young woman urges, "Flee, my beloved, run like a gazelle [*tz'vi*] or a bounding deer, to the hills of spices" (8:14), one anonymous midrash interprets this as addressed to God, being urged to ascend to the angelic heavenly hosts [*tzava*], who praise God with one voice and one melody, on the celestial hills of fragrant spices. Another reading (*davar acher*) proposes the meaning, "Flee from the *Galut* [places of exile] where we reside, corrupted by our transgressions, make us pure like the gazelle, and accept our prayers on account of the sweet scent that is the merit of our patriarchs, like the Garden of Eden, which is the hill of fragrance" (m. Shir 8:13).

The national-historical-spiritual nexus is well represented in the Aramaic Targum of Song of Songs, a translation and commentary from the seventh century CE that was exceptionally widely read and translated into numerous languages, including Latin. Honoring Solomon's poem as the ninth and finest of the "songs" sung by the world, and inspired by the "*ruach kud'sha*" (holy spirit), the Targum posits that it will be followed by a tenth song, to be sung by the Israelites redeemed at last from exile, as promised in Isaiah 30:29. In this text, it is the community of Israel that says to the other nations, "I am dark because false prophets led me to follow your practices, prostrating myself to the sun and moon." The house to which the lover takes his beloved (2:4) is, in this reading, the House of Study at Sinai so as to learn Torah from Moses, and the holy commandments are the "banner" of love over the beloved. The lover's morning call to the beloved (2:10) to "arise and go" is read as God urging the exodus from enslavement, part of an unfolding narrative that sees in the lines of the poem a chronicle of Israel emerging to be a fit lover of God. It is the community of Israel that God praises as "My sister," celebrating her love as more precious than that of the proverbial seventy nations, and the good name of her righteous (the *tzadikin*) sweeter than spices (4:10). Her two perfect breasts, like twin gazelles (7:4), are metaphors for both Moses and Aaron as well as the promised redeemers, Messiah son of David and Messiah son of Ephraim. For the commentators of the Targum, the poem concludes with a vision of the eschaton, the end of time, when the Shekhina—the divine presence—will withdraw from the world to dwell in heavenly purity. At the same time, it asks that the tribulations of Israel be remembered and regarded mercifully until the nation is redeemed from exile, brought to Jerusalem, and there the priests will again burn the incense for offerings, thus explaining the "hills of spices" (8:14).

Not all allegorical interpretations have been directed toward expounding on the Jewish people's national or communal experiences and aspirations. Many such interpretations, especially beginning in the Middle Ages during an era when spiritual autobiographies were cultivated in many cultures, sense subtle implications about the spiritual life of the individual in the poem's textual details. To some interpreters, the poem traces metaphorically Solomon's exploration of his self-awareness and craving for more profound perfections of spirituality as a model of inner growth. Others find in the work a kind of drama in which either God or the lover of the spiritual life leads his beloved "maiden" (usually, the individual or the soul) to a more complete, fully committed relationship transcending the ordinary social dimension of life. Particular readers may find in word choices or situations in the poem a "hint" (*remez* in Hebrew) or glimpse of a meaning beyond the literal, for instance by perceiving references to "*Sh'lomo*," i.e., Solomon, as suggesting *sh'leimut*, "wholeness."

This nexus between the literal and figurative is apt because the lovers' words express inner desires, attractions that can be expressed through physical images and that hunger for experiential fulfillment but are nonetheless driven by ineffable feelings. For instance, when the young woman says to her beloved, "Draw me after you, let us run" (1:4), a spiritually minded interpreter will discern the soul's desire for closeness with God or with the deep essence of Truth. When she describes herself as "dark yet comely," she is not alluding to her physical appearance but (for instance) to her, or the soul's, dual inner nature, where "dark" might imply hidden, obscure, unknown, or bad, yoked with attractive qualities.

The poem's love story is thus read as the story of the soul yearning for its own improvement and transcendence. The soul is drawn from its baser physical nature by its desire to be united with the higher being of the beloved, which is perfection. It craves that union, although such a "marriage" is not easily obtained; however, the lover's affection for the beloved draws her on, encouraging her spiritual and psychic movement toward greater refinement. The poem depicts spiritual development allegorically through images from the natural world; external perfections, and for that matter imperfections as well, stand for internal ones in ways discernible to the thoughtful, reflective interpreter.

An even more esoteric approach is expressed by the interpretive approach known in Hebrew as *sod*, or "secret." The great mystical work, the Zohar (probably thirteenth century CE), is the best known but not the only or earliest work exploring Shir ha-Shirim, among other biblical books, for its insights into the hidden mysteries that precede and surround creation as well as the nature and processes of divinity itself. Arcane readings of the poem that can be found in diverse mystical writings, many of which have never been translated or edited to make them accessible to non-specialists, tend to develop as continuous interpretations of an unfolding narrative or spiritual revelation instead of isolated glosses on individual images, verses, or episodes in Shir ha-Shirim. However, sometimes because of problems in the transmission of the texts and sometimes because some of the teachings were meant to be understood only by a coterie of the adept students, the connections between the biblical text and the mystical insights about it are often difficult to discern. Consequently, these readings are less amenable to selective quotations for interpreting diverse spots in the poem. Rather, if they are explored continuously, they delineate the soul's strivings toward union with the divine, through various impediments, distractions, and encouragements; or else, they describe the inner life of sacred energy, the dynamic interplay between pure essential spirituality and the embodiment of spirituality within physical matter.

Even though brief extracts will not adequately represent how they construct a covert dynamic drama through the poem, a tiny sampling of readings from those culled by Fishbane will indicate what these interpretations contribute to our grasp of the poem's power. So, the much-discussed image of dark comeliness (1:5) might imply that the soul's beauty and wholeness (*sh'leimut*) are covered by our physical and material being, which must be controlled so that we can more fully realized our inward nature, which is in the divine image. Recognizing the supremacy of God the King "on his couch" (i.e., the divine throne), the soul emits an outpouring of divinely given love back to God, from whom that love came; thus, "my nard gave forth its fragrance" (1:12), understood here as a spiritual or psychic outpouring, a fragrance because it is more refined than visual, auditory, or tactile phenomena. The obstacles to our connecting with the divine include not only our physical beings but also the aspects of our carnal natures that prevent us from fully expressing our spiritual essence, and the obstructions of ego, pride, and self-interest, all of which require discipline; the chastisements of the watchmen (5:7) who wound and strip the feminine soul are necessary afflictions on our path toward perfection. Being called to "turn back" (7:1), the Shulamite (the seeker of *sh'leimut*) is urged to self-reflection and self-examination while negotiating the "Makhana'im dance" between the physical and spiritual aspects of life. At the end of the poem, the soul still waits for harmonious integration with the divine, but it does not wait passively; rather, echoing its previous words of passionate longing, it earnestly expresses urgency and desire. An especially powerful expression of the book's rich fusion of sensuality and spirituality can be found in the modern dance "Song of Songs" created in 2022 by the choreographer Pam Tanowitz, incorporating elements from Jewish folk dance along with her own aesthetic vocabulary and set to a 2014 vocal and instrumental score called "just (after song of songs)" by the composer David Lang that uses brief mesmerizingly repeated English phrases evoking passages from the biblical text.

Shir ha-Shirim is one text but many poems, not only because there are diverse poems within the book but because any one poem is simultaneously its own primary accessible lyric (*p'shat*) along with the overtones and harmonies comprised of its additional varieties of meaning that essentially transform it into, so to speak, a different poem but with the same words. We may read it many times, perhaps each time hearing one or several of the other "poems" resonating with the one we thought we were engaging. It remains a gorgeous love poem in every register or dimension. But a poem from whom? To whom? And celebrating what kind of love?

4

Book of Ruth

The narrative line of the Book of Ruth is compellingly direct and clear. Without a great deal of editorial intervention, the story can be told to youngsters and appreciated as well by adults who enjoy a romance with a happy ending. Of all the Bible's multitudinous stories, this is the ultimate feel-good tale. There are, admittedly, three deaths, but they occur discreetly offstage, involving characters we do not care about or even know except by name. We encounter grief and hardship, but in a way that evokes Psalm 30:11, "You turned my mourning into dancing." A major female character, a poor widow, who under duress places herself in situations that could be dangerous or compromising finds succor and safety, being treated with exemplary courtesy by the male protagonist. The critical decision that will resolve the entire plot provides a dramatic moment of short-lived tension worthy of a Jane Austen novel. An apparently simple narrative of an apparently random family undergoing various tribulations concludes with a marriage of two mature people who seem destined for one another, followed by a happy childbirth and the critical link to Israel's greatest dynasty.

How does this come about? A family of four fleeing a famine moves from the land of Israel to a neighboring country, Moab, where the two sons marry. Over the course of several years, all the men die, childless; the famine ends, and the older woman, Naomi, decides to return home, accompanied at first by her two daughters-in-law. Naomi tries to dissuade them, pointing out that she has nothing to offer them in return for their companionship. One of them chooses to go back to her own country, while the other, Ruth, affirms her commitment and journeys on with Naomi. Naomi's former neighbors are shocked that the woman whose name means "pleasantness" has changed so much for the worse. "God has dealt harshly with me," she complains; "now call me Marah [bitterness]" (1:20). Resourcefully, Ruth offers to join gleaners in the fields to find food for herself and Naomi, though it is hard labor and potentially dangerous for a woman, especially an unmarried immigrant. However, the landowner, Boaz, praises her for her loyalty to her mother-in-law; he also protects and helps her, so that she returns to Naomi with plentiful food and harvest gatherings. Amazed at the bounty, Naomi asks where Ruth gleaned, invoking blessings of whoever the benefactor might be. With an exquisite sense of dramatic timing, Ruth replies at the end of an unusually long twenty-five-word verse that "the name of the man with whom I worked today is Boaz" (2:19).

This is the moment that a modern audience might call The Big Reveal, with appropriate musical underscoring. Naomi explains that Boaz happens to be a relative with legal obligations (in biblical terms, a "redeemer") to rescue them from their difficult situation. She advises Ruth to make herself presentable, return at night to Boaz, and follow his instructions. He does not (apparently) take advantage of her vulnerability but rather again praises her loyalty and devotion, though also saying that another relation has a stronger family obligation toward Naomi's kin. Seemingly the next day Boaz approaches the other relative, formally and properly offering him first the opportunity to claim Naomi's inheritance and, second, marriage to Ruth as well, which would entail securing the lineage of her late husband. The other man promptly accepts the first (a dangerous moment for our protagonists) but balks at the attached latter condition, allowing Boaz to take his place and marry Ruth. She subsequently bears a son, who is welcomed by Naomi and celebrated by her neighbors as if he were her own. The triumphally happy ending concludes by identifying the child of Ruth and Boaz as a progenitor of King David. Not quite a "Cinderella ending," but a story that seems very much like a fairytale.

Is Ruth a historical book or a literary one? In the Tanakh, where the megillot are printed in the third section (Ketuvim/Writings), Ruth is the second text in the group of the megillot, following Song of Songs. That order is primarily liturgical, based on the sequence of Jewish holidays, though we may also deem it literarily sensitive.

Of course neither of those designations precludes a historical reading as well. Like Esther, the Book of Ruth is taken by many readers as historical, which is reflected in its placement in Christian editions of the Bible right after Judges, an editorial choice surely influenced by the opening reference in Ruth to the historical period of the Judges. A further historical connection is suggested by the Babylonian Talmud, Bava Batra 14b, which presents an order of biblical books that does not group the five megillot together but lists Ruth at the beginning of the Writings/Ketuvim, followed by Psalms, an arrangement no doubt based on linking the genealogy that concludes Ruth with the conventional ascription of the psalms to the authorship of King David, who is identified as Boaz and Ruth's great-grandson and the last-named offspring in the book's list of forebears and descendants. (In that talmudic passage, Job and Proverbs come next, followed by Ecclesiastes, Song of Songs and Lamentations, with Daniel and Esther as the subsequent pair, both set in lands of exile following the destruction of Jerusalem mourned in Lamentations.)

However, most modern scholars do not support taking the story as a historical account. Albeit strands of historicity doubtless inform the text, it presents too many perplexities and implausibilities to be regarded simply as factual. To begin, we have the obvious problem of the narrative voice. Who is telling this story? How would the narrator, distant enough in time from the events to be cognizant of David, know crucial moments of indelibly precise and eloquent dialogue from conversations between two private individuals such as Naomi and Ruth, or even more strikingly, the words uttered between Ruth and Boaz in the nocturnal intimacy of the threshing floor? Notwithstanding possible factual bases for the incidents, the Book of Ruth comes to us as an immaculately crafted short story.

The narrative's artfulness shows the author's literary sophistication. The book's major episodes develop like scenes in a drama, while the major events rush by. In the first chapter, Elimelekh's death is noted in the third verse, and then, as ten years pass in a phrase, the two sons also die, all of them gone before we even meet them. In the fourth and final chapter, the denouement takes merely one verse: "So Boaz wed Ruth and she became his wife, and he went to her; and God allowed her to conceive, and she bore a son" (4:13). In between, the focus tightens so that we listen to dialogue, usually conversations of two figures, occasionally punctuated by what might be called choral pronouncements from the townswomen or elders.

As we shall see, its three main characters—Ruth, Naomi, and Boaz—are individuals, precisely delineated for us and at times noble and ingenious, yet each somewhat enigmatic, their motives and emotions most often hidden beneath the inscrutable narrative perspective of this scroll. The story is shaped by someone who has decided cannily what needs to be explained and what is simply to be taken for granted, someone willing to posit minor characters and discard them casually at will, even the crucial person (the "nearer redeemer") cheekily referred to simply as *ploni almoni*," not a real name but a Hebrew phrase that we could render as "What's-his-name." Cinematically, this story unfolds in a series of long takes, each one bounded by a fade-out, fade-in or a jump cut; there is not a wasted episode or superfluous character, not even Orpah, Naomi's other Moabite daughter-in-law, who chooses to turn around rather than continue the journey to Eretz Yisrael / the land of Israel.

Also like the Book of Esther, this narrative unfolds by tantalizingly misdirecting our attention from the title character. That is, the book named after Esther first seems to be a story about Ahasuerus, then one about the soon-elided Queen Vashti, before shifting to Mordecai and only afterward to foregrounding Esther herself. The book named after Ruth begins as a tale about "a man from Bethlehem, his wife, and two sons" (1:1). The male characters succumb within the first five lines, shifting the focus then to Naomi, subsequently to her and her daughters-in-law, and within another few lines, more tightly to her and Ruth. Eventually, another major figure emerges: Boaz. By the time the book concludes, it seems that either Naomi or Boaz might well have been its title character. Though we cannot be certain when or from whom the work acquired the name by which it has always been known, by its title the Book of Ruth announces itself as a tale about the Moabite immigrant, not the native Israelite figures. Nevertheless, the shifting centers of focus reveal something essential, that this is (again, like the Book of Esther) not a work primarily about an individual but a story of relationships. It is a tale about a small group of interrelated people and a dynastic line, all held together by the eponymous pivotal character, whose two most significant relationships turn this book also into an unconventional love story as well as a tale about making a family.

We find those focal shifts in the main scenes of the book. The first is the three-way conversation in which Naomi, Ruth, and Orpah sort out their futures. Next is an interlude in which the women of Bethlehem react to Naomi's return—the "call me Marah" episode. Then, as Ruth gleans a field to feed the two of them, Boaz emerges as the landowner who takes a particular interest in the immigrant woman. Naomi stage manages the ensuing climactic scene that takes place between Ruth and Boaz on the threshing floor, although Ruth emerges once again as someone capable of deciding and acting for herself. That is followed by a pair of brief paired vignettes, one between Ruth and Naomi as they discuss Boaz's reaction, the other between Boaz and his relative, *ploni almoni*, that will decide the plot's outcome. Lastly, we have the conclusion of the narrative, "how the story turns out," along with the essential genealogy that sets the whole book in a historical and, we might say, teleological frame.

The ending of Ruth is as momentously resonant as the conclusion of the Torah itself. Deuteronomy/Devarim, which ends as Moses dies overlooking the land toward which he had taken his people, concludes with the words that there was never again a prophet like him "among all Israel" (*kal yisra'el*). With a similar sense of attaining the dramatic climax, Ruth leads at last to a genealogical overview stretching back through seven generations of Boaz's lineage to Perez, the son of Tamar (Genesis 38:29), but more importantly three generations forward from Boaz and Ruth to the most nostalgically remembered monarch of ancient Israel, with whose name the book triumphantly finishes: "and Jesse begot David." As if completing a circle, the tale that originates with Elimelekh, "a man of Bethlehem in Judah," reaches its conclusion with David, "the son of an Ephrathite of Bethlehem in Judah" (1 Samuel 17:12). We might assume that the author of the New Testament's Gospel According to Matthew remembered the rhythm of that passage when composing the genealogical lineage for Jesus. While one might consider the possibility that the megillah's genealogical coda was a late addition grafted on to a pre-existing narrative, we can nevertheless recognize that the little Hebrew storybook called Ruth is craftily plotted for pathos, suspense, and finally transcendence. In short, it is a literary masterpiece of the ancient world.

How ancient? That question baffles scholars, who have placed it variously from around 950 BCE to 500 BCE, an almost absurd span of time. The work's literary sophistication combined with its integral (that is, not merely appended) concluding genealogy mean that it cannot be earlier than David's reign, which began around 1010 BCE. Its artistic refinement suggests that it was composed by someone experienced in the craft of literature; and while we might associate that with a courtly urban milieu such as could have existed in David's Jerusalem and thereafter, the work is also steeped in agrarian life from famine through bountiful harvest. This is not pastoral so much as georgic: its central characters are not lyrical shepherds piping in arboreal shade, nor sophisticates pretending to be "mere shepherds" but agricultural gleaners laboring to bring in the barley harvest. Neither linguistic evidence nor cultural clues offer more precise guidance for the date, meaning that speculations have been based largely on suppositions about some political motivation for the composition. The earlier date posits this story as a celebration of David the king, suggesting that his values were presumably rooted in the personal ideals exemplified by the three protagonists. The later date, occurring after exiles from Babylonia returned to Jerusalem, finds in it a promising reward for returning exiles along with perhaps a polemic countering Ezra's vigorous preaching against exogamy with a recollection that the fabled Davidic monarchy itself descended from the marriage of an Israelite with a member of the abhorred Moabites. We shall return later to this viewpoint.

Furthermore, its uncommon, nuanced focus on three female characters might suggest female authorship, much as the late nineteenth-century writer Samuel Butler hypothesized that the author of Homer's *Odyssey* (composed presumably around the eighth century BCE) was a woman. At the very least we must say that the work shows great insight in treating women's relationships with one another and their life options, unique in the biblical canon and arguably in the extant literature of the ancient world, save for the Greek poems of Sappho, who lived in the late seventh to early sixth century BCE.

The opening words of the book set it in an era far enough removed to be closer than "once upon a time" and yet not quite datable: *b'ymei sh'fot*, "In the days of the judges," or "when the chieftains ruled." The phrase evokes the pre-monarchical time prior to the first two kings of Israel, Saul and David, therefore before about 1000 BCE. In so doing, it is likely to remind the biblical reader of the phrase characterizing the putative loose standard of conduct at that time as formulated in the Book of Judges/Shof'tim: "In those days there was no king in Israel; everyone did whatever they pleased [literally, that which was right in their own eyes]" (Judges 17:6; 21:25). If that is an appropriate framework for this story, then the Book of Ruth counters this view of amoral unruliness with a romanticizing representation of rural wholesomeness. Instead of the lawlessness and arbitrary behavior denoted by the condemnatory line in Judges, here we find the major figures conducting themselves with decency and compassion. In its pre-monarchical environment, there is no mention of Jerusalem, judges, priests, or prophets; and although there is what might be called halakhic behavior, there is no appeal to halakhah (Jewish law) per se. While Shavuot, the festival on which it is read, celebrates the giving of the Torah, the Book of Ruth honors the receiving of Torah: it is living Torah.

In addition to its personal ethos, the story respects the Torah's legal teaching to attend to the needs and rights of the poor, the widow, and the "stranger" or resident alien; it follows the obligations regarding the *go'el*, the obliged "redeemer" of a family in need; and it ultimately turns on a practical decision sealed with a ritual similar to *halitzah* by which a man releases himself from the duty to perpetuate a deceased male relative's lineage by marrying his widow so as to sire children that will be accounted the children of the deceased. If we want this depiction to fit coherently into a narrative also celebrating the roots of David's monarchy, then we might propose that the values expressed through the behavior of Ruth, Boaz, and Naomi are the foundation of royal benevolence presumably exemplified by David, the former shepherd who becomes king through both divine favor and his own prowess, rather than someone born into nobility or raised in luxury.

According to the Jerusalem Talmud (Hagigah 2:3) Shavuot was the day of David's death, and some say it was also his birthday, offering additional insight into the association of the Book of Ruth with Shavuot and David. However, the Book of Ruth, with its simmering sexual tension in the scenes between Boaz and the title character, might also remind us that David's personal history was marked by sexual transgression (recorded in 1 and 2 Samuel) that led eventually to the de facto murder of Bathsheba's husband, a crime that deprived David of the right to build the Jerusalem Temple, a task by which his son, Solomon, was honored. Also, at the beginning of the genealogical line recounted in Ruth we find Perez, the first of the twin sons born of the surreptitious sexual encounter between Judah and his widowed daughter-in-law Tamar (Genesis 38), another reverberation of sexual transgression against which the account of Boaz and Ruth plays out.

Especially in congregations observing Shavuot in traditional ways, reading Ruth or at least discussing some of its major themes is a highlight of the holiday. Since this festival has other special poetic texts associated with it and the traditional biblical reading for Shavuot includes the

Exodus chapters (19 and 20) leading up to and including the Ten Commandments, Ruth might be the focus for an adjacent sabbath, a special program, or even a second day of Shavuot in those congregations that observe the festival for two days. When recited in Hebrew, the book is chanted in the same modal pattern as Shir ha-Shirim and Qohelet, the two other pilgrimage holidays.

Coming as it does in the late spring, Shavuot is often celebrated in Jewish congregations as the end of the religious school year and graduation from religious school, using agricultural and floral decorations not otherwise customary in Jewish houses of worship. Synagogues or school auditoriums may be decorated with floral arrays, flowering plants, and sheaves of grain, especially wheat; even students might be garlanded or carry floral bundles in processions. Perhaps because of the holiday's agricultural associations, or perhaps because the giving of the Torah suggests "milk and honey," dairy foods (and therefore, not meat) are traditional albeit not obligatory for Shavuot meals; otherwise, the holiday has no special home observances associated with it, which might account for it being less widely marked across Judaism's spectrum than the other major holidays.

Shavuot nonetheless is not just the next biblical festival after Passover: it completes Passover. Being liberated from oppressive servitude is a reason to celebrate but it is not sufficient for life. Freedom without purpose and without structure can devolve into chaos or anomie. We are "free" but free to do what? Shavuot is the answer to that. The purpose of the liberation is to become a holy people, *am kadosh*, through observing the revealed Torah and its explications. Shavuot is the purpose of the exodus. The birth metaphor implied in the exodus story may be complemented by another metaphor, not just of birth but rebirth.

We can think of the forty-nine days linking Pesach to Shavuot as similar to another forty-nine-day period, the transitional stage of forty-nine days that the Buddhist Book of the Dead calls the *bardo*, beginning at death and ending with the soul's reincarnation. At the exodus, the descendants of Isaac pass out of a death-centered, death-shadowed kingdom of Egypt, the place of being hemmed in and constricted, the meaning of the Hebrew word *tzar* in the root of the Hebrew name for Egypt, *Mitzrayim*. They left a country where the burial pyramids, mausoleums, and sarcophagi monumentalize the culture's obsession with what follows this life, a country stained with blood-red rivers (the *dam* or blood of the Passover seder's litany of plagues) and with the death of the firstborn that at last opens the border for Israel's departure. In leaving *Mitzrayim*, the Israelites pass through the parted waters that will engulf and swallow their Egyptian pursuers. Subsequently, they are cautioned against trying to return to the place they left. Through the bardo-like forty-nine days of interregnum, the descendants of Joseph, still nostalgic for what was left behind (the free fish, cucumbers, melons, onions, leeks, and garlic they nostalgically recall in Numbers 11:5), must learn and reconcile themselves to not returning, much as the soul in the bardo must accustom itself that, like Eurydice, it cannot return to where it was. At Sinai the Israelite people become reborn as a nation with a purpose that looks forward, not back.

The Book of Ruth is also a narrative that takes us from death to rebirth. It begins amid a famine in Israel that precipitates a reverse exodus of sorts. This family (can they have been the only one?) deserts the "promised land," and specifically Bethlehem (*Bet-lekhem*, the seemingly ironically named "House of Bread") for neighboring and historically hostile Moab. In the story's accelerated narrative time, the third verse tells us that the husband died in Moab; in the next verse, the two sons marry Moabite women, Orpah and Ruth, and live there around ten years; and then, in the fifth verse, they are both dead, leaving the widow and her two widowed daughters-in-law. The men fled death by starvation in their homeland but met death in what had seemed the place of refuge, leaving behind no offspring of their own. Naomi is left, according to the sixth-century-CE midrash of Ruth Rabbah 2, "like the leftovers of the sacrificial grain offering." Hearing that Israel's famine is over, the older woman, accompanied by the daughter-in-law Ruth, returns to her former home, where she insists that she should bear a new name: not "Naomi" (*pleasant*) but Marah (*bitter*), for God has soured her life and embittered her as well. "I went away full but return empty." Before the book ends, the child born to Ruth will rejuvenate her mother-in-law, who holds him to her breast; the other women proclaim, "a son is born to Naomi," as if the woman who declared herself barren of pleasure had been revitalized. The vitiated lineage that seemed to have died out with the deaths of Elimelekh and his two childless sons, Makhlon and Kilion, finds new life, grafted onto the vitality of Boaz, who never left the land of Israel, and effected through the fertility of Ruth, who has in a sense rebirthed herself by embracing Naomi's home and love. The once-starving nation is again fruitful. With the concluding genealogical summary of the male line that passes through Boaz and Ruth, the rebirth motif culminates in the crown of David, scion of a foreign womb.

The names in this story tantalize with allegorical possibilities. Not only *Bethlehem* and *Naomi* but most of the other proper names resonate. The name of Naomi's husband, Elimelekh, literally means "my God is king," like "Bet-lekhem" an ironic appellation for someone who flees Israel for Moab because of a famine. Their ill-fated sons, Makhlon and Kilion, are named "Sickness" and (perhaps) "consumptive." *Ruth* is aptly "compassionate friend," while *Boaz* means "strength is in him." We even have the throwaway albeit crucial character dubbed "*ploni almoni.*" Yet if we were to build on these hints to pursue an allegorical reading of the entire text, we would be puzzled by the obvious inconsistencies, for while some names are literally apt, others are paradoxical. If they reflect a constructed narrative by a literarily sophisticated artist, rather than a recounting of archival facts, then we might conclude that the author did not have complete aesthetic control of the tempting onomastic material. While that is certainly possible, it might be fairer to imagine otherwise. One of the fourfold interpretive strategies articulated many centuries later in rabbinic literature is termed *remez*, "hint." The hint may be numerological, for example, or linguistic; it points to a deeper layer of meaning beyond the text's surface. The names in Ruth might be examples of such a technique. Rather than direct equivalences or a straightforward chronicle of historical facts, perhaps they intend to signify to the story's audience that the events have a more abstruse level of meaning, one that we might variously term literary, ethical, or sacred. That is, names in most allegories map out a network of alternative readings of the text. In Ruth, they might hint that the story's significance is not confined to the literal.

As happens in this book, naming also situates the text in a liminal region overlapping fact and fiction. No sooner than Elimelekh and the sons are named, they are all dispatched through sudden deaths. Why (one might ask) bother to name characters if they are introduced only to die, thereby rapidly turning the three female characters into widows? Certainly their names give what Gilbert and Sullivan's Pooh-Bah calls "artistic verisimilitude" to the narrative, though the only important thing about them is whom they married. One might almost say the same about Orpah, seemingly introduced to be the antithesis of Ruth, to be the one who chooses not to journey with Naomi but to return to her birth family in Moab. So little importance is given to the men that the late Elimelekh is remembered only as the kinsman of Boaz, and (almost comically) the identity of which son was married to which Moabite woman becomes clear only late in the story when Boaz publicly and formally announces the quasi-levirate marriage through which he espouses "Ruth the wife of Makhlon" (4:10).

Three times, Naomi admonishes Ruth and Orpah, "Turn back" / *shavna*, urging them to return to their families. It is prudent advice from an impoverished widow beyond childbearing years who is unable to protect them or meet their future needs. Yet we perceive that it is also one of the characteristic responses of a clinically depressed person to push away would-be helpers because they feel themselves to be lost causes. Her three attempts to deter them (1:8, 1:11, and 1:12) are cited subsequently in rabbinic literature as the source for dissuading a potential convert to Judaism three times, a teaching of Rabbi Shmuel bar Nakhmani in the name of Rabbi Yudan bar Rabbi Khanina (Midrash Ruth Rabbah 2:16). Though the practice never became religious law, across centuries it has often been followed by rabbis dealing with potential converts and frequently leads to the impression that Judaism discourages conversion.

So far as the Tanakh is concerned, Orpah exits the scene at this point, leaving her mother-in-law with a kiss, and never to be mentioned again. However, Naomi refers to her as having returned to "her people and her gods" (1:15), a phrase that the Jewish oral interpretive tradition seizes upon. For if Ruth, the loyal daughter-in-law, becomes David's progenitor, then the one who rejects Naomi, Israel, and Israel's God by returning to Moab and its gods must give birth to Israel's foes. And no foe more apt than David's legendary antagonist, Goliath, said to be one of Orpah's four gigantic and ill-fated sons, whom she putatively conceived in hedonistic abandon with multiple fathers (indeed, according to one particularly nasty midrash, a hundred men and a dog). Orpah's name may derive from the Hebrew *oref*, nape of the neck, and has been interpreted to refer to her turning away after giving her mother-in-law a tearful parting kiss. From the standpoint of Jewish spiritual homileticists, she made the carnal choice. Her reward is to have physically imposing sons who will be slain by David and his faithful followers in Israel. As the Talmud (b. Sotah 42b) puts it, "The Holy One, blessed be, said, 'Let the sons of the kissed one fall by the hands of the sons of the one who cleaved.'"

The rabbis and scribes who developed and compiled midrash, and biblical commentators influenced by them, had no notion of being expositors of literary exegesis as we understand it. They were looking for a homiletic truth, approaching the texts as keys to religio-legal observance (halakhah) and records of Israel's history, assuming that even minor characters or seemingly random details were recorded because they connected somehow to the story of the Jewish people in covenantal relationship with God. Like much homiletically driven biblical commentary, this interpretation of Orpah reads the story as history rather than literature, and it is eisegetical, a counterfactual imposition of meanings on the written material. For taken by itself, Orpah's brief biblical narrative does not condemn her choice.

Granted, unlike Ruth's, it will not be described in terms of Rabbi Abraham Joshua Heschel's resonant phrase, "moral grandeur and spiritual audacity." Rather, it is understandably safe and prudent of her to return to what she knows and where she is known, to her homeland where she has a family of origin along with a defined social place. Furthermore, it is a choice she makes with tears of sorrow and seeming reluctance, urged to it by Naomi's earnest delineation of her own inability to provide a secure future for any of them in the land that the daughters-in-law do not know. After Naomi's first admonitory "Turn back" and her parting blessing of them, Orpah joins with Ruth as both cry and promise to stay with the older woman. Only after her third urging of them to turn away does Orpah part from the other two women to make her way back to her family and homeland.

Perhaps readers or listeners of the time would have understood those three pleas for them to go back as merely a formulaic cultural ritual, like offering refreshments to a visitor three times before they accept or persist in declining, but to modern ears they surely sound earnest. When she insists that she has no future to offer them, there is no reason to dispute her and Orpah accedes. William Blake, in his 1795 watercolor *Naomi Entreating Ruth and Orpah to Return to the Land of Moab*, depicts the oppositely curved figures of the two younger women mirroring one another: Ruth clasping Naomi in an enfolding embrace as a bowed Orpah departs, hand to her head in a gesture that has been read as grief or as shame.

Ruth, on the other hand, does not go back, and because of her choice and its consequences, she has been regarded as an ideal convert, perhaps the first convert in Israel's sacred literature. In both Judaism and Christianity, Ruth is often imagined as a paradigmatic spiritual hero who makes a faithful commitment to adopt as her own a people and faith new to her. That view of the character in Jewish tradition is a product of midrash, for no one knows what "conversion" would have meant in pre-rabbinic times. Of course there had been other examples of the *b'nei Yisrael* (literally, sons of Israel/Jacob) marrying someone not of the extended tribal or familial network. Joseph, for example, married Asenath, daughter of Potiphar, the priest of the city of On; their two sons, Ephraim and Menasheh, are still evoked as paragons of male Jewish identity when traditionally observant Jewish parents bless their sons on the Sabbath, despite there being no biblical evidence that Asenath was in any sense Jewish. Similarly, Moses married Zipporah, the daughter of Yitro (Jethro) a Midianite priest; she becomes the mother of his two sons, Gershom and Eliezer, both accepted as Jewish though the Torah never posits that their mother had somehow become a Jew.

Based on biblical evidence, we might hypothesize that in the absence of any recorded official process, patrilineal descent was accepted, and what passed as conversion was that a non-Jewish woman who married a Jewish man accepted his religious practices, perhaps alongside her own, thereby becoming fully integrated into Jewish society as if a native-born member of the group. However, according to the midrashic Ruth Rabbah 2, the early sages known as amoraim transmitted the teaching of Rabbi Meir, that the sons "did not convert . . . nor immerse" (*lo girum v'lo hitbilu*) their wives to make them members of the community of Israel but married them despite the prevailing law (Deuteronomy 23:3) against intermarrying with Moabites or converting them. At some point, as attested in the Talmud, Yevamot 76b, that prohibition became limited to Moabite men, through a highly literal (and grammatically dubious) reading of the Deuteronomy text. In Ruth Rabbah, one commentator proposes that *ploni almoni* refuses to wed Ruth because he is not learned enough to know that the halakhah had changed to permit Moabite women.

By contrast, if Ruth somehow "becomes" Jewish, it is through a purposeful series of clearly articulated choices. Her "conversion class" so to speak began when she wed a son of Naomi. Her formulaic pledge of allegiance, stated in concise and eloquent parallel phrases, is throughout a pledge of devotion to Naomi and all that Naomi is connected to. Her succinct statement probably makes explicit the ways in which, during pre-rabbinic Jewish history, someone could become integrated into the Jewish familial community.

In the most familiar English translations, Ruth responds to Naomi's urging that she, like Orpah, should return to her original home, by protesting, "Do not *entreat me* to depart from you" (1:16). The Hebrew verb *tif'g'i* (*p-g-i*) can mean entreat or supplicate, but it can also have a more hostile sense, to assail. That is how Ruth Rabbah interprets it: do not attack me by making me go back. That is, Ruth regards Naomi's imprecation as if she were being thrust away. According to this homiletic interpretation, Ruth conveys her desire not only to journey with Naomi but to convert, preferring to do so under her direction than with another. At that point, the midrash argues, Naomi sets forth "*hilkhot gerim*," the laws of conversion, each of which Ruth affirms. We may divide her promises to highlight their sequence:

> Wherever you go, I will go;
> wherever you lodge, I will lodge;
> your people shall be my people
> and your god, my god. (1:16)
>
> Where you die, I will die,
> And there I will be buried. (1:17)

Read in sequence as markers of a life in brief, Ruth's commitments are all-encompassing. They are sometimes used in modern wedding ceremonies. Reacting viscerally to them, we may not even notice that they make no allowance for Ruth to have a future spouse. Again, the traditional Jewish commentaries interpret her pledges as commitments to halakhic living according to rabbinic precepts articulated many centuries later. For example, in Ruth Rabbah, Naomi is said to explain, "My daughter, Jewish women do not go to the gentiles' theaters and circuses (*teatriyot v' kirkiyot shel goyim*)," prompting the response, "Wherever you go, I will go." That is, they deem that through these succinct pledges, Ruth promises to abide by the laws that regulated personal and domestic practices, to follow Jewish teachings about limiting travel on the Sabbath and other holidays, to embrace the Jewish concepts of community, and to respect Jewish penal statutes mandating punishment for religious violations. The culminating "your god, my god" thereby implies acceptance of the entire body of commandments (*mitzvot*).

However, considered by themselves without the traditional glosses, Ruth's affirmations seem to depict something different. First, she promises lifelong companionship. Second, she promises they will live together always. Third, she more broadly embraces Naomi's "people" as her own and, fourth, similarly Naomi's god, by which we should probably understand Ruth to mean Naomi's worship and cultic practices. Lastly, Ruth pledges a spouselike companionship even in death.

But what, we might ponder, is that to Naomi? In the biblical text, after Ruth speaks, Naomi does not reply verbally, instead responding with silence. "When she saw how intent she was to go with her, she said nothing more to her" (1:18). That verse has often been translated as, "she ceased arguing with her," though some read it as, "she stopped speaking to her." Either is possible, depending on what we make of Naomi's attitude and state of mind at this point. Perhaps she prefers to return by herself, unencumbered with her widowed, penniless Moabite daughter-in-law, who sensed that she was being rejected and resisted it. Perhaps she accepts that the younger woman's feelings have overridden her own prudent advice. Clearly, she is resigned to Ruth accompanying her. But it is surely as a marginalized, almost phantom presence; for when they arrive in Bethlehem and Naomi is recognized, her response that she should be called *Marah* (bitter) because "I left full and God has returned me empty" shockingly ignores the presence of the devoted Ruth alongside her. We might ponder whether it is artistic license or the imagined effects of traumatic losses that has caused Naomi to forget that she has family property that could be claimed and some kinsmen (such as Boaz) who could redeem both the property and the younger widow.

This episode centering on Ruth's succinct, powerful words of commitment is widely felt to be the most memorable and significant in the book. For whatever reasons, the Book of Ruth has only infrequently attracted creative explorations in music, drama, or the visual arts (e.g., some Rembrandt sketches, a Poussin landscape), but one of the few musical examples is a short cantata, based entirely on this passage, composed in 1947 in the United States by the Italian-born Jewish composer Mario Castelnuovo-Tedesco for soprano, women's chorus, and accompaniment (originally piano, later orchestrated), significantly called *Naomi and Ruth*, in which Ruth's lines are sung by the chorus because the composer deemed them "universal."

Of all these statements, poignant and beautiful as they are, the most significant for its wording is the fourth: *v'elohaiyich elohav / and your god, my god.* Four times—once indirectly, three times directly—Naomi has referred to her God as YHVH, but she used a more generic Hebrew word for "god" (*elohei*) when referring to Orpah's religion. Remarkably, given Ruth's subsequent reputation as the convert par excellence, she does not proclaim (for example), *YHVH shall be my God*. She does not attest her belief in the God of Israel (*sh'ma Yisrael / hear, O Israel YHVH eloheinu YHVH only*—Deuteronomy 6:4) as mandated in modern Jewish conversionary affirmations. Rather, using the same word *elohei* that Naomi chose in speaking of Orpah's decision to return to her home and her gods, Ruth pledges to Naomi that *your god shall be mine*, making this a bond of allegiance formed through Naomi and because of her, not what we might call Ruth's spiritual awakening to a new religious understanding of God. When in 1:17, for the first and only time, she uses "YHVH" in pledging to Naomi, "Everything and all may YHVH do to me if anything other than death parts me from you," she implicitly accepts the authority of this Hebraic god in the context of binding her allegiance to her companion.

If we understand "conversion" in its root sense to mean "turning around," we might say that there is an ironic tension between the figurative and literal events at this point in the story. Ruth is notably not as Keats poignantly misremembered or misrepresented her: "Perhaps the self-same song that found a path / Through the sad heart of Ruth, when, sick for home, / She stood in tears amid the alien corn" ("Ode to a Nightingale," 65–67). The biblical Ruth never expresses nostalgia for Moab or "home." Literally, Ruth "converts" by moving forward with Naomi to whatever that will bring, rather than turning around and returning with her sister-in-law. We can also say that what she does internally seems best understood as her voluntary absorption into a new social construct as well as a commitment to a new home.

Hebrew also poses a terminological play of word and concept regarding the alien and the convert. A stranger in a strange land, as Moses was in Midian, Ruth is a *ger*, a stranger or foreigner, though the synonym that she uses for herself in speaking to Boaz is *nokriya*, "foreign woman." The word *ger*, which occurs frequently in the Torah, came to mean a convert, though we do not know when that change or expansion of meaning occurred, much less what was meant in that era by conversion (in Hebrew, *gerut*). By the time of the Talmud, there were two forms of *ger*. One was the *ger tzedek* or righteous convert, who went through formal processes of conversion before a rabbinic panel (a *bet din*), obligating the convert to all Judaism's practices and laws. The other was the *ger toshav*, what we could call a resident alien, who chose to live permanently among the Jewish people in the land of Israel and was thereby obligated to observe some but not all of Judaism's commandments; rabbis greatly differed in judging which commandments were obligatory. Essentially, the *ger tzedek* was a "stranger" who was no longer a stranger, a stranger who had become part of the people Israel and was to be regarded as an Israelite. The *ger toshav* was technically a stranger, not an Israelite, but a largely assimilated one who was guaranteed some basic protections by the same Torah laws that safeguarded widows, orphans, and the poor in general. Ruth, continually called "Ruth the Moabite" by the narrator as well as by the characters in the story, seems to remain a *nokriya* but also seems to be treated as a *ger toshav* for most of the book.

That changes when Boaz formally announces at the city gate that he, rather than *ploni almoni*, is taking "Ruth the Moabite, the wife of Makhlon, as my wife, to perpetuate his name in his estate" (4:10), at which the transformation in her status to *ger tzedek* is announced implicitly by all present in celebrating the betrothal. "May God make the woman coming into your house like Rachel and Leah, who built up the House of Israel" (4:11). Their formulaic-sounding language links "Ruth the Moabite" to the wives of Jacob as exemplary matriarchs of the Jewish people. Notably, when Boaz marries her, the text does not call her "Ruth the Moabite" but simply "Ruth." At this point, through the marital pledge of Boaz and the promise to her late husband's lineage, Ruth is clearly accepted by the local Jewish community as one of them and a crucial link to the Jewish future. The women of the community, who apparently greeted Naomi's embittered return from Moab without resentment or Schadenfreude, ratify that communal acceptance of Ruth when they subsequently celebrate the birth of Boaz and Ruth's son: *vayikrei sh'mo b'yisrael*, "may his name be known in Israel" (4:14). Fittingly, in what might point to a communal practice, the son's name, Obed, is bestowed on him by these women.

In the midrashic collection Ruth Rabbah (ch. 2), Rabbi Zeira poses this rhetorical question: since *Ruth* teaches nothing about the fundamental halakhic behavioral categories, specifying for instance what is clean and unclean or what is forbidden or permitted, what is its religious purpose? He answers that it exists to teach that there are great rewards for *gom'lei hasidim*, acts of lovingkindness. While Ruth evinces lovingkindness toward Naomi, the older woman does the same toward her, in effect making Ruth her adopted daughter, whose fortunes will shape the future of them both. Both are rewarded by Boaz, whose overtures to Ruth speak not of love or dynasty but appreciation of her kindness toward her mother-in-law.

At the heart of this text is a theology of affectionate relationships, which develop in either harmony or tension with personal interests. For instance, in the divergent choices of the two younger women, we see that Orpah's affectionate relationship with Naomi (and perhaps also with her sister-in-law) conflicts finally with her self-interest, while Ruth finds harmony between the two, choosing a commitment to Naomi that we can see as altruistic (i.e., motivated by *hesed*, lovingkindness), though one might just as well argue that it profoundly fulfills her. Although the agricultural subject matter is most likely the critical link between the Book of Ruth and the revelation of the Torah on Shavuot, the book's value system of *khen hesed v'rakhamim* / goodheartedness, lovingkindness, and compassion seems to exemplify the Torah's central concept of loving another like oneself.

Furthermore, at the heart of this exposition is someone especially vulnerable among the vulnerable: a female immigrant working in the fields, an impoverished widow whose only companion and guide is a local native but otherwise in the same situation as she, and a generation older. Interestingly, although Ruth understandably addresses Boaz deferentially from the standpoint of a vulnerable supplicant, a foreigner who presumes no entitlement and represents herself as grateful for every consideration, she is nevertheless an adult woman. Widowed after some years of marriage, she is presumably at least in her late twenties, her one advisor and confidante being her mother-in-law, a generation older. Ruth Rabbah 6 cites talmudic notables alleging that at the time of their meeting, Boaz was eighty years old and Ruth forty, both of them childless until their union is blessed by the righteous in the story. As with the putative lifespans of figures in Genesis, these imagined ages of the main characters in this book deserve more than a grain of salt; still, they usefully remind us that we are not dealing with Romeo and Juliet but with mature adults, at least one of whom has been previously married. (As noted below, one midrash speculates that Boaz himself was newly a widower.)

It is hard, maybe even impossible, for us to read this story outside our modern frames of reference. However, the narrative itself points to the relevance of our concerns. It is Boaz who admonishes his field hands not to interfere with Ruth. Ruth Rabbah 4 explains that Boaz notices Ruth's diligence and modesty, meaning (as the midrash proposes) that she works without raising her skirt or socializing with the men the way the other women do, and confining herself first to the public gleaning areas, not between the sheaves. Similarly, our minds and the rabbinic homiletic mind react quite differently to Naomi's advice to Ruth, "wash and anoint yourself, put on fresh clothing, and go down to the threshing floor where Boaz sleeps." We most likely hear this as dating advice. By contrast, to the sages of the midrash, bathing implies washing away the stain of astrology and idolatry, anointing means adorned with *mitzvot* and righteousness, while changing clothes indicates shabbat/Sabbath raiment. In telling Ruth to go to the threshing floor, Naomi furthermore assures her also that "my merit" will accompany the younger woman.

The traditional commentary treats Boaz similarly. Boaz ate and drank and his heart was merry, the story tells us. We think we understand the behavior of a successful, hard-working man enjoying life at the conclusion of his harvesting labors, stopping at the tavern for a few drinks before going to sleep. Midrash elaborates with various other explanations: he was merry because he had blessed his food, or because he ate dessert after his meal and was therefore inspired to speak words of Torah, or perhaps because he was seeking a wife. Even lying down by his pile of grain is treated as a mark of righteousness because he did not follow the supposedly common path of promiscuity at that time by spending his earnings on prostitutes. Instead, he questions the woman lying at his feet to ascertain that she is unmarried and ritually clean (*tahor*), indeed, the midrash asserts, the cleanest of the clean.

Boaz, according to these traditional interpretations, lives up to the meaning of his name, literally, "strength," by defeating the evil impulse (*yetzer hara*) that urges him to have sex with Ruth, or worse, even to show his "mastery" by raping her. Instead, he assures her safety, swearing an oath "as God lives," while he tells her to stay the night, promising to resolve her status legally in the morning. Midrash even explains that Boaz spent the night in prayer, pledging to God that he never touched Ruth, whose covert departure before daybreak is effected so as not to desecrate the divine name with the appearance that they behaved improperly.

In all their interactions, Boaz and Ruth speak and act in ways that may remind a modern reader more of courtly than rustic behavior. Boaz continually addresses Ruth as *bati*, "my daughter," the same word as Naomi uses for her, implying his protective care rather than erotic intentions.

Ruth in turn calls Boaz *adonai*, "my lord," (2:13), using a term that most often refers to God.

While the biblical narrative depicts Boaz as behaving with almost chivalric propriety, midrash also imagines that his restraint did not come easily. Maybe the midrash authors want to assure us that Boaz's self-control does not mean that he lacks virility or that the perfumed and adorned Ruth is not desirable. Whether we imagine their respective ages as eighty and forty, or we suppose that Ruth might be closer to thirty and Boaz older though not elderly, this midrash seems to admit that we cannot overlook the sexual tension, or the potential for manipulation and exploitation in the scene. Not unexpectedly, Marc Chagall, in his lithographic biblical illustration *Boaz Wakes Up and Sees Ruth at His Feet*, depicts a young, lithe, round-breasted Ruth, smilingly turned toward the viewer while completely nude save for a beaded necklace to adorn her, the standing sheaves of wheat between her and the looming, almost soaring Boaz hinting at fertility. Chagall's interpretation makes quite clear the sexual excitement in which Ruth would implore the man to spread his cloak, and likely also himself, over her.

Throughout the tale Boaz regularly invokes God's blessing, God's name, or God's protection, using the *shem hameforesh* / Tetragrammaton YHVH. While one can certainly argue that these are conventional formulaic phrases or even that he uses them purposefully to portray himself as virtuous, the effect (readily embraced by traditional commentaries) cloaks him in religious reverence complementing Ruth's decency. He is not necessary a life-long bachelor at this point; a midrash (Ruth Rabbah 3) alleges that when Naomi and Ruth reach Bethlehem, crowds have gathered already to do acts of kindness (*gemilut hasidim*) because Boaz's wife had died that day. While there is no textual support for this idea in the biblical narrative, it allows imagining Boaz as a recent widower reacting not to Ruth's physical attractiveness (which in fact he never mentions) but, as he himself says, to her kindness, dedication to work, modesty, and familial devotion. In this midrashic reading, a widower is responding to the mature merits of a widow.

When Naomi greets Ruth, returned from visiting Boaz, she asks the surprising question, "Who are you, my daughter?" (3:16). The midrash points us to her real meaning: Has your status changed? There being no simple answer to that question, Ruth must explain by telling what had and had not happened that night, as well as showing the bountiful quantity of barley Boaz bestowed so that she would not return empty-handed "to your mother-in-law." With that simple one-word acknowledgment, Boaz registers both his generosity (or perhaps canny appeal for Naomi's favor) and his respect for the existing family tie between the two women.

One textual oddity has been a focus of varying explanations, reflecting readers' different views of authorial control as well as interpretations of Ruth's character. When Boaz first encourages and aids Ruth, he specifically tells her to stay close to his "young women," *na'arot*, as she works (2:8), promising that he has warned his men not to harass her. Later recounting the episode to her mother-in-law, Ruth specifically says that Boaz told her to "stay close to my men [*na'arim*]" (2:21), leading Naomi to advise instead that she would be safer to remain with the women (*na'arot*). In midrash, Rabbi Chanin bar Levi (Ruth Rabbah 5:1) interprets this altered wording as a remnant of Ruth's origins among an allegedly decadent people, saying about this passage, "Indeed, a Moabitess," implying that her mind swerved toward desire for the young male harvesters. Some modern scholars interpret Ruth's change of words as minimally significant, either the error of the foreign-born Ruth not recognizing a grammatical distinction between male and female or simply Hebrew's default use of the masculine word form regarding groups containing both men and women. Others more plausibly imagine that Ruth is testing Naomi's reaction to the possibility that her son's widow might find another husband among these working men, perhaps at the cost of their bond.

We do well to recall that Ruth is indeed a woman who has been married before, not a naïve youngster. She is old enough and experienced enough to recognize that Boaz's attentiveness to her, while protective, may also be proprietary as he urges her, practically bribes her, to keep apart from the male field hands and not to glean in anyone else's field. Furthermore, the sentence we are considering immediately follows Naomi's revelation that this landowner is in fact closely enough related to redeem these two widows who otherwise have no visible means of support save for the common means of charity that the Torah provides. Consequently, we might understand Ruth's change of noun endings as a way of testing her own instinct. If Naomi agrees with the statement as Ruth has delivered it, presumably she thinks that Ruth's best chance of finding a man to take care of them is among the harvesters. If instead she advises Ruth to work only alongside the women (essentially affirming what Boaz actually told her), then Naomi also believes that Boaz's consideration for Ruth comes from this prominent man's personal interest in her. That is exactly

Naomi's reading of the situation: stay away from the male field workers and do not glean anywhere else.

The scene between Boaz and the other potential redeemer is meticulously staged so that it is not a private conversation but a carefully established legal proceeding in public before the elders of the town, a group constituting not merely two witnesses that might be expected according to biblical practices but a minyan, a quorum of ten men representing the community at large. To modern readers, virtually every aspect of the transaction is problematic, first because what takes place is at variance from Torah law, second because Boaz's strategy is unclear, and third because an absolutely crucial word has been interpreted and emended by Jewish tradition differently from the written text (a practice known in Hebrew as *qere-ketiv*, literally, "read" and "written").

The Torah law regarding a "redeemer" (*go'el*) simply concerns property. As articulated in Leviticus 25:25, if an Israelite (such as Elimelekh or his widow) must sell land because of financial need, a close relative is obliged to redeem that property so that it stays in the family. Ruth, in her appeal to Boaz on the threshing floor, may have implicitly joined that obligation with another one, stated in Deuteronomy 25:5–6, that pertains specifically to a brother of a deceased, childless married man. According to the law there, the surviving brother is obligated to marry the widow for her to have a child that will preserve the dead man's lineage and inheritance, or else to relinquish that formally and visibly by the removal of a shoe.

The first element, marrying the widow so that she will bear a child to transmit the lineage of the dead husband, is recalled indirectly in the closing verses of Ruth through the reference to Perez, the son born to Tamar. Widowed, Tamar had next been wed to Onan, who did not want to get her pregnant, thereby impairing his own legacy while preserving his late brother's; consequently, he ejaculated outside of her during intercourse (thus, the literal meaning of onanism) and was punished by God with an early death for failing to accept his obligation. The ceremony enacted between Boaz and the other redeemer as a ritual of transference resembles the Torah's mandated *halitzah* ritual but differs significantly from it. According to the Deuteronomic ritual, in the presence of a *bet din* (a panel of Jewish authorities), the rejected widow removes the shoe of the brother-in-law who has declined to wed her and spits toward him. Instead, our narrator presents the rite in the Book of Ruth as an old Israelite practice in which a deal was sealed by one person removing his shoe and giving it to the other party. There is extensive debate in the commentaries over which person's shoe is removed, who removes it, and what the symbolism implies, but while the uncertainties cannot be resolved, none is truly consequential.

What are the other perplexities here? Ezekiel 16:8 represents God spreading a cloak over Israel's nakedness as a betrothal. On this basis, scholars hypothesize that this was a recognized ritual or formula of legal betrothal, so that when Ruth asks—or directs—Boaz to "spread your robe over your handmaid, for you are a redeeming kinsman" (3:9), she is asking him for both marriage and redemption of Naomi's inheritance. However, on one hand the Torah's obligation of *ge'ulah* (that is, the act of redeeming property) does not itself imply any obligation to marry a widow who is involved with the property. On the other hand, the levirate marriage (from the Latin *levir*, meaning brother-in-law) as detailed in Leviticus seemingly applies only to a brother, not to any more distant male relative such as a *go'el* could be. Yoking the two as Ruth does looks to be ad hoc. We simply do not know whether the story reflects a cultural expectation of that time or whether it is really a dramatic gambit by a woman who sees the opportunity to secure her own future and her beloved mother-in-law's as well.

Also problematic is Boaz's presentation of the facts to the other potential redeemer (the one who will not redeem) in this scene. A landowner of substance, who confidently takes charge in this episode with the compliance of the town's elders, Boaz might well have little interest in claiming Naomi's field for himself; therefore, first offering it for purchase to *ploni almoni* presents no problem for him even when the man promptly agrees. Boaz however has great interest in Ruth, so adding marriage to her as the mandatory second part of the deal is exceptionally risky. Suppose the other man accepts. But nobody wants Ruth to be married to *ploni almoni* rather than Boaz, least of all Ruth and Boaz themselves! This looks like a moment when the action is driven mainly by the author's desire for dramatic tension (will he or won't he?) or perhaps idealization of character by showing Boaz offering a magnanimous gesture of selfless integrity (despite our not understanding from where the legal obligation to marry Ruth derives).

This is the moment to consider a critical verbal detail. Hebrew texts are commonly written in consonantal form only, which can lead to ambiguities over word forms and meanings. To the engaged reader, such moments open a path to exploring alternative readings, many giving rise to midrash. At times in the transmission of Hebrew biblical texts, scribes and sages have provided widely accepted alternative spellings (*qere* forms) in the margins in place of the written (*ketiv*) ones, intending to clarify meanings. In this instance, according to the *ketiv*, Boaz tell *ploni almoni* that when you acquire the field, I [*kaniti*]—not "you" [*kanitah*]—will acquire Ruth the Moabitess as a wife to preserve the lineage of the deceased Makhlon. The ancient sages who edited the biblical text perhaps thought that when *ploni almoni*, having already agreed to redeem the field, turns down the deal so as not to impair his own estate, he does so because of the provision that a child with Ruth would eventually mean an inheritance for Makhlon's lineage and not his. Therefore, their *qere* emendation ("you will acquire Ruth") was intended to explain that nuance by making *ploni almoni* the one faced with the mandate of wedding Ruth as well as claiming the field. However, if we accept the original *ketiv* reading, we might imagine that the rival sees a step further into the future: supposing he redeems the field from Naomi, if Boaz marries Makhlon's widow and has children with her, then that field will pass to those heirs anyway.

Of course when considering "motivation," we may get so immersed in the characters that we forget they are just that: characters in a story. Regardless of whatever is historically true in the Book of Ruth, the tale that has come down to us, told from the viewpoint of an anonymous narrator, involves figures constructed on a page. We are therefore dealing not with an account of the thought processes or motives of (for instance) a real man called Boaz but with a plotline shaped by an author looking for the maximum effect from the ways in which the characters are presented and the events unfold. Similarly, the author is not interested in telling us how, not to mention where, the impoverished widows Naomi and Ruth lived in Bethlehem. After working, Ruth returns "home," though what and where that home might be remains a blank. Their practical circumstances register in our consciousness only when Ruth, by announcing her intention to glean in some field with the hope of receiving compassionate permission, implies that they are living with meager resources.

The beautifully conceived scenes involving Boaz and Ruth carefully yet succinctly develop their growing mutual interest in one another. We first see and hear that Boaz, clearly a prosperous farm owner (an *ish gibor* or prominent man as the narrator terms him), notices the strange "girl" (*na'arah* rather than *isha*, "woman") gleaning in his field and expresses curiosity about her. He obviously likes what his foreman tells him, that is, that this Moabite came from Moab with the returning Naomi, asked permission to glean behind the reapers, and has been working almost constantly from the morning onward. Seemingly at once, Boaz instructs Ruth to glean nowhere else but to remain close to "my girls." Addressing her as *bati*, "my daughter," Boaz essentially extends his protection over her. Surely, we should imagine that he says this loudly enough for the overseer and others to hear, for he also has ordered that she be treated respectfully and allowed to drink at will from the water drawn by the workmen. Essentially Boaz is doing little more than ratifying the rights to which the Torah already entitles Ruth, indeed, three times over as a widow, a poor person, and a *ger* or resident foreigner. But his proprietary care for her includes his concern that she not be harassed by the men either in the field or when getting a drink of water. We might recall Exodus 2:17 in which Moses, having fled Egypt into Midian and thus also become a stranger in a strange land, chases off the herdsmen who interfere with Zipporah and her six sisters as they attempt to draw water, an episode that eventually leads to Moses and Zipporah marrying. Boaz is obviously aware that sexual harassment is part of the fieldwork culture, but he is determined to shield Ruth from it with a grand gesture of protection that he announces publicly. It is left to us as readers to conclude whether he is nobly motivated by his appreciation of her loyalty to Naomi and willingness to work hard for her living or whether he also (or instead) is driven by personal interest in this woman, who is presumably attractive and, though known to be a widow, still young enough in appearance for him to refer to her first as a "girl" and to address her as "daughter."

For her part, Ruth reacts to him not with simple thanks but with a question, not merely a rhetorical exclamation but a direct inquiry that engages him in conversation. Prostrating herself with her face to the ground, in a gesture that can be read as supplicatory or worshipful, she inquires, "Why is it pleasing in your eyes [*khen b'eynecha*] to pay attention to me when I am a foreigner?" (2:10). We might suspect that it is Ruth herself who is pleasing to Boaz's eyes. In any event, this interesting combination of a humble posture with a forthright question demands a reply.

Boaz's response, which pays tribute to her character and behavior, suggests that he has already heard a great deal about her, though one must always remember that events and information in the narrative follow the needs of storytelling rather than historical plausibility. In particular, he notes her care for Naomi and her willingness to leave her parents and country to come to a foreign land. In keeping with his characteristically pious language in this episode, Boaz also wishes that she will be fully rewarded by this God, having taken refuge "under the wings" (*takhat kanafav*) of "YHVH, the God of Israel" (2:12). The scene thereby reverberates against Naomi's earlier plaints that "the hand of God has struck against me" (1:13) because "I went out full and God has brought me back empty," therefore God has "embittered my life" (1:20–21). Naomi's experiences cast in an ironic light Ruth's affirmation that "your God shall be my God." Does the Moabitess widow have a stronger faith in this God than the Israelite widow, or do we rather perceive her statement as attesting how fully she embraces life with Naomi. Boaz, at least, presents himself as both a believer and an adherent of God and the Torah.

If we suspect that Boaz is wooing Ruth during the gleaning, his pursuit is conducted indirectly yet openly; he does not hide his preferential treatment of her but addresses himself to her needs and wellbeing, presenting himself as thoughtfully attentive. Sit here and join in the reapers' meal, he beckons, as though she were one of his own hired workers, and he gives her more than enough to eat so she has food left over. When she returns to work, he instructs his reapers not merely to let her glean at will but also pull out some stalks to leave for her, without chastising her for what she is taking. Thus, while she has a biblical right to glean, he goes well beyond the legal requirement of the Torah.

It was Ruth who proposed the idea of gleaning for their survival. Returning to Naomi, Ruth astonishes her with an exceptional bounty, leading the older woman to wonder aloud whose fields Ruth worked and to exclaim a blessing for his generosity. After learning that it was Boaz, Naomi bestows an equivocally worded blessing that has produced two significantly different readings. "Blessed be he of God (YHVH), who has not failed in his kindness to the living or the dead" (2:20). The controversy, of course, is whether Naomi's dependent clause ("who has not failed . . .") refers to God or to Boaz. Many readers and translators choose the former: the woman who earlier complained that God had sent her home empty now learns to praise God's faithful generosity. However, if this were the intended meaning, the customary phrase would be simply, "Blessed be God." Instead, her phrasing seems more naturally to refer to Boaz, honoring him for his kindness to the living (Ruth and Naomi) as well as to the dead (their deceased husbands, who are Boaz's kin).

Throughout the book, while religious language hints at a divine context like a deep background in which the story unfolds, the action depicts human agency motivating and directing what transpires moment to moment. In the relationship between Naomi and Ruth, the narrative shows each woman at times taking the lead. Through these exchanges, we become increasingly aware of Ruth's resourcefulness. At first, Naomi is the one to initiate action along the road by imploring the younger women to return home, with Ruth persevering to overrule her through the book's most famous speech. Later, it is Ruth taking the initiative, declaring her intention to glean in the fields being harvested, to which Naomi quickly and laconically acquiesces, "Yes, go, my daughter." The succinct simplicity of her reply, unadorned with advice or concerns, may hint at their urgent need, while also revealing the closeness that has developed between them when Naomi now addresses Ruth as *bati*, "my daughter," just as Boaz will.

This is also one of the hints of some cosmic economy at work: the woman who came back "empty" (1:21) having lost a husband and two sons has gained a daughter and will eventually gain more than that. Perhaps this verbal embrace, so to speak, counterbalances that earlier scene in which the newly returned Naomi bemoaned her emptiness even as she was accompanied by the daughter-in-law who had left behind her family and country of origin, solemnly pledging her fidelity to her late husband's mother. Naomi's self-pity could be forgiven more easily were it not for the attendant insensitivity to the situation of Ruth, who is accompanying her, also without a husband or a child and now a stranger in a strange land, presumably standing alongside her as Naomi bemoans returning with nothing.

One of the oddities in Naomi's disconsolate plaint to her friends is that she refers to God by two names, YHVH (i.e., God, Lord, Yahweh, Adonai) and Shaddai (usually translated as "Almighty"), a much less common term within the biblical canon, though used several times in Genesis and widely throughout Job, where many scholars take it to be deliberately archaic. In fact, God tells Moses in Exodus 6:3 that El Shaddai was one of the names by which the patriarchs Abraham, Isaac, and Jacob knew of God but that they did not yet fathom the meaning of YHVH. Perhaps such archaizing is the author's intention in Ruth as well, suggesting that there is something primal in Naomi's response to what has happened to her.

Later, when Ruth returns with her bounty, we find the testing interplay in which Ruth claims to have been told to stay near the harvesting men and is then "corrected" by Naomi, who advises her just as Boaz had done to remain by the other women. Leading up to the climactic encounter at the threshing floor, the older woman, explaining that "I must find you a husband," counsels Ruth as to how to prepare herself for Boaz, who will tell her what to do; the younger responds, "I will do everything that you say." Naomi takes charge; Ruth expresses a subservient role; we could say they are mentor and mentee.

As the subsequent scene unfolds on the threshing floor, though, Ruth (not an inexperienced youngster, we recall) manages the confrontation and becomes the one to direct Boaz as much as she is able. (The complication of there being another redeemer with priority is one she could not have anticipated.) Instead of awaiting instructions from Boaz, she uncovers and thereby awakens him. But that is not enough. As he awakens, startled, and then seemingly alarmed to find a woman crouching by him, he is not the one to give instructions as Naomi had imagined. Rather, Ruth demands that he cover her with his cloak, apparently enacting their betrothal, and furthermore insists at the same time that he take the responsibility of redeemer.

A modern reader contemplating this dramatic scene will likely feel a swirl of mixed emotions. What Ruth does in going to the sleeping Boaz in the middle of the night, when she knows he has eaten and drunk enough to have laid down "merry," is more daring, more risky, more edgy, and more morally ambiguous than anything else anyone in the book has done. If she was bold earlier in her quest to glean, she has gone much further now in risking her reputation along with her personal safety. We also understand Boaz's surprise and alarm at thus being awakened, when he thought he was sleeping in solitude, by someone who has suddenly uncovered part of his body, and that person proves to be a woman accosting him. His amazement could give way to resentment, violence, or lust.

And yet, our modern point of view also allows us to read this episode as a comical reversal of the expectations we have developed through centuries of stories. The young woman, instead of being the sleeping potential victim of a lurking male assailant, is the covert and aggressive one, almost literally throwing herself on the unaware and perhaps intoxicated man. Whether we imagine her pleading or insisting, it is she who demands that he commit to her, though the relationship between them is tenuous at best, and one in which he appeared to be in charge. And it is he, the man who strode confidently into the story not long before, grandly bestowing blessings and largesse, commanding his field workers even in the way that they had to treat this same indigent foreign woman, who initially reacts to her with obvious fear and confusion. We may well believe that he is accustomed to being in charge and has never encountered a woman so assertive. The humor is situational rather than verbal: nothing said here is funny, though the action might seem so. Yet even as we perhaps are also amused to find that Ruth is possibly "trying too hard" in thrusting herself on Boaz in the middle of the night, we also understand that she is driven by the urgency of her and Naomi's need for necessities of life in the short term and financial security in the longer term.

Again she returns to Naomi, once more laden with grain given her by Boaz, and again she seems to alter the narrative, now claiming that Boaz told her not to return without something for her mother-in-law. While we might imagine Boaz saying that "in real life" in a snippet of conversation not transcribed into the report of the evening, the more significant fact is that since this detail was not previously mentioned, the narrator springs the statement on us as an apparent invention by Ruth. Do we read it as another example of Ruth's abiding care for Naomi—in other words, he gave this to you, not to me? Does she want to convey that Boaz is a compassionate man who will not neglect Naomi if he manages to wed Ruth? Is she deliberately covering the fact that he did not actually say anything about Naomi, let alone send her a generous present? Is she embarrassed because the bounty, if given only to her, might imply that uncovering his "feet" was a periphrasis for a sexual act for which Boaz compensated her by lavishly bestowing this grain?

In typical biblical fashion, commentary is withheld. Any or all interpretations are possible; at any reading, we may find ourselves modulating between them, sometimes preferring one, other times embracing ambiguous possibilities. The same is true of course about Boaz's nature and intentions. Are his interest, concern, and generosity driven by altruism and piety? Are his actions intended to woo or to seduce Ruth? Is he manipulative? Is there evidence that the character Boaz is even conscious of his own motivation? If he is, then that is most clearly reflected when he quickly regains his composure in Ruth's presence, promising to do everything that she asks for, noting that "all the elders at the gates" know that she is an "*eshet khayil*," a woman of merit, using the phrase from Proverbs 31:10 that has come to exemplify the industrious, resourceful wife whose husband thereby lauds her as exceeding the worth of all others. (In many traditional Jewish homes, a husband will recite this passage of some twenty-two lines every Friday night to praise his wife, although feminists and other readers recoil from its catalogue of seemingly unending, exhausting chores.) While it might seem odd for Boaz to evoke the esteem in which she is held by the town elders when he assents to Ruth, perhaps this is his way of implying that there would be no public objection to her as a foreigner because the community recognizes her as an exemplar of virtuous familial behavior.

As the action reaches its climax with the betrothal of Ruth and Boaz, the townspeople, including the elders, take on a choral role in which they do something more than laud "Ruth the Moabite." They transform her into the quintessential Israelite, saying to Boaz, "May the woman who is coming into your house be like Rachel and Leah, who built up the House of Israel" (4:11). Perhaps by the time of composition such a benediction was already commonplace. A version of that blessing, "May God make you like Sarah, Rebecca, Rachel, and Leah, who built up the House of Israel," is still recited for daughters in traditionally observant Jewish homes every Friday night before the Sabbath begins. Even more daringly, considering what we might term the courting history of Ruth and Boaz—have people been gossiping?—they further pray, "May your house be like the house of Perez, whom Tamar bore to Judah, by the offspring God will give you through this young woman" (4:12). Again, we cannot know whether this language is purely formulaic, but we see that it fits the story.

It is the reception of the son born to them, and the significance of his birth for Naomi and the community's other women, that now interests the narrator. The last that we read of Ruth in the book that bears her name is the verse of praise from the townswomen, announcing that she has borne a son, that she loves Naomi and is "better to you than seven sons" (4:15). For many readers, it is both disappointing and puzzling that Ruth, whose presence was so strong through most of the action, should be relegated so abruptly to the background, as if her sole function had been to produce an heir. Likely even more puzzling is the new attention directed back to Naomi, who becomes something of a surrogate mother to the child, and even more, for the women proclaim, "A son is born to Naomi" (4:17). In a sense, this formulation contrafactually implies that the ancestor of King David is virtually born of a native-born Jewish woman, Naomi, rather than Ruth the Moabite.

The talmudic passage cited earlier (Yevamot 76a-b) claims that during the era of David and Solomon, conversion was not allowed because the prosperity of the kingdom made the motives of potential converts suspect. Perhaps the end of the book reflects such anxiety over conversion itself, along with possible discomfort over the Moabite ancestry of

Israel's king. If so, we may nevertheless be uncertain about the author's stance, which might itself be equivocal. Is this a defense of the convert's value and integrity or a literary sleight-of-hand to camouflage the convert's crucial place in Israel's history?

The concluding section of the book takes us from the literary realm into the national-historical stream. Ruth has been legitimated as a mother in Israel, naturalized and adopted into the lineage of Rachel, Leah, and Tamar. The merit of her values is affirmed in the praise of her to Naomi by the celebrating women, whose words suggest that the love and goodness of this daughter-in-law more than compensates for the loss of a husband and two sons.

However, by turning our focus to the native-born Israelites—that is, Naomi, Boaz, the infant Obed, who also bears the legal ancestry of Makhlon through Makhlon's widow and thereby the legal heredity of Elimelekh as well—and concluding with a patrilineal genealogy of male offspring leading to King David, the narrator presents this tale as not only the engrossing unconventional family love story that has won our attention but a critical moment in the birth of a nation and a people. The public significance of the tale emerges when the women also exclaim to Naomi, "Blessed be God, who has not withheld a redeemer (*go'al*) from you today. . . . He will revitalize your soul and sustain your old age" (4:14–15). Especially if we perceive this book as postexilic, it becomes a tale counterbalancing Eykhah/Lamentations. The once-desolate widow, empty, bereft of her children and seemingly spurned by God, receives a redeemer, a lover and comforter; her fertility restored, she enjoys new youth and a new future. Naomi becomes Israel. And as the story looks ahead to the reign of King David, it seems to promise its postexilic audience what they would pray for through many generations: the restoration of the Davidic line.

5

Lamentations/Eykhah

How difficult it is to read this little book! Difficult because of the subject, which the heart and imagination want to resist, and difficult because of the poetic language, which is dense, and its vocabulary is uncommon. Adding to the difficulty, the commemorative day for which it is the designated special reading in Jewish liturgy, Tisha b'Av (the Ninth Day of Av), is a somber fast day that occurs in the northern hemisphere's late summer, from mid-July to mid-August, a time of year when most people recoil from burdening their spirits as they must while remembering the smoke, flames, and screams of a city's destruction so vividly memorialized in the poem, especially when the memory takes us back more than twenty-six hundred years to the devastation of the city and the Temple by Nebuchadnezzar's invading Babylonians. That Jews still do this is a measure of how important remembering is as well as how important that city, Jerusalem, is in Jewish life.

As the historian Yosef Yerushalmi argues in his slender yet influential 1982 book *Zakhor*, remembrance and history are not the same. The Hebrew—and indeed Jewish—imperative *zakhor*, "remember," is not a simple injunction to recall the chronicle of the past but to understand it as meaningful and relevant to oneself and to Jewish communal continuity. Grasping the significance of Lamentations and its commemorative role requires that we engage with what we might think of as the received narrative, or perhaps more accurately the received rabbinic narrative of Jewish history.

This foregrounds the destructions of the historic Temples, especially of the Second Temple, placing those structures, rituals, and their losses prominently in Jewish historical experience. It also places them critically at the formation of rabbinic Judaism, which supplanted the priestly sacrificial ritual mandated for the Temple with rabbinic practices of learning along with applied law, supplemented with analytic and interpretive methodologies, all resting on the authority of a coterie of rabbis and scholars ("sages"). This is not identical with modern historians' narratives of Jewish life in antiquity before and after the Second Temple; those studies follow the experiences of dispersed Jewish communities outside the land of Israel, surviving and sometimes even flourishing at various times, not heedless of events that transpired in Jerusalem and Judea yet not overwhelmed or incapacitated by them because what happened to that traditional cultic center of the Jewish people was essentially peripheral to their ongoing experience wherever they resided.

The received rabbinic narrative is transmitted in some part through the annual commemoration of Tisha b'Av (though many Jews do not observe it at all), in larger part through Jewish education, in even greater measure through daily prayers evoking the Temple rites (as well as, in the most traditional prayer expressions, calling also for their restoration) and probably most influentially through more widely experienced festival liturgies, especially those of Rosh Hashanah and Yom Kippur, which explicitly memorialize the ancient Temple rituals. Through these, most Jews have come to imagine that the Temple, even in its absence, is at the center of the Jewish religion. In fact, its erstwhile rituals are the pattern of Jewish worship even today, with each of the two daytime worship services in a traditional congregation relating to one of the ancient Temple services and the liturgy substituting for ancient offerings of material goods or animals. While some pray for the Temple to be "rebuilt," many who do not long for a Third Temple nonetheless see in the destruction of the Second the shattering of the Jewish religion's ancient core. Some traditional Jews who pray for the coming of the Messiah pray as well for the restoration of the Davidic monarchy, the return (one might say) of the once and future king. Similarly, at the heart of some Jews' Judaism also stands the once and future Temple. While not all feel that way, there is no other single place anywhere in the world that so focuses the historical imagination and deep emotional or spiritual bond for a large segment of the Jewish community and has done so for centuries.

While Tisha b'Av is obviously a postbiblical observance, the rabbis at an early stage in the development of the Oral Law (Mishna Ta'anit 4:6, b. Ta'anit 26b) sought to anchor it in biblical experience. Elaborating on chronological hints within the Torah, they posited that the Ninth of Av was the day on which the scouting party that Moses sent into Canaan returned to the Israelite encampment in the wilderness with a report so terrifying and disheartening that the people, after weeping and wailing through the night, wanted to choose a new leader to take them back to Egypt (Numbers 14:1–4). For punishment, none of that generation except the two who spoke favorably of the land, Joshua and Caleb, would live to cross the Jordan into "the land flowing with milk and honey" (Numbers 14:8). In this rabbinic model, the Ninth of Av was marked as a day of grief for the Jewish people even before there was a Temple to mourn.

Notwithstanding the more complicated picture of ancient Jewish religious life that emerges in modern scholarship, the fall of the Temples and the bitter experiences that resulted from those trials, along with other disasters occurring around the same time in the Jewish calendric year, such as the expulsion from England in 1290 and more consequentially from Spain in 1492, became part of the remembrance of the Jewish past even among Jews for whom the losses were sorrowful markers but not cataclysmic or personally damaging. For Jews later and elsewhere who themselves bore memories of the destruction of their families or even their entire communities by lawless mobs or tyrannical rulers, Eykhah with its record of devastation through iron and fire has given a voice to express communal and personal rage and grief.

Further, with Tisha b'Av occurring as it generally does in early August or at least late July, the evocation in Eykhah of a city's destruction amid smoke and flames brings to mind the 1945 atomic bombings of Hiroshima and Nagasaki on August 6 and 9 respectively. Many Jews commemorate those events as well in their Tisha b'Av services, joining the particularity of Jewish suffering with compassionate humanistic awareness of the anguish of civilians amid war's devastation.

Eykhah is a series of laments or *qinot* (singular, *qinah*) in five chapters; four of them are acrostics, each line beginning with the next letter of the Hebrew *alef-bet*'s twenty-two letters, while the fifth poem, albeit not an acrostic, consists of twenty-two verses. Following common Jewish practice the book is named for its initial word, which is an exclamatory "How": How barren, like a widow, sits the city that once teemed with people! Latin and English terminology follow the Greek title given in the Septuagint, which is *Threnoi*, Lamentations. In some sources that Greek title is *Threnoi Ieremiou* or Lamentations of Jeremiah. That is because a biblical tradition (2 Chronicles 35:25) reinforced in the Talmud (b. Mo'ed Katan 26a) ascribes the text to the contemporaneous prophet Jeremiah, thus the book has often been designated as "The Lamentations of Jeremiah." For that reason the Septuagint and Christian Bibles place the book following the Book of Jeremiah, among the Prophets, rather than with the other Megillot in the Writings.

That attribution is not taken seriously by modern scholars. Much as Qohelet was ascribed to Solomon based on his legendary wisdom, Eykhah is linked to Jeremiah because, deemed to be the author of laments, he was also the preeminent poet-prophet of the era, foretelling the collapse of the kingdom yet promising God's retribution against Babylon, concluding the Book of Jeremiah by recounting King Zedekiah's horrific end along with the Temple's despoliation and destruction. A modern editor's point of view might well question whether Jeremiah's eponymous prophetic text is the work of one visionary only; similarly, one can reasonably suspect that the five chapters of Eykhah may be by different poets working in a conventional literary technique, that is, the acrostic, and a familiar genre, the lament for a destroyed city. Sumerian culture was especially rich in verse laments, with poems commemorating the loss of Ur, Akkad, Eridu, Sumer, and other places. Notwithstanding modern doubts about authorship, in contrast to the other Megillot this one can be dated within a fairly narrow time frame: it cannot have been composed before 586 BCE, when the first Temple was destroyed, and its relentless mood of grief and horror suggests that it predates the rebuilding of the Temple, which commenced fifty years later.

Just as we do not know whether the poems were the work of one virtuosic author or a compilation of polished verses from diverse poets, neither do we know when, by whom, or how the poems were edited and formed into the composition we now have. As we shall see below, the arrangement of the five chapters seems intentional, suggesting that it is not an arbitrary sequence; rather, it is one that appears structurally coherent. That supposes a high level of artistic insight in the editing.

The literary device of the acrostic is also a feature of several of the psalms—specifically, numbers 25, 34, 37, 111, 112, 119 (which is a spectacular sequence of eight alphabetical acrostics), and 145—and in the "woman of merit" passage in Proverbs 31:10–31. Long after, it became a recurring feature of many prayers and piyyutim in Jewish liturgy, especially for Rosh Hashanah and Yom Kippur, some of them using inventive approaches such as acrostics built on some letter other than the first of each line. The technique reflects sophisticated literary sensibility, valuing technique at least as much as direct expression and suggesting a relatively cultured audience as well as authorship. It is, however, more than a literary trick. By its alphabetical organization (we would say "a to z," or in Hebrew, "*aleph* to *tav*"), it denotes the author's effort to encompass the experience completely, even exhaustively, while also implying that it takes the entire alphabet to do so.

Given the subject of Eykhah, its acrostics have an additional function. Confronting an overwhelming experience, particularly a deeply painful one, demanding verbal expression, an author likely confronts two immediate challenges. The first is structural, deciding where and how to start. This is a difficulty similarly facing any epic poet, each of whom develops a personal approach to the incipit, the beginning clause of the poem, that will tell the audience about the subject but moreover about the ensuing poem's real interests. The *Iliad* is not only about the Trojan War, it is particularly a poem about Achilles' prideful anger and it is motivated by the impulse to give voice to the story, a program compacted in the work's opening five Greek words, declaring "The rage of Peleus' son Achilles, sing, goddess." Virgil's "*arma virumque cano*" ("Arms and the man I sing") announces that the man, Aeneas, will be as significant in the poem as the war story; and it shifts the compositional focus from Homer's Thea, the inspirational divine muse, to "I," the human poet. Milton opens *Paradise Lost* with a series of prepositional phrases and subtle verbal nuances, starting with the initial "Of man's first disobedience and the fruit / Of that forbidden tree, whose taste . . ." thereby hinting at the poem's deep engagement with interrelatedness and consequences of actions along with a nuanced rhetorical style in which words are often filled with disguised implications. Through the acrostic, the Eykhah poet (or poets) has a prompt for starting that is predetermined (the letter *aleph*) and chooses an opening ("How desolate") to make explicit the subjective, emotion-driven orientation of the poem. This is not a historical chronicle of the siege and fall but a lament impelled by grief, horror, and aching.

The second challenge is how to maintain stylistic and emotional control over the work of poetry when one's emotional responses to the material might be overwhelming. The acrostic imposes a structure, and the need to adhere to that structure adjusts the balance between the expressive or descriptive content and the aesthetic form of the work. However intensely the writer might respond to the work's historical or biographical circumstance, the acrostic form imposes a demand for a particular type of verbal order that insists on its primacy or at least its significance in the composition. It impels forward motion (from *aleph* to *bet*, then to *gimmel* and so on) while it imposes restraint.

Eykhah and the Ninth of Av together are more than the recollection of the First Temple's loss. All commemoration begins with something specific that becomes the focal point for memories, much as the Japanese attack on Pearl Harbor and the raising of the flag on Iwo Jima focused American experiences of World War II. We cannot imagine memorializing "the war on terrorism" without centering it on "9/11" or the imagery of the World Trade Center towers burning. The single name "Auschwitz" has developed as metonymy for the devastation of European Jews and their communities by the Nazis and their allies, stretching far beyond the precincts of southern Poland's Oświęcim. Tisha b'Av commemorates what Jews have lost in the course of history. The date has become the focal point of many other disasters that have befallen the Jewish world on or near the same day of the same month; the Book of Lamentations has likewise become a lament for the many anguishing tribulations in Jewish history. Not least of those are the destruction by the Romans of the Second Temple in 70 CE and the devastating expulsion of Jews from Spain in 1492.

Each of these events occasioned, in addition to the great loss of lives and disruptions of entire societies, the dispersal of Jewish populations, many people to captivity, others to wherever seemed reachable and possibly safe. Some who managed to live survived as best they could, albeit sometimes at the expense of relinquishing their Judaism. At each juncture we see brutality and suffering; we see a heritage lost to its inheritors and a tradition deprived of those who could transmit and enrich it. All the more reason why we cannot turn away, and all the more reason why the Eykhah poet or poets would struggle to maintain artistic equanimity.

To begin understanding Eykhah, we need to grasp the Temple's importance. Solomon, according to 1 Kings 8:29, in dedicating the Temple that he had built, prays to God that it will be a place claiming God's attention "night and day" as the locus where "My [God's] name shall be," a sort of listening post where prayers of the devoted servant of God might resonate in heaven. Although it is not God's dwelling place, it is the place where those who pray have particular hope of their prayer reaching God. Built to sacredly imparted dimensions precisely revealed in the Torah and constructed in a divinely appointed location, the Temple seemed designed to reverberate with messages from this place on earth to "heaven your dwelling place" (1 Kings 8:39). The offerings of penitence and gratitude along with the required tithes that attested to the sustaining bond Israel and her people maintained with God were acceptable nowhere else; even prayers were doubtful with no fixed abode for them. Loss of the Temple meant loss of the earthly channel for communicating with the divine realm. The critical earthly terminal for receiving human contributions and petitions was destroyed, and there was no evident hope of restoration. Though God was still in "heaven your dwelling place," now the down-link was gone.

The core experience represented through the destructions of the First and Second holy Temples, "with loss of Eden" as Milton wrote about a primal fall, is loss of connection with the divine, which is the root of it all. If Eden means the wholeness of sanctity within the natural world, the Temple stands for the structured access linking humanity with divinity. Animal sacrifices were historically real, yet we can imagine them metaphorically as the process by which we accept and go beyond our physical needs, becoming closer to the sacred. That is what the sacrificial offering, the *korban*, was for: its purpose was *karev*, "bringing close." In various ways we now acknowledge separation. Whether we say that God is absent or dead or hidden, or that we have become secularized, whether like the mystics we yearn to bridge the gap or like Wordsworth feel that we have become mortal while "trailing clouds of glory" from a divine origin from which we have been thrust (understanding birth as the fall itself), the experience of being remote or even estranged from holiness is common.

This purpose may help us understand why, notwithstanding the continuation of Jewish worship following the destruction of both the First and Second Temple, the line connecting those historical events and other catastrophes has run through the centuries of Jewish history like an earthquake fault line. The spiritual function of the Temple seems of less concern to the Eykhah poet than the human misery resulting from its destruction. Still, that misery is theologically significant because of the presumed special relationship between God and Israel articulated repeatedly in the Torah and reaffirmed through the words of the prophets even—or perhaps especially—when they chastised the people and their leaders for abusing or disregarding that relationship. These are some of the reasons why the Western Wall of the Temple Mount in Jerusalem, sometimes dubbed "The Wailing Wall" and most often referred to in

Hebrew simply as *"ha-Kotel"* (i.e., "the Wall"), has long been a pilgrimage place, as we see from diaries of voyagers and pilgrims along with drawings and nineteenth-century photos, a place of prayer that many Jews pined for in vain when Jerusalem's Old City was barred to travelers from Israel by Jordanian authorities from 1948 to 1967.

While Jerusalem's devastation along with that of the Temple was catastrophic, of even greater long-term consequence was the corollary end of Jewish political autonomy. Admittedly, that end was temporary, but there was no way for the brutalized or grieving victims, both those in Judah and those deported as Babylonian captives, to know that at the time. Worse was to come. The voice of Eykhah is the voice of the disconsolate.

Much later, Jewish rebellions against Roman rule led to the calamitous destruction of the Second Temple in 70 CE at Tisha b'Av; a short-lived attempt led by Bar Kokhba and supported by Rabbi Akiva to establish a Jewish commonwealth by defeating the Romans militarily ended after about two and a half bloody years with the terrible massacre of the Jews at Betar on Tisha b'Av in 135 CE. These brutal defeats effectively ended Jewish national governance for centuries until the State of Israel became independent in 1948. Behind the founding of the new nation, even apart from the Holocaust of 1939–45, lay a history of traumatic events for which the date of the Ninth of Av is the calendric focus and Eykhah the eloquent voice of witnessing.

Along with the tangible losses we have been considering, this history carries with it another loss harder to quantify but of far-reaching significance. It is the loss of the communal sense of security and place in the socio-political environment. In the resulting Jewish view of the world, foreign states along with their rulers are expected to be hostile; periods of harmonious coexistence may be seen as fragile and easily broken. The watchword phrase "Is it good for the Jews?" is at once the punch-line of a joke and the sounding of an early-warning system. With ample reasons Jews have perceived their place in the world as precarious, threatened, insecure, and impermanent. This inheritance of historical trauma has had lasting political, psychological, and sociological effects through centuries of Jewish life. For at least some Jews, and certainly for the received rabbinic narrative, Eykhah is Judaism's *in memoriam*.

The expulsions of Jews from England and Spain meant the loss of community. Amid all of the other fears and horrors, tearing of the fabric of lives and relationships must be included in those caused by these expulsions and the countless others recorded through Jewish chronicles (not to mention those of other groups expelled from their places of residence or indeed their ancestral homes). Letters and other accounts of the victims record the poignant, bitter rupture of friendships and family groups. Being forced to leave behind not only homes and businesses and synagogues, familiar landscapes and neighborhoods, they also lost their communities and communal organizations, for a synagogue is not just a building with a Torah scroll. Recalling place after place after being expelled, they recorded the excruciating pain of being uprooted from what they called "the Jerusalem of . . . ," that center of Jewish civilization having become the paradigm of all others, expulsion from it being the paradigm of all others, its destruction the paradigm of all others.

Of course, this sort of disruption carries with it something yet more fundamentally universal, the loss of one's sense of safety. We know from victims of natural disasters how profoundly disturbing it is to the psyche to feel that not even one's own residence is protection, and in knowing that neither can one defend one's family's home or one's family itself. How much more frightening it is to live with the knowledge that one can be expelled arbitrarily from one's dwelling-place, indeed, banished from what one had always taken to be one's own country. No wonder that the refugees took refuge in what was most easily transportable, such as recipes that could be imitated elsewhere and in songs to be sung and stories re-told in any time or place, in the constancy of the languages that they took with them into exile and preserved wherever they went in the world. For the Jews of Iberia, that meant Judeo-Spanish (also called Judezmo or Ladino) for conversation and music, and Hebrew for learning.

We do not have to cut Tisha b'Av from its traditional moorings in Jewish history to appreciate and extend its applicability to life. Not only do entire communities live in continuing diaspora or *galut* from their home or ancestral land, we as individuals also often feel that we are uprooted or even rootless in the modern world, with no clear sense of "home." We also feel insecure. Those who grew up during the Great Depression, World War II, the Cold War, the epoch of *film noir*, the Vietnam Era—indeed, most of the twentieth century and lamentably the first quarter of the twenty-first—recognize insecurity as endemic. Magda Sorel in Menotti's 1950 opera *The Consul* gives a particular human voice to the catastrophe: "To this we've come: that men withhold the world from men."[1] And, we might add today, they withhold more of it from women.

Tisha b'Av posits that this is not a normal or natural way of life, nor inevitable, by posing that we mourn for the absence of security and the lost confidence of knowing that we are "at home" and safe being there. Consider the reorienting, potentially restorative value of that recognition, that mourning, channeled through a public and, importantly, community observance. Imagine the power of a community lamenting the ruptures in the universal or common notion of community itself!

The Hebrew *galut* is too often translated as "diaspora." This ignores a crucial distinction. The Greek word *diaspora* simply means "dispersal." A diaspora may be made up of people who more or less voluntarily emigrated for any number of reasons, but are free to return to a native land that has retained a familiar identity with them, and this may be said of their descendants as well. The Hebrew word, however, specifically denotes exile. An exile has been cast out, along with subsequent generations of the exile's family, with no inherent right to go back. The separation is so radical that even if one could physically return, as Gertrude Stein (an émigré but not an exile) remarked about revisiting the place of her birth after many years of absence, "There is no there there." Legally, spiritually, and psychologically, the differences between being outside of one's homeland and being exiled from it are enormous.

The fall of Betar was a momentous and relatively recent loss in the memory of Jewish sages of antiquity who mention it nine times in the Babylonian Talmud. The last blow in smashing Bar Kokhba's revolt against Roman rule, this defeat meant the loss of the hope for political independence. Naturally, that cannot be separated from the previously mentioned losses of home and security. We yearn for self-determination, not only in the political realm—essential as that is—but also in other aspects of human life. Rome (in rabbinic terminology, "Edom") is not only a place and an empire in chronological time. Quintessentially bearing all the worldly power that is invested in The State, it also represents coercion. In addition, because the biblical Edom is etymologically related to the name Adam and therefore also to the words for "red," "earth," and "blood," the sages associate it with physicality, emotional impulsiveness, and violence. Rome/Edom means the rule of might, the rule of the sword.

---

1. Gian-Carlo Menotti, *The Consul* (New York: G. Schirmer, 1950), 41.

When considering how to commemorate liturgically the destruction of European Jewry in what has become known as the Holocaust or Shoah, some traditionalists have argued that it should be subsumed into the Tisha b'Av observance; this is the case in many Orthodox and some Conservative congregations, which incorporate newly composed *qinot* for the Shoah to be recited on the Ninth of Av. The argument that prevailed more generally worldwide was for the singularity of the Shoah, and especially in Israel the particular relevance of it to survivors or refugees who had moved to Palestine before Independence or Israel after it, as well as to their families. For all of them, and arguably also to ethical thinkers, the Shoah in dimension and purpose was more than another in a long history of brutalities suffered by Jews, consequently it demanded its own day, Yom ha-Shoah, observed generally in Israel and in the United States on 27 Nisan, between the end of Passover and the festival of Shavuot (Pentecost). Another commemoration, International Holocaust Memorial Day, is observed on January 27, especially in Europe, for it marks the Russian Army's liberation of whatever remained of Auschwitz.

Certainly one might accept that the Holocaust was unique in Jewish experience, different from those assaults and expulsions that Tisha b'Av marks, therefore deserving of its own memorial day. Still, anyone who experiences the remembrances that have thus far developed probably cannot avoid perceiving that only Tisha b'Av has religious observances of genuine gravity and liturgical depth. The other commemorative days such as Yom ha-Shoah are predominantly secular, marked by speeches and wreath-laying, generally with the additional ritual of lighting six or more candles to acknowledge the six million murdered Jews, the reading of some victims' names and the recitation of traditional memorial prayers. When a survivor is present and able to tell even a small part of their story, that is almost certainly the most memorable, affecting part of the commemoration. In Israel the day is known as *Yom hazikaron l'shoah v'l'gevurah*, Memorial Day of the Shoah and the Resistance, a name intended to move beyond the record of victimized Jews by honoring, along with those who were killed, those who fought, resisted in other ways, or managed to stay alive. The most movingly simple observance of Yom ha-Shoah is likely to occur in Israel between 10 a.m. and 10:02 a.m., when air raid sirens wailing throughout the country bring all activity to a halt as everyone, even drivers of vehicles on the road, stops and comes to attention in remembrance of the dead.

By contrast, Tisha b'Av as traditionally observed is fully immersive and interruptive. To begin with, it is a day of fasting. There used to be more of these in the Jewish liturgical calendar; but even when there were, the two that stood apart for the extent of their observance and for the length of the fast, stretching more than a full day from sunset to sunset rather than simply from sunrise to sunset, were Yom Kippur and Tisha b'Av. Conventionally the former has been called a "white fast," the latter a "black fast," because Yom Kippur's fast is for spiritual purification while that of Tisha b'Av is for grieving.

The Ninth of Av in the traditional Jewish realm is like a black hole shaping space-time around itself. For the three-week period preceding it, marking the time when the Romans (and at a similar date, the Babylonians earlier) breached the city walls of Jerusalem, the mood is funereal. Traditionally, no weddings or musical performances are permitted; indeed, even many non-Orthodox rabbis and cantors refrain from attending, much less officiating, weddings during this period. Orthodox practitioners avoid getting haircuts or buying new clothes; from the beginning of Av, they will abstain from meat and wine until after the Ninth. They bathe for hygiene, not for pleasure—this at a time of year when countless others are crowding pools and beaches in lighthearted playfulness. The final meal before the start of the observance is a mourner's repast, with hard-boiled eggs (sometimes dipped in ashes), lentils, perhaps raw vegetables, fruits, water, and a plain piece of bread preparing for a day-long complete fast. As mourners, they will also abstain from sex on this day. If the Ninth of Av happens to fall on the Sabbath, the actual observances take place the following day so as not to violate the essential joy of Shabbat. In Israel, restaurants and places of entertainment are closed for the day according to law.

The worshiper attending a traditionally observant synagogue on the evening and morning of Tisha b'Av enters a dimly lit house of mourning. Those present may be sitting on low stools, benches, or even the floor. They do not greet one another either arriving or departing, for such moments elicit words such as *shalom* ("peace, wellbeing"). There is no casual conversation. The ark, which is the ceremonial cabinet or enclosure containing the scrolls of the Torah, will be shockingly open and even more shockingly empty, barren of its ornamental curtain and beautifully ornamented Torah scrolls that we are accustomed to see glistening with their silver ornaments; instead, it is empty, shrouded in the black cloth of bereavement or left vacant, as if thoroughly despoiled. The customary religious service will be chanted in doleful melodies. Both in the evening and the morning, Eykhah is recited in traditional melodic patterns unique to it, ranging from melancholic grieving to anguished declamation. Dirges or laments for other disasters that have occurred in Jewish communities are often added to the service. In some congregations, the lights are extinguished as the congregation departs silently. In the morning, unlike every other weekday morning, worshipers do not wear the *tallit* (prayer-shawl) and *t'fillin* (phylacteries), thereby expressing their spirits depressed in the shadow of the absent, annihilated Temple through the ritual items that are missing. Since Jewish sages regard the study of the Torah as a pleasure, on this day sad passages only are deemed appropriate for reading.

When worshipers return for the afternoon (*mincha*) service, the mood lightens toward hopefulness. To begin with, we are still here. We may be here as mourners but here and together nonetheless. Despite all that has transpired, Jewish worship continues, transformed from the forms it took two thousand years ago. The Jewish community remembers and laments its sorrows even as it adheres to commemorating the past. It also coheres, albeit beleaguered by differences, disagreements, and contentiousness.

But beyond the tenacity implied by this mere survival, an early midrash from the Jerusalem Talmud (Berakhot 2:4) suggests that this sorrowful day holds the kernel of joyous rebirth. It claims that Tisha b'Av is the birthday of the Messiah. What this might mean is not explained there. A legend? A quaint bit of folklore? We should rather think of this as a profound truth attested to by experience as well as psychology. In our deepest pain—the dark, seemingly hopeless moment, when we "bottom out"—restorative hope comes. We know how bad the worst is. When things can't get any worse, the hopeful sense of a possible better future slips into our awareness. The time of liberation from oppression will begin when we have reached the lowest depth from which any return is possible. When we have really fallen to the bottommost point of our spiritual or emotional journey, then the recovery commences. It begins even when we may feel that we do not have the will to initiate it. Call that, perhaps, divine intervention: at the last possible moment, God rescues us as a people. The principle underlying this idea has both psychological and historical validity. When we think that the situation cannot get worse—when for example the Temple is in ruins, or Europe's Jewish communities are uprooted and annihilated in the Holocaust—a movement coalesces that will make of the remnants something greater.

As if responding to this altered frame of mind, for the only time in the year worshipers may put on both *tallit* and *t'fillin* at *mincha*. The musical *nusach* or melodic framework of the service returns to normal. Subsequently, people will break their fast and, in many communities, go outside in the evening to recite the monthly blessing for the moon. Rabbi Arthur Waskow suggests that the timing of the blessing this month might be related the idea (found for instance in the Zohar) that when the Messiah comes, the feminine moon will be equal to the masculine sun.[2]

All of this is high liturgical drama. It has evolved over a long time, mostly by accretion, under pressure from vicissitudes of Jewish diasporic experience as well as developments in Jewish thought that added poetic religious texts along with nuances of imagery and meanings. For many centuries this compellingly dramatic immersion in ritual expression was more or less the way in which Jews around the world experienced Tisha b'Av, and the full recitation of Eykhah was an essential element of that commemoration, even when local practices otherwise shaped ritual practices and the choices of *qinot*. Today, Orthodox Jews customarily experience Tisha b'Av in traditional ways, as do significant numbers of practitioners from other streams of Judaism.

Granted, in our era many Jews do not undertake anything like the rituals and observances just described. Those who do not may ignore or be completely oblivious to Tisha b'Av, regarding it either as a burdensome relic of antiquated piety or a holdover from what the great Jewish historian Salo Baron termed "the lachrymose conception of Jewish history." Many may feel it to be unnecessary, perhaps even inappropriate, after the creation of a modern Jewish state. Or, now that a state of Israel exists with Jerusalem as its capital and the status of the Temple Mount (to Muslims, Haram al-Sharif) the subject of persistent internecine as well as intercultural conflicts, they may turn away consciously from ceremonies that seem to valorize the Temple. To some, indeed, mourning the destroyed Temple implies that one longs to restore its historically central status, like those eccentric cultic devotees one might meet in Jerusalem who are preparing themselves to celebrate a miraculously formed "Third Temple" on the same site, served by priests and Levites with rites precisely replicating the ones described in the Torah.

---

2. Arthur Waskow, *Seasons of Our Joy* (Philadelphia: JPS, 2012), 212.

Though Eykhah and Tisha b'Av are rooted in Jewish historical experiences, neither is bounded solely by that history. For they give voice to, or sometimes honor through silences, the griefs of other peoples as well as individual suffering. Without denying the specificity of the text that has come down to us or the particularity of historical experience from which it arises, we see that *Eykhah* gives a powerfully expressive voice to the shattering experiences of suffering, regardless of the origin of that suffering. That voice can be articulated not only through words but also melodically, keeping in mind that in ancient times poems—whether epic narratives, love lyrics, or dirges—were commonly sung, even accompanied by stringed instruments or flutes (*khalilim*). In fact, in Jeremiah 48:36 God promises that "my heart sounds for Moab like flutes, for the men of Kir-kheres like flutes" because of their destined destruction; in Isaiah 16:11 God's lament for them reverberates "like a harp [*kinor*]." Much later, the Babylonian Talmud instructs that even the poorest widower is obliged to pay for at least two flutes and one lamenting woman for his wife's burial (Ketubot 46b). The "lamenting woman" was presumably a professional mourner, skilled in techniques like *moirologia* still practiced in the Mani region of Greece.

As the introduction points out, among the books of Hebrew scripture only the Psalms and Song of Songs have been the subject of as many musical settings as Lamentations. The vast number of compositions set on this text, or rather the Latin translation of the text, are by Christian composers for church use, such as those by Lassus, Tallis, Byrd, Victoria, Palestrina, Brumel, Charpentier, Couperin, and Zelenka—very much a partial list, though a starry one spanning several centuries and nationalities—along with more recent settings for the concert hall by Stravinsky, Ginastera, Krenek, and Bernstein, only the last of whom was Jewish. Jewish worship practice hews to systems of text cantillation rather than drawing upon composed works of art; such is the practice in the Orthodox churches and was as well in the chanting traditions of the Catholic Church.

Within Western Christian church traditions, Lamentations and Psalms together form substantial amounts of the texts chanted during Tenebrae services, which take place during the three days preceding Easter Sunday, amid rituals that may include draping the altar in black cloth and extinguishing candles until the sanctuary is in near-darkness, practices echoing synagogue observances of Tisha b'Av.

The reasons for the plentiful musical settings of these texts are clear. Not only are they poetical, they originate in music: the Psalms stem from liturgical practices of the Temple; Song of Songs emerges from the corpus of love poems and erotica; and Lamentations derives from the funeral traditions of dirges and threnodies, some of them mourning destroyed cities. The lyrical language, prosodic structures, and rhetorical moods of each work encourage melodic interpretation.

Among the innumerable musical settings, those by the outstanding Elizabethan composers William Byrd and Thomas Tallis stand out for particular reasons. Catholics during a time when Protestantism in the form of the Church of England supplanted and suppressed Catholic worship and persecuted practicing Catholics, both men survived and flourished through their artistic abilities and the queen's leniency. Their Holy Week choral settings of Lamentations, based on the Latin Vulgate text, implicitly mourn not only for the crucifixion of Jesus but presumably for the ongoing tribulations of their church and fellow communicants. Along with the dissolution of monasteries, convents, and churches went the destruction of statues, stained-glass windows, and numerous choir books containing the only copies of English Catholic liturgical settings dating from the late Middle Ages and the early years of grand sixteenth-century choral polyphony. To the recusants (that is, Catholics who refused to accede to the Church of England), Lamentations was an apt expression of grief over the ruination of England's Catholic religious life and cultural legacy.

Of additional interest for the Hebrew reader, Byrd and Tallis make musical use of the initial Hebrew letters that the Vulgate carries over from the poem's acrostic structure. Each letter they select is treated to a sustained polyphonic elaboration of the vowel sound, transforming the mere pronunciation of the letter's name into an emotionally tinged, elongated moment of tonal meditation. Probably no Jewish composer would think to do that because for them letters such as *khet, tet,* and *yud* would be just that: merely letters with no intrinsic meaning other than their ordinal place as the eighth, ninth, and tenth letters of the Hebrew alphabet. To these Christian liturgical composers, the letters are opportunities for sonic expansion and sustained tension preparing for the ensuing Latin translations of the Eykhah passages.

Fittingly, many translators have not taken the opening word "Eykhah" at its literal meaning of "how" but have instead heard in it an implicit exclamation of woe, "Alas." The first syllable aptly rhymes with the English word "ache." For this first lament for Jerusalem begins with the city already desolate, ruined, and barren. Despite the intensity of emotions and even the personal drama of its exclamations, the poem's form stabilizes it through artistic coherence because the initial letters of its twenty-two stanzas, each stanza an unrhymed tercet, follow the order of the Hebrew *alef-bet*. The cumulative effect feels relentless as well as inexorable: once we recognize the pattern, we know that the tale of woe will not cease until it carries us from the initial *aleph* to the last stanza, which begins with the last letter, *tav*. The end of this chapter will not feel as if anything has concluded. Rather, it reaches its finale and stops because there are no letters left; the speaker seems to have uttered everything that can be said and finally is exhausted: "my sighs are plentiful and my heart falters."

The concluding Hebrew verb sometimes refers to a woman suffering menstrual pain, an appropriate association in a poem that characterizes the city as a desolate widow, among other feminine depictions that distinguish this chapter of the book. In Hebrew, as in many other languages, "city" is a feminine noun. Personifying cities and states in gendered terms has been a common part of linguistic convention ("fatherland" or "motherland") and the personification often casts the territory in female terms. Admired for "her" beauty, she is also property to be conquered, even ravished and "possessed."

The first chapter of Eykhah is notable, however, for the vividness with which it insists on the image of Jerusalem not just as a woman but as a bereft widow cruelly abandoned by all who could aid her. With poignant irony the poem refers to them as her "lovers" (*ohaveha*) and "friends" (*re'eyha*), who have all deserted her in favor of her enemy. Erstwhile allies scorn her while attackers despoil her. The evocations of physical (and perhaps sexual) degradation amass, compiling insistent images of thorough humiliation, both physical ("filth besmirches her skirts," 1:9) and spiritual ("barbarians have pillaged the hallowed Sanctuary," 1:10).

As gruesome as the evocations of the catastrophe are, the significance of them is heightened by the repeated theme of Jerusalem's own culpability for her misery and that of her children. The beleaguered widow is not merely an innocent victim of others' rapacity but a guilt-ridden transgressor punished for her faults. "God has afflicted her because of her many transgressions" (1:5). The city's abundant corruption leads to her humiliation and degradation: "Jerusalem heaped sins upon sins, thus she has become impure; to all who gave her reverence, she has become contemptible, for they have seen her nakedness" (1:8).

This poetic personification of the city has a remarkable consequence for the poem's balances of drama and compassion. After all, if we consider the actual circumstance, it is clear that "Jerusalem" does not exist as a moral agent; it is simply the aggregate of its inhabitants. Accordingly, if we ascribe sinful behavior to this city, the moral failings can only have been committed by those who live in it. The municipality of Jerusalem cannot itself sin. Yet in the semi-allegorized language of this biblical depiction, Jerusalem is the sinner while her residents, both high and low of status, female as much as male, children and aged alike, have become the pitiable victims of "her" misdeeds. Not theirs, hers.

Through this rhetorical stratagem, the poet negotiates a way through difficult terrain on the human ethical level and on the level of theodicy. On the human plane, if the brutal fate of the city's inhabitants is a consequence of their own moral failings, we could easily withhold our compassion for them, feeling that they brought misery on themselves, their children, and their home by what they did and failed to do. Yet compassion is exactly what the speaker feels is needed, most especially for those victims who were truly not culpable and for the once-splendid city now in ruins, but even for the guilty, given the intensity of their suffering and the wretchedness of their condition. By displacing the faults of the inhabitants onto Jerusalem the city, here personified as guilty and immoral, the poet can unrestrainedly evoke pity for those who dwelt and suffered there as victims of her misdeeds.

In contrast to the searing indictments of particular sins that the various prophets name as they denounce the faults of Israel and Zion, Eykhah leaves those sins unspecified. Recalling those incisive words of the prophets, we look in vain at these poems if we seek to know whether neglect of the poor, widows, orphans, and strangers or some other specific violation of divine commandments such as following after foreign gods should be blamed for the city's fall. The lack of specificity, rather than seeming vague, implies instead that, on one hand, the failings were many and, on the other hand, no one type of offense would be adequate to deserve this devastation.

At the same time, when the city is described as a brutalized widow reduced to desperate straits, we perforce remember the dozen times when the Torah specifically commands compassion toward the widow as an obligation. Even more evocatively: Jeremiah 7:1–7, which specifically recalls the commandment to be mindful not to oppress the widow, begins with a warning to amend one's ways rather than to call upon the holiness of the Temple of the Lord; only by behaving righteously will God allow the people to dwell forever in the land God promised to the ancestors.

The Eykhah author also needs to accommodate the devastation to the demands of divine justice. Granted, the Jerusalemites were imperfect. They violated God's commandments. Yet what place is perfect? Did all sin? And what offenses can justify inflicting this degree of suffering? We sense the relevance of Abraham's protestations when God intends to destroy Sodom (Genesis 18), "Will you destroy the righteous along with the wicked? . . . Shall the judge of all the earth not act justly?" To gainsay such an argument, Jerusalem testifies against herself, claiming responsibility for what has happened on account of her own iniquity.

However, she is not totally consumed by guilty self-abasement, for she still cries out to God, evoking sympathy in two brief interjections that suddenly disrupt what has been a third-person perspective: "See, Lord, my humiliation" (1:9) and "See, Lord, behold, for my enemy exults" (1:11). These are perhaps especially moving because they ask nothing directly, emerging simply as pleas for compassion, perhaps implicitly pleas to cease or alleviate the torment of oppression. Asking for God to "see" essentially means asking for God's consideration, which in itself implies the favor of divine attention; and if God cares enough to take notice of one in distress, then God might perhaps intervene on behalf of the once-favored city and her people, that community once chosen by God, whose nobles and children have been taken as captives while the impoverished and desperate inhabitants who remain must scrounge hungrily, bartering all they have for whatever food can be found.

The two interjections herald—without quite preparing us for—a stunning shift in narrative perspective in verse 12, beginning with the letter *lamed* in Hebrew. This occurs midway through the poem and thus midway through the alphabet. Suddenly, what had seemed a monody chanted by one speaker turns into a two-voice composition, though not a duet because the voices do not combine. One might also describe the work as a dramatic diptych: the first half evokes the scene of destruction from the vantage point of a sympathetic and horrified observer, and the second expresses the city's dirge in which she laments her own downfall, accepts responsibility for her transgressions yet also calls for divine vengeance against those who have scourged her. The poem is perfectly balanced between these two points of view, the external and the internal, the apparently objective (albeit emotionally engaged) and the explicitly subjective. Its artful structure attests to the highly developed, experienced literary sensibility behind the composition.

Beginning the poem's second half, Jerusalem offers herself as a cautionary example: "Behold, you who pass this way, and see if you know suffering such as I have suffered when I was afflicted in the day of the Lord's wrath" (1:12). We might imagine this as the anti-Ozymandias. Instead of the boast of timeless glory that is rendered vain by the literal sands of passing time, the monumental speaker of Lamentations 1 is aware of her own ruination transpiring even in the shadow of her own glory.

In keeping with the personification of the city, its physical destruction is expressed in terms of bodily suffering: "From above he sent fire coursing through my bones, set a net to entangle my feet" (1:13). Burdened by "the yoke" of her misdeeds, the city has fallen prey to enemy forces that she cannot withstand; she is bereft of comfort, her sons and daughters crushed, priests and elders dying as they searched futilely for food. Recalling the revered names of "Zion" and "Jacob [Ya'akov]" as well, the speaker bewails Jerusalem's loss of favor in a stanza (17) that seems to be an interjection voiced in the third person, breaking into Jerusalem's first-person lament by reasserting a historical context for how momentous this event is. Now, neighbors have become enemies who turn from her pleading arms; defenseless, she is spurned like a woman who is ritually impure (in *niddah*). Outside the city is the sword; at home, there too is death.

While some grammatical ambiguity clouds understanding of the second part of verse 21, the import of the poem's concluding movement emerges clearly. It is a plea to God to visit upon Jerusalem's foes the same sort of punishment as she has endured. For while she admits her own culpability for disobeying God's laws, the savagery of her attackers along with the scornful rejection by her erstwhile allies should call forth divine retribution against them. With insightful integrity, the poet ends this threnody, the first chapter of Lamentations, not with a thunderous demand for justice but with a quietly confessional note of emotional exhaustion: "countless are my sighs and I am heartsick."

"*Eykhah* . . . ." Thus begins the second chapter, just like the first. Here, however, the force of the word seems more persuasively to mean "Alas," as most translations agree. The repetition of the book's opening word has a jarring effect, especially following the conclusion to the first lament. It suggests that this is a second beginning, an alternative way of presenting the story, and so it proves to be. Even the literary form implies that the first two chapters are parallel to one another, for this one as well consists of an alphabetic acrostic of twenty-two tercets.

The first chapter suggests that God's role in Jerusalem's destruction is to remove the shield of divine protection from the disobedient city-state. In doing so, God permits the unnamed foe (i.e., the Babylonians) to besiege, starve, and at last overwhelm the place and its inhabitants with the full might of its scourging fury. That idea also appears in this chapter; however, here God is also actively Jerusalem's scourge, and this poem's tone is darker, driven less by grief than by horror of the violence and degradation and by the idea that divine wrath has been turned against God's holy city and chosen people.

In Exodus, amid the Song at the Sea celebrating the parting of the waters during the escape from Egypt, the Israelites jubilantly proclaimed, "The Lord is a man of war" (Exodus 15:3). Now, centuries later, this "man of war" has mercilessly turned divine might against "the daughter of Zion . . . on the day of his wrath" (2:1). Not the human foe but *God* has "pitilessly reduced to ruins the dwelling-places of Jacob and shattered the strongholds of Judah" (2:2). With the Sanctuary laid waste, God has ended festivals and sabbaths in Zion, abandoning both king and priests. The motif of complete loss repeats at the end of the chapter, hyperbolically asserting that "none escaped or survived on the day of the Lord's wrath" (2:22). Devastated by the might of the masculine deity, the defenseless city that was imagined as a widow in the previous poem is compared to other societally vulnerable women, this time the young: "daughter of Zion," "daughter of Jerusalem," and "maidens of Jerusalem." Even the alternating occurrences of two forms of the holy name ("*adonai*," which is written out, and YHVH, which is conventionally also pronounced as "adonai") seem to convey that Jerusalem has suffered from the full might of divine anger.

This chapter's numerous echoes of other biblical passages, evocations of Jewish religious rituals, and reminders of normal patterns of life become sometimes poignantly, sometimes savagely ironic; as they mount, they depict not only a world turned upside down but also a moral order stood on its head. Prophets failed because they gave forth reassurances that encouraged complacency in Judah instead of reform; God responded to the persistent failings by fulfilling the threat that the Temple would fall on account of Israel's sins. So it has happened. Famished mothers cannibalize their starved infants; prophets and elders sit impotent in silent mourning, their heads strewn with ashes; alien passers-by sneer and shout with satisfaction; and in the precincts of the Temple, jubilant conquerors make a joyful noise but not unto the Lord God of Israel. "You called forth, as for a festival day, the neighbors surrounding me on the day of the Lord's wrath; ... those whom I nurtured, my enemies have slain" (2:22). The king and princes are captives among foreigners; there is no Torah; prophets wait for a revelation from God. Twenty-two verses depict a brutalized, leaderless, and directionless people amid a conquered city whose gates and ramparts have been smashed and whose center is no more.

The speaker does not heap blame upon Zion or Judah for what has occurred, yet does acknowledge that Zion was guilty of *avon* (*ayin-vav-nun*, 2:14), a type of sin generally translated as "iniquity" and understood in later rabbinic interpretations as meaning offenses committed knowingly and willingly because of following one's own desires rather than God's commandments. Nonetheless, the brunt of the speaker's accusation falls upon those prophets whose vain predictions lulled the sinners into complacency rather than spurring them to improvement (obviously unlike Jeremiah). Though the speaker does not say so directly, these false prophets and counselors have failed the commandment (Leviticus 19:17) to rebuke an erring neighbor rather than incurring guilt by ignoring that person's sins.

In some moments a complementary note is sounded, a plea for God's compassion, though the speaker of this poem, unlike that of its predecessor, does not ask directly for revenge or justice. Instead, this voice of lamentation implores Zion to lament even more intensely: "pour out your heart like water" (2:19). Along with this urging goes an entreaty for God to witness the savage consequences of divine actions, not just the reduction of a once-admired and divinely favored city to ruination but the brutal conditions in which its people live and die, cut down on the day of God's wrath. Much as the first lament comes to an end with the speaker's apparent emotional and spiritual exhaustion, the second concludes with the speaker (here, perhaps Jerusalem herself) staring at an empty future: "those I bore and raised my enemy annihilated." Left implicit is the logic of this final appeal: God, since you did this damage, do something now to repair the destruction of your people and your earthly footstool.

If we expect that the first two poems have established a rhetorical pattern, the beginning of the third jolts us. "I am the man who has seen affliction." This opening, which begins in Hebrew as well with the first-person pronoun, also seems to introduce a more overtly self-aware poetic lyricism, suggested through the internal rhyme and word-play of the first four words translated above, *anee ha-gever ra'a ahnee*. Without commentary or a grasp of the original Hebrew, the nuance is difficult to capture. Because the word for "I," *aleph-nun-yud*, and the word for "affliction," *ayin-nun-yud*, are pronounced more or less identically, the verse suggests a confluence of the two, as if the speaker has not merely seen affliction but that he has become one with it. As the poem develops, we perceive that this narrator is not a personification, though he may be an exemplar. That is, he does not represent "Zion" or "Jerusalem" or any other conceptualization. If he represents anything other than a particular solitary and anonymous individual, he may be said to typify a grieving, broken-spirited eye-witness who has endured all that has happened, albeit barely. In modern parlance, he is a survivor.

Thus the sustained first-person narrative viewpoint also distinguishes this poem. As the middle of five chapters, it forms the apex or keystone of the entire work. Fittingly for a central statement, it is not only an acrostic but a triple acrostic in which the each line of every tercet begins with the same letter of the *alef-bet*. Furthermore, in usual synagogal practice, when Eykhah is recited on Tisha b'Av this *qinah* is differentiated from the other chapters by being chanted in a melancholic melody (*nusach*) completely unique to it. While the melody used for the four other poems is sadly beautiful, it also has a strongly expressive thrust, a combination of moods (though not tunes) that we might hear in some Bach alto arias. The third, by contrast, dominated by somber descending cadences and extending over sixty-six verses, establishes and sustains a depressed temperament of obsessive remembering. The repetition of the same initial letter in each line of each stanza seems to reinforce the implication that the narrator is stuck, although struggling to move forward. This is someone haunted by their experience and nearly frozen by it.

The inner desolation is so vast that we are likely startled when, at the very end of verse 18, suddenly, for the first time in this poem, we encounter the name of God, as the speaker laments, "I said, my strength and hope have perished from YHVH." That is not to say that God has not been the cause of the lament before this point. Rather, the world of woe has been brought about by the third-person "him," who is so omnipresent in the context of the story that the real identity can be assumed, sensed behind a screen of metaphors, albeit not yet directly named. He is a lurking bear, a lion crouched in hiding, an archer who has shot his arrows into the speaker, piercing his innards; he is a poisoner whose weapon is the notoriously bitter wormwood, an assailant who has "broken my teeth in the gravel, crushed me in the dust" (3:6). This unnamed foe clearly is God because the speaker also grieves that "when I cry and plead, he blocks out my prayer" (3:8). By withholding the divine name, the speakers hints that God, the lurking power behind these events, is the Unnamable as well as the inaccessible.

The point at which the speaker is able to name YHVH becomes a point of turning. "This is in my heart, so I have hope: the kindness of YHVH has not ended, nor compassion spent. They are renewed each morning—Great is Your grace!"(3:8). The last phrase, which in Hebrew is *rabbah emunatekha* and often translated as "great is your faithfulness," has been incorporated into traditional Jewish daily worship as the concluding words of a blessing of thanks recited each morning upon awakening, even before one gets out of bed. While the blessing does not explicitly quote the preceding phrase in Lamentations, which is "They are renewed each morning [*khadashim lab'karim*]," it clearly stands behind and provides the rationale for the timing as well as the wording of this benediction.

"My portion is YHVH, declares my soul; therefore I will hope in that" (3:8). This affirmation of faith introduces a passage of theodical optimism that seems to shift the mood. It is certainly a dramatic change in the speaker's outlook, proffering assurances of God's merciful ways in language recalling Exodus 34:6–7, the so-called Thirteen Attributes of God, which are quoted in synagogue liturgies and Jewish theology still today because they attest to God's abiding patience, mercy, and forgiveness.

How temporary that tonal alteration is will not be apparent until we read further in the poem. The effect is like the middle section of a Baroque or Classical musical composition with an A-B-A structure, in which the B section contrasts in tone, tempo, and frequently the key as well, before the A motif returns, with some variations and a contrasting impact because of the preceding difference in perspective. David R. Slavitt in his free translation attempts to reconcile the incongruence by treating this hopeful passage as the almost desperate expression of a tenuously maintained faith, the recollection of what one has been taught to say and believe, maybe even the urgent need to believe. In his version, the speaker opts to "somehow cling to" hope and "remember how to say" that "The Lord is my portion."[3] Slavitt's reading of the passage is boldly unconventional, yet it is a perfectly defensible way of finding tonal

---

3. David R. Slavitt, *The Book of Lamentations: A Meditation and Translation* (Baltimore: The Johns Hopkins University Press, 2001), 75.

coherence between this section of some eighteen verses and the laments that encapsulate it. We might even venture to say that his interpretation is consonant with the traditional cantillation, which does not differentiate in *nusach* between these verses professing faith in divine justice and those bewailing the battering experienced by the poem's speaker, as if the mordant tone prevailing in the rest of the third chapter should apply equally well to its ostensible assertion of confidence in divine compassion.

Believing, or trying to believe, in God's abiding goodness and justice means that we are responsible for transgressing and consequently also responsible for our punishment. Each of us should therefore look to our own behavior and turn back to God, "*v'nashuvah ad-YHVH*" (3:40). The word for "turn," *shuvah*, is often conventionally translated as "repent," though the precise sense of the Hebrew is that one has strayed from the right way and needs to correct one's behavior on the path of life. The speaker, while continuing in this vein, switches to first-person plural, voicing the people's confessions of their guilt, "We have transgressed [*nakhnu pashanu*] and rebelled [*u-marinu*]" (3:42), words that resonate across the centuries because Jews encounter them annually in the liturgies for Yom Kippur, the Day of Atonement.

The consequence, however, in Eykhah is the shattering antithesis of what we expect to hear affirmed on Yom Kippur in recompense for our confessions of wrongdoing, for the experience of the lamenting poet and public is, "*atah lo s'lakhta*," "You have not forgiven" (3:42). Rather, cloaked with anger, God has pursued and slain without pity; hidden as if behind a cloud, God is inaccessible to prayers and "we are trash and refuse among the nations" (3:45). The cloud metaphor may recall not only the many references in the Torah to the occurrence of the cloud as attesting to God's presence, safely hidden there by the cloud that will protect mortal beings from the power of the Almighty, but also ironically Isaiah 44:22, in which God promises to blot out Israel's sins and transgressions "as if in a cloud." Thus the outlook reverts to that of the first section. It is as if for a moment the clouds parted and we glimpsed the possibility of divine compassionate forgiveness, only to see the thunderheads form again and the tempest break over us.

"Watery streams pour from my eyes for the shattered daughter of my people" (3:48). The last phrase is a succinct idiom in Hebrew, *bat-ami*, that we are rendering literally, as did the sixteenth-century Geneva Bible and the 1611 King James translation also, rather than simply "people" or "poor people" as in the JPS translation. Awkward as that literal construction is in English, the feminine epithet fits tellingly in the gendered dynamic of the entire book. The lamenting speaker insists that the tears will continue until God in heaven looks down and beholds the woe for "*banot iri*," the daughters of my city. Defeated, downcast, desperate, the poet still appeals to God, "You have drawn near to me when I have called upon You and You said, 'Fear not.'" Since God must see the villainy and hear the contemptuous taunting by the enemy, the speaker at last, in the concluding words of this poem, pleads with the Almighty to deal with them according to their behavior: "give them heartache and curses. Pursue them in wrath and wipe them out from under the heavens of God" (3:66). The final sentence was incorporated centuries later into the Passover Haggadah to conclude the passage known as "*shefokh hamatkha* [Pour forth your wrath]," a malediction against those who persecute the Jews, recited (when it is included in the seder) before the Hallel psalms of praise and the invitation to the prophet Elijah to enter with the promise of impending messianic redemption.

Thus ends this central chapter of Eykhah. Taken in its entirety, this monody might remind a modern reader of an aria or extended dramatic *scena* for a solo singer whose moods are varied, though dominated by brutal experience and wounded by God's agonizing refusal to thwart the persecutors or relieve the suffering. There is misery both individual and collective. There is also recognition of one's own faults and therefore responsibility. Yet along with that is baffled anguish arising from God's withholding of forgiveness combined with righteous urgency for God to punish those whose affliction of Zion has been merciless. Mingled with the notes of lament, the outcry of anger resonates.

Eykhah—again this keynote announces the beginning of the next poem, the fourth chapter of the book, and again its meaning seems to vacillate ambiguously between the exclamations "alas" and "how." How tarnished is the gold, the finest gold now dimmed in luster, and the revered gems tossed out at the head of every street! The opening verse suggests a ruined palace or sanctuary; the second verse, however, reveals that the discarded gems and debased gold are the once-treasured offspring of Zion, now like ruined potter's vessels, cast into misery, even their children vainly begging for crumbs of bread that never come. The metaphors in these lines establish the intensely visual quality of this poem. To a modern reader the effect may bring to mind the work of a photojournalist moving through a siege city, capturing horrific images of wretched human suffering, which (rather than devastated buildings) is the poet's true subject.

The form of this lament emphasizes the grimness. It is another alphabetical acrostic, though in couplets rather than tercets. The effect seems more laconic, austere, drained, as if any expansiveness were out of reach in a forsaken city where people have become brutal in manner and appearance because they are starving. Even the elite of the community survive in desperate condition. Their skin has become dark, shriveled and dry through malnutrition; they are unrecognizable; and those who were slain by the sword were the fortunate ones because they died suddenly, not of a famine that has led even mothers to cannibalize their dead children. This, the speaker grieves, is what has become of "*bat-ami*," the daughter of my people (4:10).

Why has this befallen a city so favored of God that "the kings of the earth and all the world's inhabitants thought that no foe could enter Jerusalem's gates" (4:12)? The fault, the speaker propounds, lay in the sins of her prophets and transgressions of her priests, who are guilty of spilling the blood of the righteous (4:13). This justification is *prima facie* somewhat cryptic, for it is not clear whether the poet means that these religious leaders behaved corruptly, thereby causing the city to be spurned by God and thus become vulnerable, or whether it means that they behaved unjustly, abusing or neglecting (i.e., shedding the blood of) the virtuous.

The consequences nevertheless are clear because not only do we see devastation all around; these once-honored figures have now themselves become pariahs, soiled by blood, wandering the streets blindly, chased away by everyone, to whom they have become like lepers, "away, unclean, don't touch!" Both from the inside and from the conquerors coming from outside, the Israelite people have been rejected, hunted down, starved, enslaved or killed, even their king, Zedekiah, seemingly alluded to in 4:20 as *moshiakh YHVH*, God's anointed, or as one might also translate that phrase, the messiah of the Lord, who was unable to save the kingdom from humiliation or the people from savagery.

With biting irony the mourner for Zion bids Israel's enemy, the "daughters of Edom who dwell in the land of Uz," to rejoice, assuring them that their time of reckoning will come. Edom was, dating back to its association with Esau, the proverbial antagonist of the *b'nei Israel*, the people descended from Jacob. In this period, it was politically associated with Babylonia; in later times the name of Edom became a periphrasis for the Roman Empire and subsequently for Christianity. Uz, a region across the Jordan bearing the name of a descendant of Esau, was often associated with Edom. As both neighbor to Judea and kin to Jacob, Edom is judged in the Tanakh with particular severity for its hostility to the Israelites. The awful suffering inflicted on the daughter of Zion will expiate her offenses, but the time of Edom's punishment will come. Thus the fourth chapter ends by insisting on a moral view of divine justice, accepting the premise that Judea and her leaders were at fault while also condemning those who mercilessly assailed Jerusalem and dealt viciously with her people.

As noted earlier, modern scholars are uncertain whether all these poems were composed by the same poet, whether they were selected from a larger body of *qinot* representing the work of various writers, or how the five elegies were edited into a single collection. What seems certain, however, is that whoever edited the volume did so with considerable literary insight for juxtaposing texts and conceiving the overarching structure of the work.

The final poem is the shortest, only twenty-two lines, and each of its lines is shorter than those in the previous poems. The number of lines is seemingly an acknowledgment of Hebrew's twenty-two letters though it is not an alphabetical acrostic. Nor does it begin with the word *Eykhah*. Rather, its first word is the imperative *Zakhor*, "Remember," which is addressed to God and thus fittingly implying that this lament is a coda set apart from the artistic web constructed in the preceding descriptive poems, connected to one another through their formal characteristics.

The fifth elegy differs also in being a prayer, one whose penultimate verse is incorporated into Jewish liturgy as the concluding phrase at the end of the service for the reading of the Torah. After the scroll has been returned to its place, the ritual ends with the recitation of the line, "*Hashivenu adonai elekha v'nashuva khadesh yameinu k'kedem*," "Turn us, Lord, to You and we shall return; renew our days as of old." The same verse is an oft-repeated keynote of the prayers during the penitential service or services known as *s'lichot* preparing for Rosh Hashanah and Yom Kippur, an important theme of which is *t'shuvah*, frequently translated as "repentance" but more precisely meaning "return." In its original sense the plea means, help us return to our relationship with you, Lord, and therefore to return as if renewed to our former state of eminence in your grace and in the eyes of the world. When Eykhah is recited publicly, this line is repeated so that the reading finishes on a hopeful note, rather than the devastating suggestion in the actual final verse that perhaps God has totally and finally turned in anger from us.

The final *qinah* depicts a captive society in which the normal standards of behavior and autonomy have been obliterated. The country is occupied by foreigners, who are themselves merely pawns of the Babylonians; people's homes and farms have been confiscated; those who remain are like orphans or widows, unprotected by the Torah laws mandating attention to the needs of those who are vulnerable. The survivors are forced to buy water, as well as the wood that belonged to them. They beg for provisions from Egypt on one side and Assyria on the other. Seeking food is dangerous, but famine drives the hungry to desperate measures as their skin burns from malnutrition. Elders are spurned, once-prominent men hanged, women and girls raped, young men burdened by the manual labor better suited to animals; joy is gone, even (according to the medieval commentator ibn Ezra) the joy of worship. Recalling with irony King David's Psalm 30:12, "You have turned my mourning into dancing," the speaker here laments, "our dancing has turned to mourning" (5:15), and David's subsequent affirmation that he will praise God forevermore cannot rise to the throat of the grieving survivor of this terrible defeat.

Amid the ruins of Mount Zion, foxes (or in some translations, jackals) prowl. The scene is recalled centuries later in a midrash on this verse (b. Makkot 24b and Midrash Eykhah Rabbah 5:18). After the destruction of Jerusalem by the Romans, a group of sages weep to see a fox scamper from the place of the Temple's Holy of Holies. Rabbi Akiva, who is with them, laughs instead, giving them hope by explaining that the prophecies of Uriah about the desolation of the First Temple and Zechariah about the city's prosperity during the days of the Second promise that this later destruction will one day prove also to be temporary.

Of course even this story is less simple than it appears. For Akiva, a mystic and patriot as well as a great scholar, died as a martyr, having imprudently heralded the military leader named bar Kosiva, whom he renamed bar Kokhba ("son of the star"), as the Messiah and supported his ill-fated war against the Roman occupation that ended with the catastrophic loss at Betar in 135 CE, resulting in an enormous dispersal of Jews into Roman captivity and the end of Jewish hopes of a rebuilt Temple and of sovereignty in Judea. If one looks for the renewal Akiva envisioned, either it was more than eighteen centuries away or it has not yet come.

But restoration seems not even a dim hope at the end of Eykhah. While the poet does affirm that God is enthroned forever, from generation to generation, what is not at all certain is whether God will remember Judea with favor. *Lama: why* have you so thoroughly forgotten us and turned from us for so long? Turn us, renew us, unless you have spurned us completely in your great anger.

On Tisha b'Av we lament not being in control of our lives. That loss of control results partly from external forces, the political oppression explicitly connected with the day in history. We are subject to the power of others, whether governments or any others who have coercive influence over us. It also results in part from internal forces: we are not fully in control of ourselves but are driven by our passions, addictions, phobias, and desires. Suppose we imagine Tisha b'Av to be the occasion to lament our loss of self-control: in addition to the loss of our independence, crushed by external oppression, we defeat ourselves by yielding, even against our own will, to bad instincts. Shakespeare's Richard II facing the loss of his throne and inevitably the loss of his own life exclaims, "For God's sake let's sit upon the ground / And tell sad stories of the deaths of kings!" (III.2.155–56). On this day for God's sake we sit upon the ground and tell sad stories of the deaths of king and commoners, priests and paupers, people like us, and a homeland we called our own.

The passions of Eykhah channeled through Tisha b'Av allow lament, protest, grief, the frank recognition of horrors, brutality, and brutalization to have biblical voices. The chronically suffering, those who have been victimized along with those who cry justice for other people who have been victimized, may rarely feel empowered to express their feelings religiously. Too often they have been told that such attitudes are impious; anyone who utters them may be accused of weak faith, of not trusting sufficiently in divine providence and justice.

Tisha b'Av authenticates our plunge into grieving lament. We do so not just sympathetically and memorially, recalling what *they* suffered; but we lament empathetically, realizing that what they lost, we also lost, and therefore what they suffered is a type of our own suffering. Yes, we must see how sadly brutal the chronicle of history can be and remember the innocent victims of imperial conquests. Set aside this day to forget what can usually please and nourish the body. Forget about your physical image—never mind how you look to other people, or how you want to look to yourself. No matter how good we look at our best, we are vulnerable, every one of us. Accept how you feel when you are at your most despondent, when you suffer and mourn for all that you have lost or even all that you fear losing. Don't look in a mirror—but not because doing so is a symptom of vanity. No, avoid looking in the mirror for fear of what you might see there. For God's sake . . . for those like us, and for ourselves, creatures in the semblance of God, knowing that this day is also the birthday of the messiah, whose coming may be hastened by either the cry of human exultation or the cry of human pain, *geschrei*, Cry Out!

God is present. But does God care about us? This text, Eykhah, is always an essential one to know because it speaks with such painful honesty about our fears, guilt, anger, resentment, pain, and doubt, the fierce yearning for a reason to hope, the grief over the shattered shards of all that we have made and counted on in our lives when we see all of that ruined. Whether by war or illness, chance or error, human violence or the forces of nature, or the slow grinding down of age, we can suffer from life's vicissitudes. All of us and all whom we love are vulnerable and mortal.

This text gives us language and scriptural authority for whatever pain or anger wells up inside us and needs to be expressed (literally, "pressed out") from us. Yes, we have been imperfect; we have done wrong; but truly, we have suffered beyond measure. We bear our guilt but still we cry out for vengeance, justice, or mercy. We have nothing to believe in but God, and yet, where can God be seen or felt or trusted in the wasteland of life as it has become? And what of the future? We ask God to remember. Will God? And will God remember what we want God to remember? Eykhah leaves us in the void.

6

Coda

In the fall of 2001, when I was serving a chaplaincy internship at what was then called Wake Forest University Baptist Medical Center, the chaplain supervisors invited me to lead a worship service in the hospital's Davis Memorial Chapel, an appealingly intimate small brick and stone Tudor Gothic style building, with stained-glass windows illustrating the 23rd Psalm, that would not look out of place in an English countryside except that the chapel nestles against the towers of an expansive, ever-growing major hospital. As this was to be a Jewish-centered (albeit interfaith) event, we agreed on making it a Sukkot service. That was hardly an obvious choice for a type of event that had not been done there before; but inasmuch as I had congregational obligations for the days of Rosh Hashanah and Yom Kippur, the weeklong observance of Sukkot that starts four days after Yom Kippur offered flexible timing, along with the appealing show-and-tell possibilities for the holiday's main portable and essential symbolic elements, the bundle of palm, willow, myrtle, and citron known as the lulav and etrog.

The chapel's interior, constructed of limestone and slate, with oak for the furnishings and the gracefully vaulting roof arches from which silver light fixtures hang, could not be less like a sukkah. The flat-roofed sukkah's essence is its obvious fragility—indeed, its permeability, as exemplified by the simple and sketchy roof coverings called *skakh* that must be made of cut plant material and cannot be solid. Crucial requirements of the sukkah covering are that it will allow the sky to be visible and that it imperfectly shields whoever is under it from the elements. It would take a considerable effort of the imagination to conjure the appropriate sense of a sukkah's vulnerability in this stone edifice, especially since the chapel's front doors open onto one of the hospital's busy corridors.

But October of 2001 did not bring a Sukkot like any other. The chapel service took place approximately three weeks after the shocking 9/11 terrorist attacks. I had been in the locked-down hospital that September morning, trying like everyone else to continue functioning, ministering to the needs of patients, families, and staff, while struggling to grasp what was happening and pondering anxiously what it might mean for the future. Our supervisors checked with us to ask if we needed to leave and be with family or congregants instead. Three weeks later, perceptions of vulnerability had been transformed.

In the chapel, the stone walls around us normally feel unassailable, the roof secure and strong. The hospital's brick-faced steel towers seem as assuredly permanent as any structures one could imagine. Yet not many days before, while hundreds of miles from the actual centers of annihilation, we had watched on screens as airplanes and much grander edifices evaporated in flames, smoke, and dust, taking thousands of people to their deaths. Along with them went our perceptions of what was normal, what we could rely on, what our place in the world was. If those buildings, then so too any other building, suddenly revealed as more fragile and temporal than we would have envisioned. They were—all those mighty-seeming structures—made of dust, returning to dust. And after all, where, actually, were we?

We were in a labyrinth of interconnected buildings filled with offices, laboratories, waiting rooms, treatment rooms, and operating theaters purposefully built to deal with life's fragility and impermanence. Every day throughout the sprawling campus, human beings were contending with and striving against frailty, fears, and failings. The anxious patients did so, yes, as did their family and friends, all struggling with pains, deficits, uncertainties, worries, and tears—but so did the physicians and the nurses, the technicians and the administrators. They had to vie each day not only with the pains, limitations, and angst of those who came for diagnosis and treatment but at least as much with their own imperfections and limitations, their apprehensions about making mistakes of omission or commission, of not knowing or understanding enough, not noticing or remembering enough, while battling their personal fatigue and the stresses of their private lives, perhaps along with their own ailments, be those physical, emotional, or spiritual. So did the chaplains, like me, who would find despite our training and experience and best intentions that sometimes the right words did not come at the right time. Or worse, the wrong ones came instead.

In the hospital not only our physical health is at stake. We also confront, along with our corporeal vulnerability, spiritual and intellectual vertigo as change transforms us, undercutting our verities in swirls of unpredictability, doubt, and fear. The certainties on which we base our lives, the worldview, the truths, the hopes, the belief systems and theologies, the structure of our inner being—they were and are all at risk of sudden, shocking disruption or even devastation in a moment. We plan, imagine, hope, all in the expectation that we and everyone around us will be present in five years, five months, tomorrow, and that our lives will be much the same as we envision them at this minute. Suddenly we discover that we dwell indeed in a temporary shelter vulnerable to every element, with rain and cold seeping through the cracks in our roof, and darkness descending. In an instant, all is jeopardized; in a second, all is transformed and perhaps lost. One moment we stand, we walk; in the next, we may tumble to the ground. Now, we speak; in the next instant, words may fail to come. One moment, the convictions of our lives cover us with at least some flimsy shelter amid the changeable elements out there; another moment, that roof discloses how temporary it is by collapsing on us. We are in the sukkah, always.

That teaching became my sermon, of course, replete with words of Qohelet. Yet it was not a teaching of despair because, as Qohelet might assert, it also needed to be said that every helper (including, indeed, sometimes the patients and families, who could also be helpers) was like that *skakh*. We are not perfect shields, not impenetrable. But together, and making allowances for gaps and imperfections, we can offer some protection, more than a just a meager bit of shelter when the weather of life turns harsh. We might not be rescuers, but we may still do something worthwhile as people who tried to rescue. On good days and nights, we can also let in the sunlight and moonlight, a breath of air, a bird twitter, the glitter of stars. As Qohelet affirms, "This too I have seen."

What we often call a "life cycle" is more like a spiral, for every time the event returns, those who experience it are different. Life turns, we are altered with it, and now we see something differently, hear something we missed before. As with Qohelet and Sukkot, so with every megillah and every festival. The interpretations set forth about every text are provisional in their own ways. Here, at this moment, these meanings come through to this one reader.

For a text is thin indeed if its possibilities are exhausted through one reading or even one era. More significantly, the multiple possibilities do not exist singly or merely sequentially; they coexist simultaneously, though the light by which we perceive them shifts. At a given time, the Book of Ruth might seem primarily a story about familial dynasties or about life's second chances. From another perspective it portrays a small town's social networks and the ethical values of an agrarian community. Then we lift our gaze to the news of people fleeing famines or violence to realize that the ancient biblical story is also an account of emigration and immigration, of their causes and effects, along with the uncertainties and vulnerabilities of the migrants, especially the women. A different encounter with another life story reminds us how Naomi and Ruth's experiences illuminate widowhood along with its resulting threats of insecurity and poverty. We turn to Song of Songs and hear it speak sometimes to youthful eroticism, sometimes to the complex natural rhythms of a rich ecological system, sometimes to the sophisticated, playful edginess of urban culture, and sometimes to fervid social destabilizing and risky passion. These artistic constructions live in at least three dimensions: we walk around them, enter into them, peer through them. The light changes; shadows shift; perspectives open, then close; and that all takes place while they and we move through time.

Megillot: words inscribed onto scrolls. The nature of a scroll is that it is rolled and unrolled, turned to reveal its columns of text slowly. Each turn is like the earth's circuits, our days, months, and years that pass. That which we just read disappears as it is rolled up, and that which we are about to read has not yet emerged. Each of these scrolls summons our attention. Come and read, the text says to us. As the Talmud urges, *ta sh'ma*: come and hear, come and learn.

We began with questions that point to the ways in which these Megillot address enduring and profound human experiences in a religious context. Each in its own way invites us to explore or confront experiences or perceptions that sacred texts often disregard, such as the urgency of amorous passion, the turmoil of a devastated life, doubts about the value of whatever we do in this world, the precarity of living on the margins of society or with an identity one fears to disclose. By making each of these books the prescribed special reading for a major annual observance,

Jewish tradition places them in the mainstream of its traditional sacred writings, thereby at least opening the possibility for contemplating and discussing the issues these books present, not just one time but annually, necessarily revisiting them each year, thereby inviting rethinking and reconsideration of what each of them has to tell us. They are not simply items in the large treasury of sacred scripture's canon, included but easily ignored among the numerous other writings that one might engage with once or not at all: they are requisite reading each year for the religiously practicing Jewish person.

In the changing lights of our lives, great works of literature such as these are able to surprise, enlighten, and challenge us repeatedly, no matter how many times we have read them or how well we think we know them. That is one of the best reasons for encountering them on their own, outside the stream of holidays with their attendant religious services with which each of the megillot is associated. During the liturgical occasion in the synagogue when the books are read, we might catch a familiar phrase here or mentally spotlight a recollected incident in the story, thinking (like Honoré in Lerner and Loewe's *Gigi*), "Ah yes, I remember it well." Perhaps, unlike him, we really do, but we are likely to remember it the way we always have, so we lose the chance to encounter it anew, with a different illumination.

It is probably only when reflecting on the canon as a whole that we can recognize, perhaps with a jolt, a remarkable feature that holds these five biblical books together regardless of genre or time of composition. In every one of them, God is absent, hidden, or remote.

In that regard, they are not what we might expect for synagogal readings on major days of communal gatherings. While we can say that some of the books have "happy endings," these are not texts that reassuringly affirm, celebrate, or console us or even the characters within the texts that the hand of the divinity is providential. Neither in regard to individual lives nor regarding the welfare of a divinely favored nation do we perceive in these books the God that conveyed vast and timeless promises to Abraham on Mount Moriah or the God that brought the Israelites out of Egypt "with a mighty hand and an outstretched arm" (Exodus 13:16) or imparted to Moses a cultural treasury of teachings on Mount Sinai. While we recognize that Ruth and Boaz, along with Naomi, like Mordecai and Esther, manage to come out happy, shaping an optimistic future for themselves and their people, it appears that they really sort those futures out through their own daring. If we want to, we may say that God looked out for them; but from their standpoint, it seems more certainly their risky or enterprising gambits that brought about a successful conclusion to their narratives.

Presumably, that is one of the points of these texts. We might imagine their protagonists responding understandingly to Hamlet's affirmation, "There's a divinity that shapes our ends, / Rough-hew them how we will" (V.2.3659–60). Perhaps that will serve as a faith statement for our characters, though they seem focused less on asserting faith than on their tasks of hewing, that is, finely chiseling themselves a decisive point to conclude their tales successfully. In other words, if God is at work here, it is God operating unseen through human agency.

As we have seen, Qohelet and Eykhah—both texts that speak often of or to God—are anything but settled in faith or theology. The former swerves and dips through incisive, conflicting empirical observations, as if the would-be believer were caught in gusts of autumnal winds blowing first one way, then the other. While the book manages in the end to affirm divine providence, it does so as a leap of faith in defiance of its ample contrary evidence. In the latter work, the voices in the poetic threnodies for Jerusalem, though seemingly sure that God is somewhere in the universe, tremble in fear that the almighty God may have turned aside from the very people who had long ago been divinely adopted, appointed, saved, and led to a land promised to them but subsequently lost, perhaps at least partly through their own moral failings but also perhaps despite their innocence, amid vast destruction and overwhelming suffering. The speakers of Lamentations know to call on God, or call out to God, during their keening for the Temple, the city and its people, priests and chieftains, youth and elderly, women and maidens. They lament in guilt, misery, and outrage. Yet their voices resound in the silence or void whose meaning the mourners struggle in vain to comprehend. Even while imploring for renewal and restoration of what has been lost, they are also bemoaning the battered faith that formerly gave them confidence and hope.

More than merely being additional readings added to the already extensive liturgies of the Jewish festivals, like icing on an abundantly rich cake, the Megillot add a different theological context to the observances. Liturgically, the weekly Torah readings from Genesis through Deuteronomy as well as the specially selected Torah passages traditionally designated for every holy day present God's teachings, what is known as the Written Torah, through the exact Hebrew words transmitted by the Jewish people across the centuries "*al pi YHVH b'yad moshe*," that is, from God's mouth by Moses' hand (Numbers 4:37 and 45). The accompanying haftarah or concluding additional biblical readings that would supplement the Torah recitation on holidays impart God's teachings as mediated through the lens of warnings, challenges, and sometimes promises through passages drawn from the second section of the Tanakh, the Prophets. Taken together, the Torah and haftarah sections constitute core teachings of Jewish beliefs as they have been conveyed since the earliest times. For countless generations of synagogue attendees, the annual cycle of these readings and the sermons based on them have delineated tenets and values for a religion that eschews explicit creeds or doctrines.

In the Torah and Prophets, we are continually aware of the presence of God, the incontrovertible eternal verity that is often involved, ever watchful, constantly attentive, sometimes interventionist, always judgmental yet capable of being persuaded toward the merciful aspect of justice rather than the punitive aspect. It is the Guardian of Israel, who "neither slumbers nor sleeps" (Psalm 121:4), forgiving sins to the thousandth generation yet remembering transgressions across the third and fourth generations (Exodus 34:6–7). This is the God ascertaining that there are consequences, good and bad, for all that is done. This is the God enthroned and sanctified in biblical religious traditions, both Jewish and Christian, the transcendent deity, giver of laws, omniscient and omnipotent. In scores of Hebrew blessings and prayers, this perception of God is proclaimed *melekh ha-olam*, conventionally translated as "king of the universe."

On the five significant holy days when they are read, the Megillot suggest a third, and we might say more subtle, level of teaching about the nature and presence of God. These books hint at the possibility that God's active role in shaping our lives might not readily meet the eye but can be discerned as working latently or covertly, perhaps through actions of people as ordinary-seeming as a Moabite widow and a Judean farmer, or perhaps through the impressions and insights of any candid, observant person moving through a life that has no certain shape or promised outcome to it, save for the common outcome that ends every life.

Hungry for an even more intimate knowledge of God, Moses implores, "Let me behold your glory" (Exodus 33:18). But after replying, "no mortal can see me and live" (Exodus 33:20), God offers another way of perceiving the divine presence. "I will shelter you in a cleft of the rock and shield you with my hand until I have gone by. Then I will remove my hand and you will see my back but not my face" (Exodus 33:22–23). Perhaps this Torah passage gestures toward the theological outlook we may perceive in the Megillot. What these books show us is not the bold face of God but the after-effects of God having been present.

In the years following the Shoah/Holocaust and the use of nuclear weapons at Hiroshima and Nagasaki, many religious people sensed God had abdicated the royal throne. Not only had God not intervened to prevent or halt the massacres of the "chosen people," the ruler of the universe seemed to have left human beings to their own deadly devices. The diverse Christian and Jewish theologians exploring this idea sometimes drew upon, and sometimes were popularly associated with, Nietzsche's formulation that "God is dead," a statement more often misunderstood or distorted than read rightly in the original context of Nietzsche's thought. The nuances of these thinkers as well have often been lost in critiques or popular accounts of their ideas.

For some, the old and traditional understanding of how God affected the life of the world was no longer tenable: i.e., the familiar biblical notions of an all-powerful, all-knowing, all-wise God that intervened at will in the affairs of people and nations did not hold up to modern historical reality. For others, God had indeed once been actively engaged and conversant, in some sense, with certain human beings but since then (different thinkers would locate "then" according to their own theories) God had withdrawn from this world or at least from human history. Still others wrote of God's inscrutable, unknowable hiddenness: God might be there but not perceivable to us. Instead of honoring in awe the transcendent deity revealed in majesty through the Torah and Prophets, now we peer into the dark clouds of ash or the literally blinding flash of a massive explosion trying to perceive what is called in Latin *deus absconditus* and in Hebrew *ha-mustar*, that is, the Hidden. Once upon a time in the biblical narrative, the patriarch Jacob awoke from a nocturnal experience exclaiming, "Indeed, God is here in this place, though I myself did not know" (Genesis 28:16). For him, the hidden God became known albeit still concealed. For others, God remained hidden, though they may have been convinced somehow that God was nonetheless still there, obscured by the darkness in which we dwell.

Other religious thinkers, perhaps without rejecting any of the other theological concepts, sense that the divine is also, or instead, within us. For human beings, they would say, God's place is not preeminently transcendent but immanent. Regardless of whatever any person might mean by "God" and however God functions in organizing and governing the world's works, God dwells within us as motivator and guide but not necessarily named as God even by the person experiencing the stimuli of the divine force. For instance, faced with responding to momentous crises—through the scheme by which Esther succeeded Vashti, or Esther's daring stratagem to save Persia's Jews—Esther and Mordecai do not ask for God's help or guidance, much less pray for it. Even the fast that Esther and her community undertake appears intended for its own sake (*lishma*, one would say in Hebrew) as a kind of personal discipline or purification ritual rather than an expiatory offering to the divine. The success of their enterprises seems to be due to their own resources, not to any miraculous intervention, much less an answer to prayers. They themselves choose successful strategies.

Reading the texts in this way places us at a considerable remove from the sages who originally designated these to be special holiday readings. Of that we can be reasonably sure because, as we have seen, the burden of the early commentaries is to argue for the most pious, traditionally religious, and, one might say, theodically correct interpretations of the characters and stories. Nevertheless, the books say what they say and do not say what they do not say.

In the Megillot we are far removed from the theological world of (for instance) the Book of Jonah, which is sometimes discussed along with the Megillot because it is similar to them in length and literary characteristics, and also like them in being a designated additional holiday reading, in this case for the afternoon of Yom Kippur. Despite those similarities, it is after all placed among the Prophets rather than Ketuvim, and a closer examination reveals the crucial difference. Here, the clear theological commitment begins in the first verse of the text when God's word (*d'var YHVH*) "came to Jonah" and ends abruptly with the very words of God castigating Jonah for disregarding the sins and sufferings of Nineveh's humans and beasts. In this prophetic book, every moment and every action make explicit the workings of a deity not to be avoided, evaded, fled from, or ignored, a divinity still communicating explicitly to some selected individual and unmistakably shaping not just the story's end but the main steps along the way, be they providential natural effects such as a storm at sea and a ravenous albeit slow-digesting great fish, or a hostile foreign foe suddenly moved, from their king to the most common inhabitants, to penitence and reformation, expressed outwardly in the form of donning sackcloth and ashes. Yet by the same measure at the conclusion of each of the Megillot we are also far removed from the final scene of the Book of Jonah, which leaves the disgruntled, rebellious, sulking prophet who does not want to be a prophet somewhere on the outskirts of that great and reformed but still alien city of Nineveh, the place he did not want to save to begin with, the place he sought to avoid by taking a ship bound for the opposite direction, alone and seemingly stranded at the end of the story beneath the withered plant that no longer shelters him, far away from his Jerusalem home, hearing the chastising words of God that remind him of his ethical failure.

To know these five books from this perspective is to understand not only their coherence as a group but also to understand their inclusion in the holiday liturgies as theologically important. More than merely adding additional textual elaboration to already expansive liturgies, they place the narratives of these significant days in unexpected religious contexts. God is neither their subject nor their theme. The hand of God might be felt, as it is in Eykhah, but even there it is not a comforting hand. The workings of God might be inferred, but any miracles are wrought through human invention or inspiration. Instead, we see different varieties, different faces and facets, of lovers and mourners, seekers and strivers, trying as well as they must to shape their lives amid the losses and promises of an uncertain world, while somewhere in the dark and perhaps distant background we may hear a whisper or catch a passing glimpse of that which is great, greater than all, eternal (so far as our temporal lives can grasp that concept), that which some call, for want of better terms, God, YHVH, Ekhad, One.

7

For Further Reading

It seems impossible not to quote Qohelet: "Of making books, there is no end." Exploring these five texts may send a reader into a deep dive through innumerable volumes and countless pages, so a bit of guidance seems worthwhile. Many will have a preferred or at least accustomed biblical translation reflecting a particular religious outlook, for instance the New Revised Standard Version common to some Protestant denominations, the Artscroll editions favored by many Orthodox Jewish readers, or the Jewish Publication Society (JPS) editions preferred by more progressively disposed Jews. The works mentioned below are recommended as being particularly helpful for readers of this volume seeking additional literary, historical, linguistic, or thematic perspectives.

We are most likely to encounter the Megillot as part of the whole canon of the Tanakh or Hebrew Bible, or as separate volumes studied individually, rather than as a combined collection of the five scrolls. In light of the many linguistic and historical difficulties they entail, even a reader reasonably comfortable in Hebrew will likely benefit from a translated or bilingual text with notes and introductions.

Complete editions of the Tanakh that can be recommended for their scholarly and literary editorial contributions in their introductions and notes are the English-only *Oxford Annotated Jewish Study Bible*, eds. Berlin and Brettler (Oxford: Oxford University Press, 2014), the *JPS Tanakh Gender-Sensitive Edition*, ed. Stein (Philadelphia: Jewish Publication Society, 2023), and the bilingual *JPS Hebrew English Tanakh*, 2nd ed. (Philadelphia: Jewish Publication Society, 1999). An invaluable source for original language and translated texts of the Tanakh along with a wide range of rabbinic texts and commentaries is the website of Sefaria (www.sefaria.org), with search functions available for concepts and themes as well as the usual search categories such as names.

The Five Megilloth and Jonah, ed. H. L. Ginsberg (Philadelphia: Jewish Publication Society, 1969) is a conveniently slim, classic, often reprinted bilingual edition of the five texts, plus Jonah, with brief introductions to each.

The *Steinsaltz Five Megillot*, ed. Adin Steinsaltz (Jerusalem: Koren, 2019) is traditionally Orthodox in its outlook and frames of reference but includes a new English translation along with a verse by verse interpretation supplemented by maps and illustrations connecting the texts to the history and material culture of ancient Israel and the Near East.

A reader seeking a traditional Jewish outlook may also find appealing the analyses offered by Gabriel H. Cohn, *Textual Tapestries: Explorations of the Five Megillot* (Jerusalem: Maggid, 2017), giving special attention to Hebrew linguistic details and Jewish liturgical uses.

The classic traditional Jewish interpretations of the scrolls' history and meanings may be found in the Talmud and other rabbinic writings, especially the diverse midrash collections, most notably Midrash Rabbah, with volumes devoted to the individual books, and Aramaic versions (Targums), along with classic rabbinic commentaries from late antiquity and the early medieval period onward, as well as kabbalistic texts like the Zohar. Readers of midrash need to be aware that these texts are primarily homiletic, intended to expound religious, moral, or ethical interpretations as well as to reconcile the text with traditional Jewish practices and teachings. That is, they do not primarily intend to explicate texts literarily or provide philological and historical information in the ways that modern readers will expect.

Surveys of the Jewish festivals are likely to include some attention to the relevant megillot. Arthur Waskow's *Seasons of Our Joy* (Philadelphia: Jewish Publication Society, 2012; originally 1982) offers especially thoughtful insights about the spiritual and ethical connections between each of our books and the associated holiday.

Countless composers have set at least parts of these biblical books to music. The contemporary American Jewish composer David Lang deserves particular mention for his vocal and instrumental work called "*the writings*" that evokes each of the Megillot through short phrases, beginning and ending with texts from Ecclesiastes. Composed over many years, they are brought together as a whole in the 2022 recording David Lang, *the writings* (Capella Amsterdam, Pentatone PTC 5187 001).

ECCLESIASTES

Kohelet: A Modern Commentary on Ecclesiastes, a translation and commentary by Leonard S. Kravitz and Kerry M. Olitzky (New York: UAHC, 2003) offers the verse by verse Hebrew text accompanied by their English translation and line by line interpretations focusing on the value of the work's teachings for a modern reader.

Rami Shapiro, *The Way of Solomon: Finding Joy and Contentment in the Wisdom of Ecclesiastes* (San Francisco: HarperOne, 2000), translates and interprets the text from a Zen perspective, seeing it as teaching equanimity in the face of life's seeming contradictions or perplexities.

Qohelet: Searching for a Life Worth Living (Waco, TX: Baylor University Press, 2023) is a joint project between a Jewish artist, Debra Band, and a Jewish philosopher, Menachem Fisch. It presents illuminated paintings of the full text of Qohelet in Hebrew and English, along with a commentary on the art and a philosophical commentary in the text.

BOOK OF ESTHER

Timothy K. Beal, *Esther*, in *Berit Olam: Studies in Hebrew Narrative and Poetry*, ed. Cotter (Collegeville, MN: Liturgical, 1999) richly examines details of the text with attention to cultural and religious identity as well as gender politics.

Jon D. Levenson, *Esther: A Commentary* (Louisville, KY: Westminster John Knox, 1997) studies the narrative by sections, each introduced with an English translation of the text. The study gives particular attention to the story's formalistic patterns of language and structure.

Esther in America: The Scroll's Interpretation in and Impact on the United States, ed. Stuart Halpern (Jerusalem: Maggid, 2020) is an engrossing, varied, often surprising anthology of writings from early colonial times to the present exploring how the Megillah and its characters have figured in constructions of American politics and society, with special relevance to themes of race, identity, gender, and power.

A list of related art works may be found at http://www.textweek.com/art/esther.htm.

SONG OF SONGS

For a serious student, the *JPS Bible Commentary: Song of Songs*, ed. Michael Fishbane (Philadelphia: Jewish Publication Society, 2015) is the *sine qua non*, a magisterial three-hundred-page translation accompanying the Hebrew text, with extensive annotations and commentaries covering centuries of readings, mainly but not exclusively in Jewish sources, distilled by the editor's decades of work and organized to distinguish different levels of interpretive readings. Fishbane's compendious annotators include many that are not available in English translation.

Ellen Bernstein, *Toward a Holy Ecology: Reading the Song of Songs in the Age of Climate Crisis* (Rhinebeck, NY: Monkfish, 2024) is an imaginatively and boldly wrought translation (with the Hebrew text on facing pages) and interpretation, incorporating introductory material, commentary throughout, and endnotes, presenting the text through the lens of an environmental activist who sees the poem as a celebration of the natural world's richness and coherence.

Passages from the book will be familiar to many readers through the language of the King James Bible and musical texts using that wording. Among modern translations, two others deserve mention in addition to those above.

In their *Song of Songs* (New York: Modern Library, 2006; originally published in 1995), Ariel and Chana Bloch combine the capabilities of a scholar and poet respectively in a translation and bilingual edition of the poem supplemented by copious notes, many of them philological, engaging with the challenges and nuances of translating this frequently enigmatic poem with its often-obscure vocabulary.

The poet Marcia Falk, in her bilingual *Song of Songs: A New Translation and Commentary* (New York: HarperCollins, 1990), boldly redistributes the lines to highlight and reshape the book's dialogic and dramatic elements.

In addition to Arthur Waskow's other writings about the festivals and their texts, his web commentary on the connection between Song of Songs and the Passover seder deserves special mention: https://jewishjournal.com/commentary/blogs/128230/the-seders-innermost-secret-charoset-earth-eros-in-the-passover-celebration/ (April 8, 2014).

It should be noted that the collaboration between Pam Tanowitz and David Lang mentioned in this chapter uses a setting and text for "Song of Songs" different from the one in Lang's earlier work cited above.

BOOK OF RUTH

Todd Linafelt, *Ruth*, also in *Berit Olam: Studies in Hebrew Narrative and Poetry*, ed. Cotter (Collegeville, MN: Liturgical, 1999), interestingly explores the ambiguities and structural richness in the text, from a biblical scholar's standpoint.

Reading Ruth: Contemporary Women Reclaim a Sacred Story, ed. Cates and Reimer (New York: Ballantine, 1994) is a generous selection of essays by various commentators, many of them creative writers themselves, on seven themes from the book, accompanied by poetic responses to the text from a half dozen other authors.

Stuart Halpern's *Gleanings: Reflections on Ruth* (Jerusalem: Maggid, 2019) offers an array of essays approaching the story from wide-ranging viewpoints and contemporary topics, including immigration, conversion, communal identity, and gender.

Ilana Pardes has written insightfully on several biblical books. Her *Ruth: A Migrant's Tale* (New Haven, CT: Yale University Press, 2022) offers especially interesting perspectives regarding kabbalistic and early Zionist applications of the Ruth narrative.

For selections from, and information about, Mario Castelnuovo-Tedesco's musical work, augmented by a detailed commentary by Neil W. Levin on the biblical story as well as its various other opera and oratorio representations, one should consult https://www.milkenarchive.org/music/volumes/view/odes-and-epics/work/naomi-and-ruth/.

LAMENTATIONS

David R. Slavitt's *The Book of Lamentations: A Meditation and Translation* (Baltimore: The Johns Hopkins University Press, 2001) is a poetic *tour de force* as well as a profoundly personal reflection on the historical resonances of the poem and the destruction and consequent exile that it mourns, seen in the long shadows of Jewish history stretching through the Shoah. With Hebrew on the facing pages, Slavitt's translation remarkably replicates so far as possible the poem's complex uses of acrostics and other literary structural devices, resulting in a poem that can stand on its own in English.

Joshua A. Berman's contribution to the New Cambridge Bible Commentary series, *The Book of Lamentations* (Cambridge: Cambridge University Press, 2023), approaches the text from the perspective of trauma studies, seeing it as an attempt at therapeutic intervention for a wounded community.

General Index

Aaron, 100
Abba, R., 56
Abishag, 90
Abraham, 2
Acrostic poetry, 137–38
After-life, 10–11
Agag, 52
Akabia ben Mahalalel, 13
Akiva, R., 69, 75, 84, 97, 162
Albee, Edward, 39
Alexander the Great, 34
Amalek, 52, 53
Artaxerxes, 64
Asenath, 115
Assyria, 162
Auschwitz, 139
Austen, Jane, 103

Baal-Hamon, 94
Babylonia, 108, 134, 137, 145
Band, Debra, 177
Bar Kokhba, 141
Baraita, 5
Bardo, 110
Beal, Timothy K., 31, 177
Berlin, Adele, 27, 29
Berman, Joshua A., 179
Bernstein, Ellen, 71, 178
Bernstein, Leonard, 148
Betar, 143
Bethlehem, 111, 112
Bibi, R. 9
Billings, William, 96
Blake, William, 114
Bloch, Ariel and Chana, 93, 178

Bloch, Ernest, 16, 22
Book of the Dead, 110
Brumel, Antoine, 148
Butler, Samuel, 108
Byrd, William, 148, 149

Cantillation and nusach, xxi, 19, 42, 70, 156
Castelnuovo-Tedescho, Mario, 117, 179
Chagall, Marc , 122
Chanina bar Levi, 123
Chaplin, Charlie, 53
Charpentier, Marc-Antoine, 66, 148
Cohn, Gabriel H., 176
Commonplace book, 8
Conversion, 45–46, 118–19
Couperin, L., 148
Crescas, Hasdai, 58

Dante Alighieri, 2
Darius, 62
David, 90, 104, 105, 107, 108, 109, 132, 133, 135, 162
De Gelder, Arent, 65
Dead Sea Scrolls, 6, 34, 51
Deuteronomy , 17, 52
Diaspora/galut, 143
Ditters von Dittersdorff, K.M., 62

Ecclesiasticus (Wisdom of ben Sira), 15
Egypt, 162
Edom, 143, 160–61
Elbogen, Ismar, 43–44
Eliot, T. S., 48
Elisha, 90

Euridice, 111
Exodus, 52, 55
Ezra, 108

Falk, Marcia, 70, 89, 93, 178
Fisch, Menachem, 177
Fishbane, Michael, 75, 97, 101, 178
Flanigan, Lauren, 66
Four Species (see also lulav and etrog), 19

Genesis, 2, 23, 120
Geneva Bible, 158
Gentileschi, Artemisia, 65
"Gigi" (Lerner and Lowe), 169
Gilbert, W. S. and Sullivan, A., 112
Ginastera, Alberto, 148
Ginsberg, H. L., 176
Gold, Shefa, R., 96
Goliath, 113
Graetz, Heinrich, 9, 22

Hades, 10
Halpern, Stuart, 177, 179
Handel G. F., 65–66
Hanukkah, xiv–xv
Herodotus, 44
Heschel, A. J., 114
Hezekiah, 5
Hemingway, Ernest, 5
Hiroshima, 136, 172
Hiyya Rabba, R., 5, 69–70
Holocaust, 141, 144, 172
Homer, 108, 138
Horace, 20
Hughes, Langston, 66
Huna, Rav, 41

Ibn Ezra, Abraham, xix, 11, 14–15, 71, 162
Isaac, 96
Isaiah, 22, 37
Ishmael, 76

Jacob, 90, 96
Jacquet de la Guerre, Elisabeth, 66
James, Henry, 10
Jastrow, Joseph, 39, 68

Jeremiah, 137
Job, 22
Jonah, 173–74
Jonathan ben Eliezar, R., 6
Joseph, 49, 115
Josephus, 34
Judah, 132

Kabbalah (see also Zohar), xix, 14
Kates, Judith A., 179
Keats, John, 95, 118
Kedar, 76
King James Bible, 74, 78, 158
Kondek, Charles, 66
Kravitz, Leonard S., 177
Krenek, Ernst, 148

Lang, David, 96, 102, 176–77, 178
Lassus, O. de, 96, 148
Leah, 132, 133
Levenson, Jon D., 177
Levin, Neil W., 179
Levirate marriage, 125
Leviticus, 17, 18, 54
Linafelt, Todd, 179
Louis XIV, 88
Lulav and etrog, 18–19

Maimonides, xix
Makhana'im, 90, 102
Marx, Karl, 9
Masoretes, Masoretic, 34, 64–65, 70
Matthew, Gospel of, 107
Meir, R., 97
Menotti, Gian-Carlo, 142–43
Messiah, 100, 135, 146, 147, 160
Meyerowitz, Jan, 66
Micah, 9
Midrash Rabbah, 3, 5, 6, 9, 13, 14, 15, 29, 34, 37, 40, 41, 46, 53, 56, 60, 62, 88–89, 97–99, 113, 119–23, 162, 176
Milhaud, Darius, 66
Milton, John, 138
Mishnah, xv, 75
Moab, 103, 111, 119, 132
Moreau, Jean-Baptiste, 66
Moses, 107, 109, 115, 127, 129, 135

Nachmanides, xix
Nagasaki, 136, 172
Nebuchadnezzar, 36, 38, 134
Numbers (Book of), 54

Olitzky, Kerry M., 177

Palestrina, Giovanni Pierluigi da, 96, 148
PaRDeS, 74–75
Pardes, Ilana, 179
Passover, 28, 71, 144, 149, 159
Perez, 107, 124, 132
Pope, Alexander, 9
Poussin, Nicholas, 117
Prayerbook, 2
Proverbs (Book of), 6, 54, 69
Psalms, ix, xv, 18, 32
Purim, x, xv, 25, 33, 39, 41–44, 46,
    51–52, 54–56, 58, 61–62
Purimspiel, 65

Qere/ketiv, 126

Raba, 31, 58
Rachel, 96, 132, 133
Racine, Jean, 65–66
Rashbam, 15
Rashi, xix, 11, 13, 20, 59
Rav, 29
Rebecca, 96
Reimer, Gail Twersky, 179
Rembrandt van Rijn, 65, 117
Rome, 145
Rosh Hashanah, 9, 135, 137, 161

Sabbath (see Shabbat)
Samuel, (Book of, I), 52, 109
Samuel (sage), 37
Sappho, 108
Sanhedrin, 26
Saul, 108
Schrödinger's cat, 26
Schubert, Franz, 69
Schumann, Robert, 69
Septuagint, xviii-xix, 3, 34, 63–64, 65, 66
Shabbat, 71, 91
Shakespeare, William, 7, 23, 31, 69, 75,
    76, 81, 82, 120, 163, 170

Shapiro, Rami, 177
Shavuot, 120, 144
Shemini Atzeret, 19
She'ol, 10
Shmuel ben Nakhman, 113
Shoah (see Holocaust)
Shulamite, 90, 102
Shushan Purim, 32, 33
Sidney, Philip, 69
Simcha Bunin of Pzhysha, 2
Slavitt, David, 157–58, 179
S'lichot, 161
Sodom, 152
Solomon, 3, 5, 6, 69–70, 82, 83, 87–88,
    94, 95, 100, 132, 137
Spain, expulsion from, 139, 141
Steinsalz, Adin, 176
Stradella, Alessandro, 62, 66
Stravinsky, Igor, 148
Sukkot, 16, 165

Tallis, Thomas, 148
Talmud, xix, 2, 3, 4, 5, 13, 17, 26, 29,
    31, 33, 34, 38, 40, 45, 49, 60,
    105, 113, 115, 132, 135, 137, 148
Tamar, 107, 109, 124, 132, 133
Tanowitz, Pam, 102, 178
Targum, xviii, 9, 26, 28, 30, 34, 50, 53,
    56, 60, 99–100
Tashlikh, 9
Temple, xiv, xxii, 70, 109, 139–41, 149,
    152
Tenebrae, 148
Terezin, 66
Thomas à Kempis, 54
Tisha b'Av, xiv, xv, xxi, 145, 147, 149
T'shuvah, 161

Uz, 160–61

Victoria, Tomás Luis, 148
Victors, Jan, 65
Virgil, 128

Wake Forest University, 165
Waskow, Arthur 71, 147, 176, 178
Wordsworth, William, 140

Xerxes, 33, 44, 64

Yehuda, R., 97
Yom ha-Shoah, 144
Yom Kippur, 55–56, 135, 137, 145, 158, 161, 173
Yonatan, 37–38, 69–70

Zechariah, 162
Zedekiah, 137, 160
Zeira, R., 119
Zelenka, Jan Dismas, 148
Zipporah, 115
Zohar, xix, 14, 101, 147, 176

Ancient Document Index

Genesis
18	152
18: 27	2
23: 17	17
28:16	172

Exodus
2:17	127
6:3	129
13: 16	169
15: 3	154
15: 19–20	110
24: 7	97
30:10	55
32: 4	97
33: 18	171
33: 20–23	171–72
34: 6–7	157, 171

Leviticus
16:6–10	55
19: 17	155
23:40	18–19
23: 43	17
25:25	124, 125

Numbers
4:37	45, 171
24: 5	54
24:7	52

Deuteronomy
16:13	17
23:3	115
25: 5–6	129

Judges
17:6	108
21:25	108

1 Samuel
17:12	107
28	10

1 Kings
2:32	69
4:32	69
8:29	139–40

Isaiah
16:11	148
30:29	99
41: 8	22

Jeremiah
7: 1–7	151
48:36	148

Nehemiah
8:15	17

Psalms

30:11	103
30:12	162
118:1	18
121:4	171

Proverbs

15:4	6
19:21	54
31:10-31	137

Song of Songs

1:1-2	68
1:3-4	72-73, 100
1:5	74, 98-99, 101-02
1:6	73, 76
1:7-8	76-77
1:9-14	77-78
1:12	97, 102
2:1-4	78-79
2:4	99
2:5-7	79
2:8-9	79-80
2:10	100
2:14-17	80-81, 95
3:1-5	81-82, 86
3:6-10	82
4:5	84
4:14-16	84
4:16	83
5:1	84-85
5:2	85
5:4-6	86
5:7	102
5:8	87
5:16	85, 87
6:1	85
6:2-4	87-88
6:3	71-72
6:5-11	88
6:12	89
7:1-2	89-91, 102
7:3-14	91
7:4	100
8:1-5	92
8:6-7	93
8:9-12	94-95
8:13-14	9-5, 100

Ruth

1:1	106
1:8-12	113
1:15	113
1:16-17	116-18
1:18	118
1:20-21	104, 128, 129
2:8	123
2:10	127
2:12	128
2:13	122
2:19	104
2:20	128
2:22	123
3:9	125
3:16	122
4:10	113
4:10-14	119
4:11-17	132
4:13	105
4:14-15	133

Lamentations

1:1	136-37
1:8-10	150-51
1:9-12	152-53
1:13	153
1:19	153
1:21	153
2:1	153-54
2:2	154
2:14	155
2:19	155
2:22	154-55
3:1	155-56
3:6-8	157
3:18	156-57
3:40-45	158
3:48	158-59
3:66	159
4:10-13	160
4:20	160
5:1	161
5:15	162

Ecclesiastes

1:1–2	2–3, 16
1:5	5
1:7	13
2:14	8
2:16–17	11
2:23	20
3:4–5	11–12
3:20–21	11
3:22	20
4:1	8
5:9	6
5:16–17	7, 20
6:6	10
7:1	8
8:12–14	12
8:14	7
8:16	8
9:7	18
9:8–9	20
9:10	10
9:11	12
9:13	8
10;7	8
11:1	9
11:8	20
11:14	8
12:1	13–14
12:3	10
12:6	10
12:8–9	15, 16
12:12	14–15
12:13–14	4

Esther

1:10	51
1:12	39–40
1:16	40
1:22	41
2:5	35, 50
2:9	47
2:15	36
2:17	37
2:20	49
2:21	26–27, 44
3:5	37
3:7	54
3:12	27
3:13	54
3:15	28
4:1	28–29
4:11	29, 57
4:13–14	56–57
4:16	32, 57
6:13	32, 50
7:9	42
8:8	57
8:17	44
9:3–4	44
9:16	36
9:20	33, 50
9:22	32–33
9:23	58
9:27–28	50
9:29	36
10:3	49–50

2 Chronicles

35:25	137

Mishnah

M. Yedaim 3:5	75

Talmud

bT Shabbat

30b	4
88a	58

bT Megillah

7a	4
7b	51
12b	38, 40
13b	45, 48, 49
16b	50
19a	60

bT Mo'ed Katan

26a	137

bT Yevamot	
76b	115, 132
bT Ketubot	
46b	148
bT Sotah	
42b	113
bT Gittin	
68b	3
bT 'Eduyyot	
5:3	4
bT Bava Batra	
14b	105
15a	5
bT Sanhedrin	
37b	2
bT Makkot	
24b	162

bT Yedayim	
3:5	4, 75
Tosefta Sanhedrin	
12:5	69
Shir Rabbah	
1:5	5, 98
2:9	98
8:13	99
Ruth Rabbah	
2:16	113
Esther Rabbah	
4:12	41
6:2	60
8:3	62
Midrash Qohelet	
11:1	9
12:1	14

www.ingramcontent.com/pod-product-compliance
Lightning Source LLC
Chambersburg PA
CBHW021730220426
43662CB00008B/783